THE MEANING
OF METAFICTION

INGER CHRISTENSEN

THE MEANING
OF METAFICTION

A Critical Study of Selected Novels
by Sterne, Nabokov, Barth and Beckett

UNIVERSITETSFORLAGET
BERGEN · OSLO · TROMSØ

© UNIVERSITETSFORLAGET 1981
ISBN 82-00-05692-9

A.s Centraltrykkeriet, Bergen

Distribution offices:

NORWAY
Universitetsforlaget
Postboks 2977, Tøyen
Oslo 6

UNITED KINGDOM
Global Book Resources Ltd.
109 Great Russell Street
London WC1B 3NA

UNITED STATES and CANADA
Columbia University Press
136 South Broadway
Irvington-on-Hudson
New York 10533

Published with a grant from
the Norwegian Research Council
for Science and the Humanities

The cover illustration, Velázquez's «Las Meninas» (1656) is
an example of meta-art. The painter focuses on himself and
the scene of which he is a part, and he includes the specta-
tor, the courtier, observing the situation from a distance. The
supposed theme of the artist's portrait, the royal couple, is
only presented as a reflection in the mirror on the wall.

Table of contents

JAN   1983

Preface

I first read John Barth's *Giles Goat-Boy* as an existential quest novel, but as such the work as a whole did not make sense to me. Thus my interest in metafiction was aroused. I was surprised to discover later that Laurence Sterne's *Tristram Shandy*, written some two hundred years earlier, contained even more "modern" narrative devices than Barth's novel.

In this way, I became more and more aware of the importance of metafictional elements in the works of various novelists, and I developed a clearer notion of the nature and function of metafiction. It was thus natural for me to wish to explore such novels more systematically in order to clarify how various authors made use of metafictional elements. It was not my desire to categorize the works I selected for closer study, but rather to illuminate what I felt to be significant features of their narrative structure. In surveying modern metafictionists, I found that in the work of some novelists, such as, for instance, Thomas Pynchon, the metafictional element was not a major concern. I have therefore not considered such novelists in this study, although they are of some interest to my general theme.

Chapters of this work have been discussed in research seminars at the Department of English, the University of Bergen: I would like to thank my colleagues and other participants for stimulating criticism and helpful advice. Academic Librarian Maya Thee deserves special thanks for her conscientious assistance in reading and criticizing parts of the manuscript. Ms Penny Mietle and Ms Ragnhild Linchausen were of great help in typing the manuscript. I am also grateful to Ms Mietle and Ms Judy Kennedy for generous advice in linguistic matters.

Bergen, 1981   I. C.

*By hearing ye shall hear, and
shall not understand*
                    Matt., 13, xiv

Introduction

The works discussed in this study, the novels of Sterne, Nabokov, Barth and Beckett, belong to a trend which has come much to the fore in Western art in the latter half of the 20th century. Meta-art, which turns its attention upon the work of art itself, is prevalent in all media and art forms. To mention just some areas: In painting it is represented by the works of Georges Braque and in drama by Pirandello. Meta-art occurs in film (Fellini), music (J. W. Morthenson), and even in literary criticism (Thomas R. Whitaker). In fiction one finds among the practitioners of meta-art novelists like Borges, Grass, Lessing and Simon. A closer look at some representatives of metafiction may therefore create greater understanding for a general trend, not only in literature, but in contemporary art as a whole.

The novels of Sterne and the 20th century writers are here classified as metafiction. The term has been coined fairly recently, while this kind of literature has a much older tradition. One has to distinguish accordingly between the origin of the term, designating the phenomenon, and the origin of the phenomenon itself. Also one has to consider the occurrences of the attempts to define this kind of literature, and in that connection "metafiction" is just one of the terms used.

A discussion of the origin of metafiction falls outside the scope of this study. Obviously, *Tristram Shandy* does not mark the beginning of this kind of literature, which was, for instance, prominent in 17th century Spain, and was represented by writers like Lope de Vega and Cervantes.[1] To my knowledge, the term metafiction first occurs in an essay by William Gass where he refers to the works of Borges, Barth and O'Brien: "Indeed, many of the so-called antinovels are really metafictions."[2] Like Gass, I prefer metafiction to anti-novel as the more appropriate term. To approach a definition of metafiction other terms used about metafictional works have to be examined.

In Joseph T. Shipley's *Dictionary of World Literary Terms*, *Tristram Shandy* is referred to as an example of the anti-novel, which is explained as a "protest against the conventions of novelistic forms ..." Also *Don Quixote* is mentioned as an anti-novel, because it was written as a reaction against books of chivalry.[3] The meaning of anti-novel seems too wide to serve as a description of metafictional works, because a not inconsiderable number of novels appear as protests against established artistic norms without possessing metafictional characteristics. Larry McCaffery, finding that anti-novel is too broad a term, because it includes all works that appear unconventional and experimental, points out the explicit features of metafiction: "the defining characteristic of metafiction, however, is its direct and immediate concern with fiction-making itself." Anti-novels may also deal with the making of fiction, but in an indirect way. In metafiction this has become the main subject.[4]

John Fletcher and Malcolm Bradbury use the phrase "the introverted novel" about the works of, among others, Vladimir Nabokov, Muriel Spark and Günter Grass: by the turn of the century the novel seems to have no other field left to develop and therefore "it turned in upon itself". Fletcher and Bradbury distinguish between "narrative introversion", which characterizes the 20th century novels, and "the mode of self-conscious narration", which belongs to the 17th and 18th century novels. Thus a book like *Tristram Shandy* wants to draw attention to "the autonomy of the narrator, while the later techniques drew attention to the autonomy of the fictive structure itself."[5] To me, *Tristram Shandy* appears to bring into focus not only the autonomy of the narrator but also that of the narrative as well as of the narratee. I find greater likeness than dissimilarity between 18th and 20th century metafiction, and the expressions "the introverted novel" and "the self-conscious mode" seem equally as applicable to *Tristram Shandy* as to *Molloy*.

In his article "Metafiction" from 1970, Robert Scholes tries to explain "the nature of contemporary experimental fiction" by four directions in literary criticism, which he classifies as formal, structural, behavioural, and philosophical.[6] Scholes links the various manifestations of metafiction to these critical schools, finding Barth's fiction mainly formal; Barthelme's behavioural, etc. Scholes is one of the first to employ the term metafiction, but he does not give an explicit definition of it. In a later article Scholes describes metafiction, or "self-reflective fiction" as he also calls it, as: "a fiction which, if it is 'about' anything, it is about the possibilities and impossibilities of fiction itself . . ."[7] This is too sweeping a definition to be helpful in indicating the distinctive nature of metafiction.

Stanley Fogel presents an explicit and quite comprehensive definition of metafiction: "Metafiction entails exploration of the theory of fiction through fiction itself. Writers of metafiction . . . scrutinize all facets of the literary construct – language, the conventions of plot and character, the relation of the artists to his art and to his reader."[8] This definition, nevertheless, leaves out what to me is an essential aspect of metafiction – the novelist's message. Fogel emphasizes the formal side of metafictional creation. This illustrates the general tendency of the reader to overlook the message of the metafictional work.

10

In this study metafiction is regarded as fiction whose primary concern is to express the novelist's vision of experience by exploring the process of its own making. This definition indicates that only those works are considered metafiction where the novelist has a message to convey and is not merely displaying his technical brilliance.

This examination will deal with selected novels of four representatives of metafiction. Of these, only Sterne's *Tristram Shandy* belongs to the 18th century, while the works of Nabokov, Barth and Beckett represent the 20th century. The choice of novels needs some justification and particularly two questions have to be dealt with: why this emphasis on 20th century fiction and Sterne as the only representative of the 18th century? And secondly, why is the 19th century left out?

In the context of the 18th century English novel, *Tristram Shandy* presents itself as an astoundingly unique work of metafiction. Its appearance becomes less mysterious when seen against the background of Sterne's literary influences; Cervantes, Rabelais and Robert Burton are the writers most frequently referred to by the critics.[9] Wayne C. Booth ascribes Sterne's use of the intruding narrator and comments to the readers to comic novels like the anonymously published *Charlotte Summers, the Fortunate Parish Girl*, and he finds that Sterne drew on Montaigne's *Essays* for the device of the narrator's commenting on his composition during the very act of writing.[10] However, in 18th century English literature *Tristram Shandy* stands out as the most weighty specimen of metafiction. Sterne's work is an obvious choice if one wants an 18th century work to set the 20th century novels in relief, as is my purpose. Seen against the background of the earlier novel, the contours of 20th century metafiction should become clearer.

The lack of a 19th century work is partly explained in the preceding paragraph: my analysis will focus on the 20th century metafictionists, and the examination of *Tristram Shandy* serves mainly to set off the features of the later novels. The answer is also that in 19th century narrative art, metafiction is not in vogue – a circumstance noted by several critics. Robert Alter refers to the "almost complete eclipse of the self-conscious novel during the nineteenth century" and he sees this as due to the "imaginative involvement with history."[11]

The affinity between the fiction of the 18th and the 20th centuries has been pointed out by, among others, Bergonzi. He claims that while the 19th century English novelist is concerned with presenting his vision of life, the fiction of the 18th and 20th centuries discloses an interest in "craft and convention".[12] Jocipovici also remarks on the similarity between modern novels and fiction before the 19th century, which he ascribes to the dominant conception of art as artifact in contrast to the 19th century view of art as imitation.[13] To some extent this may explain why metafiction, a rather form-oriented literary trend, occurs in these periods while it is neglected in the 19th century.

Nineteenth century fiction may take up themes typical of metafictional works. Some of Hawthorne's novels, for instance, centre on questions concerning the artist's isolation from mankind, his difficulties with communication. A comparison between Hawthorne's *The Blithedale Romance* (1852) and Barth's *The Floating Opera* (1956) will disclose the thematical relatedness as well as structural differences between metafiction and the 19th century "Künstler-roman".

Both Hawthorne and Barth's novels have the first person narrator and deal with the artist-writer's existential situation: in Hawthorne's novel, Coverdale, the narrator, presents himself as a poet. Barth's narrator, Todd Andrews, works as a lawyer, but in the novel his role as writer is given the main emphasis. In both novels the narrator-protagonists' relation to other people is damaged by the detachment due to their task as novelists or poets, which is inevitably bound up with a certain aesthetic distance.

The Blithedale Romance reveals Coverdale's detached attitude through descriptions of his behaviour towards, and his remarks about his companions, and in addition by symbolic devices. Thus Coverdale discloses his remoteness by constantly referring to his associates as actors in a play with Zenobia as the prima donna and by observations like "I began to long for a catastrophe."[14] The artist as an individual removed from life is expressed symbolically by Coverdale's perch in the tree where he writes poetry and observes his fellows from a distance (p. 432) and further by the comparison of poetry to wine distilled from the grapes of reality (p. 432 and p. 595).

Barth employs similar symbolism in *The Floating Opera* but to a much lesser extent, depending more on structural devices and the narrator's direct comments to the reader.[15] While Hawthorne stops after having described his narrator-protagonist's existential dilemma, Barth goes on to disclose Todd Andrew's difficulties in writing the very book in which he figures as the narrator. By revealing the technique of *The Floating Opera* in the novel, Barth stresses the parallelism between the narrator's difficulties as an artist and as a man.

Hawthorne discusses the narrator's problems as a human being but does not, like Barth, deal with them in terms of the technical or practical aspects of the narrator's craft. Even Coverdale's true situation, his self-chosen distance from life and the complications this choice brings with it, is expressed so obliquely in the novel that the reader may get nearly to the end without discovering that this is not chiefly a book about Zenobia and Hollingsworth. The last chapter containing Coverdale's confession of his secret love for Priscilla makes one realize his dilemma: how he has lived vicariously through the lives of the other characters.

In Barth's book, on the other hand, the narrator constantly stresses his intentions by turning directly to the reader. *The Blithedale Romance* does not in any way explore the process of its own making, an important requirement according to our definition.[16]

Before one enters into a closer discussion of *metafiction*, it is necessary first to question the fundamentals of *fiction*. A consideration of the "basic situation" of story-telling as delineated by Wolfgang Kayser seems here highly appropriate if one is not to get "lost in the funhouse" of metafiction: "Die epische Ursituation ist: ein Erzähler erzählt einer Hörerschaft etwas, was geschehen ist."[17] The relation of narrator-story-audience delineated by Kayser exists in every narrative whether it is oral or written.

Kayser draws attention to some additional factors of the written narration in which fiction is included: the author and the historical or actual reader. He regards the narrator as a part the author puts on and warns against confusing the two or regarding the narrator as identical with the author.[18]

The distinction between narrator and author has been thoroughly debated in recent criticism.[19] But Kayser's view of the reader as part of the fictional world has received much less attention: "Wie können wir ... die ungezählten und völlig verschiedenen Leser Formelemente des Romans sein? ... Der Leser ist etwas Gedichtetes, ist eine Rolle, in die wir hineinschlüpfen und der wir uns selber zusehen können."[20] In this way Kayser differentiates between the reader *within* the work of fiction to whom the narrator may address himself, the narratee, and the reader, the you and I *outside* the book who adopt the part of that other reader created for us in the novel.

The relation of narrator-story-reader is expanded in the fictional situation to encompass: author-narrator-story-fictional reader (audience) – actual reader. Kayser regards the author and the actual reader as external elements in the fictional world, to which the other three elements belong as integral parts.

Seen against the background of Kayser's description of the fundamentals of the narrative situation, the differences between a work of fiction and one of metafiction become obvious. In the latter the novelist focuses on "Die epische Ursituation": this functions as the theme of the book. Secondly, the author places himself inside the fictional world and figures as a structural element in the novel. The historical author will of course always exist outside and apart from the work itself, so that metafiction only operates with an additional factor: fictional author.

Metafiction deals with questions essential to any novelist: the narrator's conception of his own role and art, and of the reader. Writers are, to a greater and lesser extent, conscious of these relations, but the metafictionist differs by making these questions the subject of his work. Thus metafiction sheds light on fundamental issues in connection with fictional creation in general.

Further, writers of metafiction focus on questions of primary importance not only to novelists, but to man in general. Daily, the average human being acts out the basic situation of story-telling drawn up by Kayser in the way that he makes use of words to impart his thoughts and past experiences to others. In this situation man will find how words very often do not give an adequate expression to what he wants to say. In addition, every user of words knows how frequently others misunderstand one's utterances. The metafictionist deals with these fundamental issues of communication by directing attention to the narrator, the narrative, and the narratee in his work.

On the basis of Kayser's fundamental elements of the narrative situation, the analyses of the individual novels will in each chapter focus on: I. The narrator's conception of his own role; II. Notions of the narrative as expressed in the novel; III. The significance of the narratee. The attitude towards narrator, narrative, narratee expressed in the novel has its foundation in the author's view of existence. Thus an analysis of these elements will in the last instance reveal not only the writer's relation to art, but to reality as a whole. Ultimately, the meaning of metafiction depends on the novelist's vision of experience.

I. Laurence Sterne's *Tristram Shandy*:
A Plea for Communication

The Russian critic Victor Shklovsky was the first to draw attention to the metafictional[1] qualities of *Tristram Shandy*. In his essay on the novel, which appeared in 1921, he claims that "awareness of form constitutes the subject matter of the novel . . ."[2] and that a prominent feature of Sterne is to " 'lay bare' his technique."[3] Further he points to his way of opposing "literary" to ordinary time, and device of "defamiliarizing" or "making strange" familiar objects and events in order to draw the reader's attention towards the form of the novel. In Shklovsky's opinion, Sterne's intentions with his book were purely aesthetical: "Sterne thought such [aesthetic] motivation an end in itself."[4]

Most recent criticism recognizes Sterne as a writer of metafiction, but this is generally considered one aspect of *Tristram Shandy*.[5] J. M. Stedmond's substantial contribution to Sternean criticism does not concern itself chiefly with *Tristram Shandy* as a work of metafiction, though this critic makes it clear that Sterne, like Joyce, Flaubert, and Beckett, stresses "the book as book" exploring the rules and limits of novel writing, chiefly through his manipulation of the time aspect.[6]

In contrast to previous criticism – with the exception of Shklovsky – Robert Alter considers *Tristram Shandy* solely from the point of view of metafiction.[7] As his definition of the "self-conscious novel" indicates, Alter's analysis of Sterne's book concentrates on the author's concern with mimesis. The present examination will also consider the aesthetic and formal aspects of *Tristram Shandy* but intends to probe deeper into Sterne's purpose with his display of structural devices. This study centres on the exploration of Sterne's vision or message, which I hope to show concerns the problems of human intercourse in its ethical and aesthetic consequences.

1. Narrator as Entertainer

The picture entitled "Thos. Bridges and Lawrence Sterne as Mountebanks"[8] gives some indication of the opinions which the public in Sterne's time formed of the author of *Tristram Shandy:* Sterne is portrayed as a quack, offering his goods for sale, hat in hand and smiling slyly. Richard A. Lanham argues that in Sternean criticism two conceptions of the novelist prevail: some of the critics see him as "venial jester" and the others cherish him as "existential philosopher" while Lanham himself suggests a reconciliation of these opposite views: Sterne has both seriousness and humour in store for his reader.[9] The last approach to Sterne seems most reasonable and comes close to the view of the narrator that will be presented here.

Before one considers the narrator's role and motivation, it is necessary first to stress the distinction between author and narrator to be found in the novel. Wayne C. Booth draws attention to the fact that "in *all* written works there is an implied narrator or 'author' . . . " but in *Tristram Shandy* the narrator's role is underlined and his self-consciousness developed to the extent that his intruding comments to the reader concern himself not only as one of the characters, but in his specific role as the teller of the tale.[10]

Sterne insists that Tristram is not to be confused with himself. This is revealed for instance in the footnote with corrections of "Mr. Tristram Shandy" 's spelling,[11] which may be taken as a kind of editor's comment and an attempt to satirize a conventional device. But the point of interest here is that the distance between narrator and actual author is underlined at the same time as one more element – the fictional editor – is placed between them.

The disparity between narrator and author is also emphasized by Tristram, who points out the fictional quality of his nature. The narrator exists only inside the covers of the book and on an equal footing with the characters of the novel. When he has finished his task of narrating the story, his existence must come to an end as well: "as long as I live or write (which in my case means the same thing)" (p. 121). In the same way as Tristram speaks of "that future and dreaded *page*" (p. 343; italics mine) when Toby is gone, he tells the reader: "Let us leave, if possible, *myself*: – But 'tis impossible, – I must go along with you to the end of the work" (p. 336).

Tristram, then, does not in any way figure as Sterne's *alter ego*; on the contrary, it is emphasized that he has a part to play like the other characters of the novel. He only wears a somewhat special mask, that of the narrator. How is this role presented in the novel? What is Tristram's own concept of his role?

Henri Fluchère finds that Tristram adopts "the mythical role of court jester . . ."[12] Repeatedly, he refers to himself as a clown: "I triumph'd over him as I always do, like a fool" (p. 162). Thus Sterne's image among his contemporaries as a smiling charlatan does not differ much from Tristram's picture of himself. And in accordance with his role as the fool, he wears the harlequin's dress: "Here – pray, Sir, take hold of my cap, – nay, take the bell along with it, and my pantoufles too" (p. 139).

By bestowing the name of the fool in *Hamlet* upon the warm-hearted but eccentric clergyman in *Tristram Shandy*, Sterne gives a pointer to his estimation of the fool's calling. According to Melvyn New, Yorick serves as a foil to the members of the Shandy family; he has his weaknesses but unlike the others he is aware of them.[13] Tristram holds Yorick in high esteem: "I have the highest idea of the spiritual and refined sentiments of this reverend gentleman" (p. 17). Yorick embodies the traditional fool: the wise clown behind whose jokes a serious intent is hidden. This is how Tristram portrays Yorick and how he sees his own role as a narrator.

Tristram expresses his intention with the words: "I sat down to write my life for the amusement of the world, and my opinions for its instruction" (p. 159). The novel is meant to provide its readers with something more than mere entertainment. In Sterne's *Letters* one gets a glimpse of his purpose behind the jokes and humour of the book. He expresses his "hopes of doing the world good by ridiculing what I thought deserving of it ..."[14]

Sterne also admits that the writing affords him pleasure: "so much am I delighted with my uncle Toby's imaginary character, that I am become an enthusiast."[15] One may therefore draw the conclusion that besides possessing a satiric intent, his narration serves as an antidote to the cares of life, which stem, in Sterne's case, chiefly from his incurable consumption. The dedication makes this explicit (cf. p. 2). Though the novel contains criticism, satirizing for instance in "Slawkenbergius's Tale" (pp. 183 ff), the alleged learned dispute over nothing; it is primarily written to make its author – and consequently also its readers – forget the sore realities with the help of laughter.

A correspondence exists between Tristram's and Toby's situations because they both obtain relief from their cares through substitution – the one on the bowling green; the other at the writing-desk.[16] The books on sieges and demolitions of towns Toby "would read with that intense application and delight, that he would forget himself, his wound, his confinement, his dinner" (p. 68). His wound makes him unfit both as a lover and in warfare, and he concentrates his activities in a play war.

Tristram finds a means in his writing – and what juicy bits does it not contain – to compensate for his impotence and lack of involvement in real life.[17]

However, he is well aware that he lives vicariously in his writing: "I who must be cut short in the midst of my days, and taste no more of 'em than what I borrow from my imagination" (p. 377). By writing in the way he does he may keep his woes at a distance. But he cannot fool himself to the extent that he confuses the laughter evoked by his writing about life with the joy stemming from actual living. In his situation the role as clown-narrator becomes the only possible escape if he is not to go insane like "poor Maria" (cf. pp. 483ff.).

Volume VII of *Tristram Shandy* illustrates rather aptly how Tristram writes both for instruction and amusement but concentrates on the latter. According to Lewis Curtis, this part of the novel was written as a parody on the French guidebook in vogue at the time,[18] and it satirizes also the usual way of making the grand tour through Europe. At the same time Tristram makes it a description of his flight from death, and this he significantly enough "turns into a festive dance".[19] In addition he applies the travelling motif as a metaphor both of the passage of life itself and of writing:[20]

> How far my pen has been fatigued like those of other travellers, in this journey of it, over so barren a track – the world must judge – but the traces of it . . . tell me 'tis the most fruitful and busy period of my life; for as I had made no convention with my man with the gun as to time – by stopping and talking to every soul I met who was not in full trot – joining all parties before me – waiting for every soul behind . . . arresting all kinds of beggars, pilgrims, fiddlers, fryars . . . In short, by seizing every handle, of what size or shape soever, which chance held out to me in this journey – I turned my *plain* into a *city* . . . (p. 409)

By this account of his way of travelling, Tristram gives a rather exact delineation of his method of writing and a description of the novel as a whole. He keeps an eye open for seemingly insignificant details, recommending the inn-keeper's daughter in Montreuil as the "one thing . . . in it at present very handsome" (p. 373). Tristram concerns himself with people, and one consequence is that the writer's task never grows dull, but becomes a source of variety and pleasure.

The other characters, to the extent that they try to express themselves orally or in writing, throw Tristram's way of narration into relief. Concerning his fellow travellers through France on his grand tour, especially Walter's situation is illuminated, and also in his case there is a correspondence between his method of travelling and the way he conducts his life (cf. p. 391).

Walter goes to see the sights recommended in the travel books. Ironically enough, the only part of the travel described in some detail is his visit to some saintly mummies in an abbey. What interests Walter is not the saints or the stories of their lives. The *name* of one of them, "Saint *Optat*" (p. 393), fires his imagination and he notes it down with great glee. Walter's visit to the dead, his excitement at names and disconcern for the individuals that the names after all denominate, shows a great difference in life style and interest between himself and his son.

Walter reveals the same peculiarities in the field of writing. His narrative differs, especially in intention and method from Tristram's. Walter's *Tristrapaedia* is meant as a source of instruction for his son. Tristram states that it was written "so as to form an INSTITUTE for the government of my childhood and adolescence" (p. 281). His intention does not correspond to Tristram's who considers *his* work first and foremost as an entertainment. Walter approaches his task "with the most painful diligence, proceeding step by step in every line,

18

with the same kind of caution and circumspection'' and his work becomes "torture to him" (p. 282).

While Tristram lets himself be distracted into pursuing every whim that occurs to him, Walter makes a point of withstanding the temptations that will make him diverge from his true intentions, and he compares his writing to warfare (cf. p. 283). This underlines the difference between Walter on the one hand and Tristram and Toby on the other. Walter's war with words causes him pain, as it is a losing battle. Toby enjoys his play war to the full as does Tristram *his* hobby-horse, the narrator's role.

Tristram emphasizes further the difference between Walter and Toby and himself by revealing their attitudes to matters of sex, which in the novel connotes another creative process, the activity of writing.[21] Here again Walter puts up a resistance: "My father, as appears from many of his papers, was very subject to this passion, before he married – but ... whenever it befell him, he would never submit to it like a christian; but would pish, and huff, and bounce, and kick, and play the Devil, and write the bitterest Philippicks against the eye that ever man wrote" (p. 446). Toby does not fight against the attacks of love: "My uncle *Toby*, on the contrary, took it like a lamb – sat still and let the poison work in his veins without resistance" (p. 446).

Tristram's narrative shows that in matters of love he takes after his father only in the way that for him too love leads to sublimation, to the act of writing. However, Tristram considers his writing as a game and a source of pleasure. He has no scruples about yielding to his inclinations, regarding both writing and the passion of love. Thus, on his tour through France he could not pass "by a woman in a mulberry-tree with out commending her legs, and tempting her into conversation with a pinch of snuff" (p. 409).

The following passage also indicates how the disparity between father and son in their views on writing is bound up with different attitudes to sex: Walter

> never used the word *passions* once – but *ass* always instead of them ... I must here observe to you, the difference betwixt
> My father's ass
> and my hobby-horse – in order to keep characters as separate as may be, in our fancies as we go along.
> For my hobby-horse ... 'Tis the sporting little filly-folly which ... a man makes a shift to get a stride on, to canter it away from the cares and solicitudes of life ... But for my father's ass ... 'tis a beast concupiscent – and foul befall the man, who does not hinder him from kicking. (p. 450)

By loading the words *ass* and *hobby-horse* with the double connotation of passion and writing and expressing his preference for the last-mentioned animal, Tristram gives here a vivid illustration of how he regards the narrator's task. In contrast to his father, he has indeed been *"wrote-galloping"* (p. 367) with great enjoyment to himself.

Playing the role of the entertainer, whose task it is to keep himself and the reader happy, the narrator removes himself somewhat from his object. Without a proper distance, the observer would not be able to see the humorous side of things. His laughter would inevitably give way to tears. Such a remote attitude in the narrator bears great likeness and may be compared to the position of a god. Stedmond finds this to be the case in *Tristram Shandy*: "From a god's eye view, man *is* comic, as Swift's Lilliputians are comic."[22] Thus by acting the part of an entertainer, the narrator also plays the role of a god, because laughter places him above his object and makes him in a way independent in relation to what he laughs at.

Tristram repeatedly stresses his autonomy as writer or teller of the tale. His practice of doing "all things out of rule" (p. 211) forms a contrast to those adhering to rules either in their behaviour like Walter or in their writing like Slawkenbergius, who "tied down every tale" (p. 199) in accordance with Aristotle's rules. Tristram demonstrates his independence by, for instance, writing chapters 20 to 25 *before* the 18th and 19th in volume IX. He explains that this is meant simply as an example of his privilege as narrator to write as he pleases: "All I wish is, that it may be a lesson to the world, '*to let people tell their stories their own way*'" (p. 485).

Though Tristram's liability to regard reality in a humorous light removes him from his creation and makes him feel his autonomy as a narrator, his independence is in no way absolute: "But this is neither here nor there – why do I mention it? – Ask my pen, – it governs me, – I govern not it" (p. 316). Kayser has pointed out the paradox of the writer's situation: "der Dichter schafft die Welt seines Romans – aber es gilt auch: diese Welt schafft sich durch ihn, verwandelt sich zu, zwingt ihn zum Spiel der Verwandlungen, um dadurch wirklich zu werden ..."[23] Tristram illustrates to some extent Kayser's paradox. He may, like Toby "make himself so far master of his subject, as to be able to talk upon it without emotion" (p. 67). But the creational process presupposes *some* kind of involvement, even if he feels himself superior to literary conventions.

Because it is Tristram's intention to provide entertainment, his commitment exists on an intellectual level. His emotional detachment as a narrator corresponds to a similar independence as a man. An incident in Toby's life makes this clear:

Whilst a man is free – cried the corporal, giving a flourish with his stick thus –

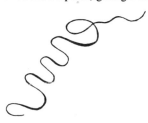

> A thousand of my father's most subtle syllogisms could not have said more for celibacy.
>
> My uncle *Toby* look'd earnestly towards his cottage and his bowling green. (p. 465)

Even unsuspecting Toby realizes that a marriage to Widow Wadman may very likely curtail further campaigns on the bowling green.

As discussed above, Toby's play war corresponds to and has the same function as Tristram's narrative. His role as narrator substitutes other possible roles, other kinds of involvement in life. He possesses a freedom as a man, a non-commitment to his surroundings without which he could not carry through his task as an entertainer. And his novel represents a manifestation of his freedom, his ability to laugh in the face of distress. The corporal's flourish does not only persuade Toby of the bachelor's advantages; it becomes a visible symbol for the reader of the narrator's independence and originality.

Tristram's emotional detachment, which characterizes him as a man and as a narrator, brings with it various problems. Repeatedly, he refers to his difficulties: "What! are not the unavoidable distresses with which, as an author and a man, thou art hemm'd in on every side of thee – are they, *Tristram*, not sufficient, but thou must entangle thyself still more?" (p. 419). What he deplores is his tendency to lose himself in digressions.

Tristram explains his weakness as originating in his mother's impulsive question to his father at the moment of his conception: "Pray, my dear ... *have you not forgot to wind up the clock?*" (p. 4). His mother's momentary "unhappy association of ideas which have no connection in nature" (p. 7) implants in her son a life-long similar inclination.

Without refuting Tristram's explanation, one may at least point to another connection to account for his digressional method of writing. This is related to his tendency to approach the world from an intellectual point of view. Not to let anything drive you off the beaten track indicates a mental restrictedness:

> Could a historiographer drive on his history, as a muleteer drives on his mule, – straight forward ... he might venture to foretell you to an hour when he should get to his journey's end; – but the thing is, morally speaking, impossible: For, if he is a man of the least spirit, he will have fifty deviations from a straight line to make with this or that party as he goes along, which he can no ways avoid. ... All which both the man and his mule are quite exempt from. (p. 28)

By driving straight on the muleteer exhibits a singleness of purpose and a complete commitment to his task. Indirectly, he is compared to his beast; the point for both of them is to get to the end. With his ready mind Tristram cannot withstand the temptation to look into matters as he goes along.

However, Tristram finds it necessary to justify the frequent occurrence of digressions in his narrative. "Digressions," he asserts, "incontestably, are the sunshine; – they are the life, the soul of reading; – take them out of this book for instance, – you might as well take the book along with them'' (p. 55). But the ideal book should contain a balance between the story and the digressions, between the "digressive and progressive movements'' (p. 55). This, he argues, may be found in his narrative where the "two contrary motions are introduced ... and reconciled'' (p. 54).

To some extent the opposing factors of digression and progression in a narrative correspond to the dichotomy between wit and judgement in the narrator. Tristram finds that these qualities should also exist in equal proportions in a narrative, and he hopes that the reader will discover that this is so in his book (cf. p. 146). In his discussion of the terms *wit* and *judgement*, Alter finds the view predominant in *Tristram Shandy* that the function of wit is to procure entertainment – a conception Alter asserts Sterne inherited from Locke.[24] When Tristram calls for equal proportions of wit and judgement as well as digressions and progression, it may be possible to see this in relation to his motivation, his intention to amuse *and* instruct.

But however much Tristram may wish to create a balance, the digressive side of his narrative outweighs the progressive one, and his work amuses far more than it instructs. Tristram sometimes laments the "thousand distresses and domestic misadventures'' (p. 175) which he has to come to terms with, thanks to his special inclination. However, he carries through his role as entertainer with immense delight. The resulting work shows that he has obtained at least part of what he intended: "to fence against the infirmities of ill health, and other evils of life, by mirth'' (p. 2).

2. Fiction as Artifact

The relation between art and reality is indeed a usual novelistic concern. However, the extent to which their work may try to reproduce the external world varies from novelist to novelist. Realistic writers find it important to create an imitation as objectively and accurately as possible. Other authors wish to make their art expressive of their personal feelings and impressions. Where should one place a work of metafiction on a scale reaching from an objective to a subjective presentation of reality? The question is somewhat irrelevant, because metafiction does not concern itself with its ability *per se* to imitate reality. It focuses on the difference between art and reality and displays its consciousness of this distance.

In a work of metafiction the concept prevails that art can never become a true copy of reality. This fact the novelist takes into account, and instead of hiding the disparity between fiction and the external world, the writer exposes it:

> A different way to come to terms with the discrepancy between art and the Real
> Thing is to *affirm* the artificial element in art (you can't get rid of it anyhow), and
> make the artifice part of your point instead of working for higher and higher fi . . .
> That would be my way.[25]

These are Barth's words, but a similar conception may be found in Sterne's novel.

Tristram Shandy displays the difference between "art and the Real Thing" first in its concept of language in general. The Greek motto on the title page of the first volume of the novel indicates Sterne's awareness that the source of men's disagreement may very often be ascribed to the fact that an object gives rise to various and conflicting meanings: "It is not things themselves that disturb men, but their judgments about these things" (p. 1). To arrive at one meaning seems an impossible task and this pertains not least to the significance of words.

In *Tristram Shandy* innumerable misunderstandings arise out of the char acters' disparate interpretations of each others' utterances: The word *bridge* holds different meanings for Toby and Dr. Slop: the one the doctor is making he intends for Tristram's nose and not for Toby's play town. Critics ascribe Sterne's preoccupation with the meaning of words to the influence of Locke: "In fact – and this is a Lockian theme *par excellence* – words do not represent reality, they are merely 'the signs of men's ideas', signs often impure . . . and unstable . . . of such ideas of reality as we can make for ourselves."[26]

In *Tristram Shandy* the disparity between art and reality is expressed not only through different uses of language, but also by the characters' approaches towards the interpretation of reality. Toby has been present at the siege of Namur, but when he has to recount what really happened, how the battle went, he meets with difficulties "as to make his company fully comprehend where and what he was about" (p. 63). Tristram underlines that what complicates Toby's account is "the unsteady uses of words" (p. 67).

To put matters straight, Toby gets hold of a map of Namur, which leads to his study of military books and later to the creation of the model town on the bowling green. This saves him from "a world of sad explanations" (p. 65), and he overcomes his difficulties in making clear to himself and his audience what really took place. What matters to him is to arrive at a truthful representation of reality, and this can be obtained only through a study of facts. His method, then, must be described as empiric, and his work – the model on the green – constitutes a piece of realism if ever there was one.

Toby and Trim go to nearly ridiculous extremes in making the world on the lawn as exactly like the original as possible. And it is important to note that they take the play war as seriously as if it were a real war:

> When the town, with its works, was finished, my uncle *Toby* and the corporal
> began to run their first parallel – not at random, or any how – but from the same
> points and distances the allies had begun to run theirs; and regulating their

approaches and attacks, by the accounts my uncle *Toby* received from the daily papers, – they went on, during the whole siege, step by step with the allies. (p. 338)

Toby and Trim confuse their constructed world with reality.

Trim displays the same tendency on another occasion when he is reading from Yorick's sermon. One part of it deals with the evils of the Inquisition, and Trim mistakes this for an actual report about Portugal, even believing it to be an account of his brother's misfortunes in that country. Walter tries to point out to him that his supposition is wrong: "I tell thee, *Trim*, again, quoth my father, 'tis not an historical account, – 'tis a description. – 'Tis only a description, honest man, quoth *Slop*, there's not a word of truth in it. – That's another story, replied my father" (p. 105). With his last remark, Walter has a fling at Dr. Slop as a Roman Catholic, but his comment also discloses that he recognizes that a written text may be true in a sense other than a factual one.

Compared to Toby and Trim, Walter has just the opposite idea of how to grasp the truth of things. Toby is suspicious of the ability of words to give an adequate interpretation of reality; he turns to "the first springs" (p. 479) of knowledge, to the world of facts itself. Walter has a great trust in words, which he shows, for instance, by his grief when his son is christened Tristram instead of Trismegistus. "His opinion, in this matter, was, That there was a strange kind of magick bias, which good or bad names, as he called them, irresistibly imprcss'd upon our characters and conduct" (p. 38). Toby, whose reasoning is always practical and down to earth, admits: "For my own part, *Trim* . . . I can see little or no difference betwixt my nephew's being called *Tristram* or *Trismegistrus*" (p. 220).

The truth exists for Walter in the words or names themselves, not in what they designate: "of the influence of Christian names . . . he was systematical, and, like all systematick reasoners, he would . . . twist and torture every thing in nature to support his hypothesis" (p. 41). In Walter's case, his not inconsiderable learning forms a barrier between himself and the world. He interprets reality through a mass of set hypotheses. In the same way as "his rhetoric and conduct were at perpetual handycuffs" (p. 150), his writing has little affinity to the external world, though it is in accordance with the rules of rhetoric and discloses Walter's konwledge of the classical authorities on science.

The difference between Trim's empiric approach to reality and Walter's *a priori* knowledge is indicated in Volume V, where Trim (ch. XL) and Walter (ch. XXXVI) give a discourse upon the same topic, "the radical heat and radical moisture within us" (p. 300). Walter, reading from his *Tristrapaedia*, quotes Aristotle, while Trim draws on his experience at the siege of the city of Limerick where the "setting [of] fire every night to a pewter dish full of brandy . . . took off the damp of the air" (p. 304). Dr. Slop satirizes Trim's speech, finding it "emperic" (p. 304). His opinion is fully supported by the rest of the audience who regard this as an indisputable fact.

Walter, on the one hand, and Toby and Trim, on the other, have different approaches to reality which their interpretations and recreations of it disclose. The latter turn to the world of facts, and their view of life stems from their experience and observations. For Walter there exists a short cut to knowledge through systems, and he has great faith in the power of words to get at the truth of reality. But none of them is aware of the disparity between reality and their respective copies of it. Toby and Trim mistake their substitute world for the real one. Walter thinks he has discovered the "North west passage to the intellectual world" (pp. 305-306) in his theory of the auxiliary verbs, and thus he seems to be subject to the same error as his brother and the corporal. They do not recognize that their grasp of the truth can never be absolute, and that a difference between life and art will always remain.

In his narrative, Tristram demonstrates his consciousness of the distance between art and reality, and he discards both Walter's way of approaching reality through words and systems and Toby's empiric method and attempt at a faithful reproduction. Sterne suspects *a priori* knowledge in general. In a letter he points out part of his plan for *Tristram Shandy*: "taking in . . . the Weak part of the Sciences . . ."[27] One may be justified in seeing Sterne's view here as corresponding to Tristram's, because the novel heaps much ridicule not only on Walter's quasi-scientific reasoning, but also on the scientists by profession. He shows how the real world contains just as much ridiculous "learned" dispute by inserting in the novel the authentic "*Memorandum* presented to the Gentlemen Doctors of the *Sorbonne*" (p. 46), which debates baptism "by injection" (p. 44) of the unborn child.

Tristram levels his criticism not least against the connoisseurs of art whose "heads, Sir, are stuck so full of rules and compasses, and have that eternal propensity to apply them upon all occasions, that a work of genius had better go to the devil at once, than stand to be prick'd and tortured to death by 'em" (p. 134). Tristram, then, pays little attention to rules and conventions in his narrative. He even anticipates the criticism levelled against him on this point:

And what of this new book the whole world makes such a rout about? – Oh! 'tis out of all plumb, my Lord, – quite an irregular thing! – not one of the angles at the four corners was a right angle. – I had my rule and compasses, &c. my Lord, in my pocket. (p. 134)

Tristram spurns convention in several ways, for instance by placing his dedication not at the beginning, but in the middle of the third chapter of the first volume.[28] Of greater interest here is his satire on literary practices that aim at giving the fiction in question an appearance of reality. Thus he makes a point of finding the exact date of his conception and showing that the time can be no other than the one he mentions (cf. p. 7). The fact that the date concerns his conception and not his birth suggests that the point here is to ridicule the scrupulous presentation of details in fiction as a means of proving its own authenticity.[29]

Tristram is further poking fun at the idea of the narrator as the teller of truths in his discussion of Yorick's name (cf. p. 18). Tristram here ridicules the device of referring to documentary sources, and thereby pretending that the story is true in a factual sense.

Tristram dismisses Walter's method of going by set rules, and he does not follow Toby's and Trim's example in trying to make his art a faithful imitation of reality (cf. pp. 69-70). Especially in his treatment of time, Tristram shows the impossibility of making the fictional representation equal to the actual experience. Shklovsky describes how Sterne manipulates time in *Tristram Shandy* by impeding the action, and the novelist directs the reader's attention towards the difference between literary and ordinary time, using "the arbitrariness of 'literary time' as material for a game ..."[30]

The following passage makes clear that Sterne operates with several kinds of time experience and that he uses this to ridicule the "truthful" presentation in conventional narratives of his period:

> It is about an hour and a half's tolerable good reading since my uncle *Toby* rung the bell, when *Obadiah* was ordered to saddle a horse, and go for Dr. *Slop* ... so that no one can say, with reason, that I have not allowed *Obadiah* time enough, poetically speaking ... both to go and come ... If the hypercritick will ... measure the true distance betwixt the ringing of the bell and the rap at the door; – and, after finding it to be no more than two minutes ... should take upon him to insult over me for such a breach in the unity, or rather probability, of time; – I would remind him, that the idea of duration ... is got merely from the train and succession of our ideas, – and is the true scholastic pendulum, – and by which, as a scholar, I will be tried in this matter, – abjuring and detesting the jurisdiction of all other pendulums whatever ... [despite the risk of] rendering my book, from this very moment, a profess'd ROMANCE, which, before, was a book apocryphal. (pp. 78-79)

Fluchère points out the difference in this passage between poetic time, time experienced by the characters (Obadiah, etc.), by the reader, and "Time of the history of humanity, whose moments add up to eternity."[31]

The essential disparity, however, exists as Shklovsky has shown, between reading time, which goes by the clock, and Tristram's, the narrator's, idea of time, experienced as duration; an expansion of the moment into eternity. Because of his way of presenting time, Tristram compares his book to a romance, a kind of fiction that was often regarded as false or untrue, due to its imaginary character.[32]

A comparison between Walter's and Toby's ideas of time reveals how the brothers are representatives of the two notions of time: passing, clock-regulated time and time as eternal duration. Walter asserts:

in our computations of *time*, we are so used to minutes, hours, weeks, and months, – and of clocks (I wish there was not a clock in the kingdom) to measure out their several portions to us ... that 'twill be well, if in time to come, the *succession of our ideas* be of any use or service to us all.

Now ... in every sound man's head, there is a regular succession of ideas ... which follow each other in train just like – A train of artillery? said my uncle *Toby*. – A train of a fiddle stick! – quoth my father ... (p. 141)

Toby has few or no ideas about time whatsoever; "of all men in the world, [he] troubled his brain the least with abstruse thinking; – the ideas of time and space" (p. 140). But one may perhaps infer from his intrusive remark, "A train of artillery", that after a life of subjection to military drill, clock-regulated time dominates his existence and his thinking. Toby represents the matter-of-fact, the conventional view of time. In the same way his model town symbolizes the kind of conventional fiction that aims at a close reproduction of reality.

Walter shows that he distinguishes between the two ideas of time. Despite his awareness of and his longing for an existence without the dominance of clocks, Walter has slavishly submitted to a clock-bound regulation of his own life. However, in his writing he finds that clock-time does not work: "He imagined he should be able to bring whatever he had to say, into so small a compass, that when it was finished and bound, it might be rolled up in my mother's hussive – Matter grows under our hands" (p. 282). In his book of instruction for Tristram, Walter tries to keep step with life, but Tristram grows at a greater rate than his father's book about him. Walter is not willing to compromise with his notions about *Tristrapaedia* in his actual writing of it. He struggles on, loyal to the ideal of his thoughts. Consequently he is unable to complete his work, a task performed by his son: "That, in order to render the *Tristrapaedia* complete, – I wrote the chapter myself" (p. 290).

Tristram is willing to "trespass against truth" in his narrative. He is writing a kind of *Tristrapaedia,* but ridicules the idea of keeping his narrative in step with his life which forms the subject matter of his novel (cf. pp. 214–215). The "common writer" referred to by Tristram would at least make an attempt not to let his work be outstripped by life or pretend that no difference exists. Tristram makes explicit his awareness of the disparity between life and art, and that he will not try to reconcile the two in his narrative.

Unlike Walter, Tristram makes terms with life in his art. He settles for less than the ideal, admitting: "There is but a certain degree of perfection in every thing; and by pushing at something beyond that, I have brought myself into such a situation, as no traveller ever stood before me" (p. 393). He here refers to the circumstance that he may visit three places at the same time in his imagination. However, he soon finds that this sort of travelling has to be abandoned: "Let me collect myself, and pursue my journey" (p. 394). He may play with the thought of reaching for perfection, but all the time knowing that such an aim has to be given up. Instead of a complete correspondence between life and art, Tristram advocates a medium position for his narrative, half-way between reality and pure fancy.

Similarly, he maintains that a novel should contain a "just balance betwixt wisdom and folly, without which a book would not hold together a single year" (p. 472). Though he may wish for a maximum quantity of wit and judgement for himself (and his reader) so that he might be able to create a work of the greatest merit, he sees that this would not be the result: "Bless us! – what noble work we should make! ... but oh! – 'tis too much ... 'tis more than nature can bear! – lay hold of me ... I'm dying, – I am gone. – Help!" (p. 144). Such an amount of wit and judgement the writer cannot stomach; he dies and leaves his work incomplete. Thus Tristram again underlines how the creation of ideal art, possessing the utmost of wit and judgement or having a perfect correspondence to reality, does not fall to the lot of any man.

3. Reader as Narratee

The reader constitutes the third element of Kayser's basic situation[33] and in metafiction he usually plays a prominent part. The author of a work of metafiction exhibits his awareness of the reader's participation in the creative process. The reader is not considered merely a passive receiver of the narrative, but shares in the making of the work. To the extent that he is drawn inside the work, appealed to and taken notice of, his role changes from the more passive one of *reader* to that of the *narratee*,[34] sharing at times in the compositional task. Kayser distinguishes between the reader outside the work and the reader, playing a part inside the fiction. In his discussion of *Tristram Shandy*, John Preston has pointed to Sterne's differentiation between "these imagined readers, the lady and the critic" and the reader outside the fiction.[35] By designing the term *narratee* for the reader inside the work, it becomes easier to distinguish between the two.

Tristram takes considerable notice of the narratee. He recounts how his writing has been used as curl papers by the mistress of a house where he has been staying:

> ... so without any idea of the nature of my suffering, she took them from her curls, and put them gravely one by one into my hat – one was twisted this way – another twisted that – ay! by my faith; and when they are published, quoth I, – They will be worse twisted still. (p.405)

Tristram manages here to joke about a matter that concerns him deeply; the reader's conception of his novel. However, when describing Yorick's situation, he displays more directly that he regards the audience's or readers' often distorted opinions as not merely a matter for jests, but of painful consequences to the author (cf. p. 18). Tristram's situation does not fully correspond to Yorick's; he has managed to establish a better relationship with *his* audience, but he takes care that what he wants to say is really brought home to the reader (cf. p. 145).

Tristram's deep concern for the reader's comprehension of his work may perhaps originate in the fact of Sterne's profession as vicar in the Church of England. Central to a preacher is the problem of transmitting a message to the audience. This question will be prominent during the preparatory work with a sermon and influence its writer in deciding its formulation and structure.[36] A preacher is in a unique position compared to that of a writer of narratives; he is present and may watch the congregation's reception of what he has written.

A dramatist's situation corresponds somewhat to that of a preacher in the way that during the process of writing he will take into consideration the effects his play may have on the audience. Tristram compares himself to a playwright: "I have dropp'd the curtain over this scene for a minute . . . the curtain shall be drawn up again" (p. 109). This shows that Tristram considers his task not unlike that of a dramatist, keeping an eye on the audience. However, the congregation in a church may play a more active role than people in a theatre, changing the shape of the sermon in the course of its deliverance. This depends on the preacher's ability to perceive the audience's reactions. A conscientious preacher will at least be able to draw experience from his trials and failures in the same way as Yorick "for it was *Yorick*'s custom . . . on the first leaf of every sermon which he composed . . . to add some short comment or stricture upon the sermon itself" (p. 324).

In the episode where Trim reads Yorick's sermon (vol. II, ch. XVII) the audience, consisting of Toby, Walter and Dr. Slop, plays an active part, interrupting and commenting on Trim's performance and on the sermon itself. Especially the two last mentioned serve as a parallel to the narratee's role in *Tristram Shandy* as a whole, forming two opposing parties. Dr. Slop finds the writer of the sermon too frivolous and not at all in agreement with his own conception of what a priest may allow himself. On one occasion he deplores "the liberty of the press" (p. 95) that gives free scope to such a person. Then he states that the author could need some chastisement from the Inquisition: "in such a case as this, he would soon be taught better manners" (p. 94).

During Trim's reading, Dr. Slop falls asleep – perhaps the most serious proof of his negative attitude. He finds the sermon dull. However, Dr. Slop's behaviour and opinions reflect upon himself: with his sloppy brain, fixed opinions and closed mind, the physician becomes a caricature of the unsympathetic critic whom Tristram fears so much. Walter, together with his brother, represents the opposite party, the positive readers. They listen eagerly, trying to understand what the author has in mind, and on the whole Walter defends him against Dr. Slop's attacks. Thus Walter and Dr. Slop illuminate how the perception of a narrative largely depends on the reader, his qualities and background.

Another aspect of the reader's situation is the narrator's qualifications and abilities to reach him with his message. In the novel this is illustrated not only through Tristram's case. Besides Yorick, Walter and Trim represent the most conspicuous orators in the novel. Their capacities in the field of communication have received considerable critical attention. It has been pointed out that Walter has little success in getting other people to understand him; this difficulty is expressed by his sexual failures.[37] When the news of his son's death reaches him, he makes a speech that defers to conventional oration, but is not at all expressive of his feelings.[38] On the same occasion, Trim moves his kitchen audience to tears with simple words and gestures. He speaks from the heart and awakens the others' compassion.[39] Walter uses an intellectual language and nobody understands him.

Critics agree that the central message of the novel is a call for sentiment or sympathy as the basis for human intercourse and understanding.[40] Robert Alter mentions wit as another means by which communication may take place.[41] Involuntarily Walter demonstrates this. He tries to communicate on an intellectual level, but his speech has one effect not aimed at by himself – laughter. In one episode he reads a passage from *Tristrapaedia* about the use of auxiliaries to instruct children and he chooses a white bear for his example (cf. pp. 307-311). His audience reacts in two ways: Toby, as far as he understands his brother's speech, rejects it. Yorick also expresses his doubts about Walter's method, but he cannot help smiling. So too with the readers outside the work, the you and I. Walter's gestures and words are so studied, such a discrepancy exists between his feelings and their expression that in any observer but his emotionally involved brother, his behaviour and manner of speaking provoke laughter.

Like his father, Tristram appeals to the intellect of his audience. But he does this consciously; with his narrative he intends to make the reader laugh. This effect he wants to enlist from the actual readers outside the novel. A closer look at Tristram's comments to the narratee reveals how he regards the relationship between the actual reader and himself and what qualities an ideal reader should possess from a narrator's point of view:

> Was I left like *Sancho Pança*, to chuse my kingdom, it should not be maritime . . . no, it should be a kingdom of hearty laughing subjects . . . I should add to my prayer – that God would give my subjects grace to be as WISE as they were MERRY; and then I should be the happiest monarch, and they the happiest people under heaven – . . . (pp. 255-256)

Tristram wishes the relationship between narrator and readers to be similar to that existing between a king and his subjects, because in the position of a king he would be endowed with more or less absolute power over the welfare of his subjects. He would be more able to ensure the happiness of the inhabitants of his kingdom than what he may hope as a narrator to create for his readers.

Walter also has designs upon the throne, and he too is concerned about the happiness of his imaginary people, but his means differ from Tristram's:

> "Was I an absolute prince," he would say, pulling up his breeches with both his hands, as he rose from his arm-chair, "I would appoint able judges, at every avenue of my metropolis, who should take cognizance of every fool's business who came there; – and if . . . it appeared not of weight sufficient to leave his own home . . . they should be all sent back, from constable to constable . . . to the place of the legal settlements." (p. 36)

One may infer that Walter, by enforcing laws and regulations, would not only have less chance of making his subjects happy than Tristram, but would arrive at the opposite result to what he intended.

In the relationship between reader and narrator, Tristram considers the latter the dominant part. He is responsible to the reader who has shown him confidence by listening to what he has got to say:

> But courage! gentle reader! – I scorn it – 'tis enough to have thee in my power – but not make use of the advantage which the fortune of the pen has now gained over thee, would be too much – No –! . . . ere I would force a helpless creature upon this hard service, and make thee pay, poor soul! for fifty pages which I have no right to sell thee . . . I would browse upon the mountains . . . (pp. 370-371)

The narrator must not misuse the reader's confidence by boring him with tiresome and learned talk. The reader will constitute the receptive and consequently the more passive party, swayed by the narrator's fancy. Tristram finds that the ideal reader trustfully and of his own free will places his imagination at the mercy of the narrator: "I would go fifty miles on foot . . . to kiss the hand of that man whose generous heart will give up the reins of his imagination into his author's hands, – be pleased he knows not why, and cares not wherefore" (p. 135).

Wolfgang Iser asserts that Fielding and the other 18th century English novelists laced their books with apostrophes to the readers to secure their co-operation. Otherwise the newness of the novel genre might offend and become a barrier to the readers' understanding of it.[42] When the first volumes of *Tristram Shandy* appeared in 1759, the new genre seems already well established by the works of Defoe, Fielding, Smollett and Richardson. In Tristram's comments to the narratee one cannot trace any real anxiety that his book might be misunderstood because the public is not used to fiction.

Tristram worries more about the reader's willingness and ability to appreciate his particular originality and inventiveness. *Tristram Shandy* was published over a span of eight years (1759-1767), and Sterne would study the reactions of the public and even give the critic tit for tat when writing later volumes. In Volume II, chapter 2, Tristram gives an example of his method of bringing the critics to silence: after having invited them to the "party" he engages them in a conversation, refutes their objections, and thereby justifies his own manner of writing (cf.pp. 65ff). By thus exposing the gravity and stupidity of his critics, he forestalls future criticism.

In some of Tristram's comments to the narratee, he pleads for his sympathy: "As you proceed further with me, the slight acquaintance which is now beginning betwixt us, will grow into familiarity; and that, unless one of us is in fault, will terminate in friendship. ... Therefore ... bear with me" (p. 8). But on the other hand Tristram knows that all readers cannot be won over to his side. He even once severs his connection with the critical part of his audience all together: "As for great wigs ... peace be with them! ... mark only, – I write not for them" (p. 150).

Tristram concentrates on the friendly reader. By various means he involves him in the novel: "as we have got thro' these five volumes ... let us just look back upon the country we have pass'd through. – What a wilderness has it been! and what a mercy that we have not both of us been lost, or devoured by wild beasts in it" (p. 311). Tristram uses the pronoun *we* about himself and the narratee, stressing the close relations that exist between them. He entices the sympathetic narratee to make common front with him against the nasty critics.

Tristram may compare the narrator's task to that of an absolute king; the readers become his subjects abandoned to his mercy. Though he sometimes regards this as an ideal situation, on the whole he harbours a more democratic view of the reader's role:

> Writing, when properly managed ... is but a different name for conversation: As no one, who knows what he is about in good company, would venture to talk all; – so no author, who understands the just boundaries of decorum and good breeding, would presume to think all: The truest respect which you can pay to the reader's understanding, is to halve this matter amicably, and leave him something to imagine, in his turn, as well as yourself.
> For my own part, I am eternally paying him compliments of this kind, and do all that lies in my power to keep his imagination as busy as my own. (p. 83)

Tristram takes so much notice of the reader because he is chiefly concerned with communication. What matters to him is that his message gets through to the reader. He uses the word conversation to describe their relationship; a successful intercourse cannot be one-sided, but has to work both ways in a dialogue, in a continual process of give and take. Tristram's frustration with his critics originates in the circumstance that he feels himself misunderstood; his words do not get the intended response and no real conversation can take place. His narrative becomes a meaningless monologue in that case, and he finds it best to break the connection with these readers.

Tristram, however, lives in the hope that the participation of the friendly readers in his narrative will increase. One way of securing this he himself points out; the narrator must not tell all, but make room for the reader's imagination. According to Alter, Tristram all the time deals in double meanings and leaves it to the reader to discover the hidden significance, which is mainly sexual.[43] Preston asserts that Sterne induces the reader to play a part in the fiction by his use of asterisks or by leaving a blank page in which he may draw a picture of Widow Wadman (cf. p. 357).[44] One may also note that the narratee is asked to swear in an empty space (cf. p. 404).

But to be sure of a proper participation, Tristram warns his narratee – in this case "madam" – to take her time and read in an attentive way that allows for thinking things over:

> 'Tis to rebuke a vicious taste which has crept into thousands besides herself, – of reading straight forwards, more in quest of the adventures, than of the deep erudition and knowledge which a book of this cast, if read over as it should be, would infallibly impart with them. – The mind should be accustomed to make wise reflections, and draw curious conclusions as it goes along . . . (p. 43)

Besides teaching the narratee how to read to get the most out of the narrative, this passage also serves as an explanation, and an admonition to approach this kind of narrative on its own terms. Thus, the sympathetic, the ideal reader may share in the final formulation of the narrative simply by his reading of the work.

However, the reader also participates in giving shape to the narrative in another way. He may influence the narrator in the very act of creation. This depends on the extent to which the narrator is willing to pay attention to the reader's situation. In a work of metafiction, where communication constitutes a major theme, the narrator possesses a sharpened consciousness of the reader's significance. Tristram admits that consideration for the reader decides his technique. He explains why he ends a particular chapter though he is in the middle of the story. The narrative has to be served to the reader in a way that pleases him, and the narrator consequently shapes his story in agreement with the reader's wishes (cf. p. 69).

Tristram finds it important that the reader should not be able to foretell the turn of events in his narrative. Perhaps his digressional method may to some extent be ascribed to the narrator's wish to be unpredictable to the reader (cf. p. 59). Because of the digressional method of story telling, the narrator has to take certain precautions out of concern for the reader's comprehension: "when a man is telling a story in the strange way I do mine, he is obliged continually to be going backwards and forwards to keep all tight together in the reader's fancy" (p. 351).

3

Thus, Tristram secures the reader's participation not merely by leaving matters unsaid or half-said and forcing him to use his imagination, but also by forming his narrative in a way that makes his meaning as comprehensible as possible to the reader. These are the means Tristram uses to ensure that the reader takes part in the narrative.

Conclusion

One characteristic feature of the narrator's role in *Tristram Shandy* is the emphasis placed on the difference between author and narrator. This distinction is brought to light by, for instance, "editorial" comments on Tristram's narrative and by reference to the narrator's or Tristram's fictionality. In the novel the narrator presents himself as acting the part of a clown, and this becomes another means of stressing that the narrator plays a role. By arraying himself in the fool's dress, the narrator indicates that first and foremost he intends to procure entertainment, and his task provides a way of escape from the evils of life.

The narrator's calling is illuminated metaphorically through methods of travelling and views on sex. In accordance with his role as clown-narrator, Tristram exhibits an easy-going attitude, free of established conventions. By laughing at reality, he creates a distance between himself and life. Though Tristram underlines his autonomy and independence, a commitment exists on the intellectual level, and the digressional method may be ascribed to the alertness of his intellect. Even if *Tristram Shandy* does not keep the exact balance between story and digressions which the narrator sees as the ideal, he succeeds in realizing his intention of amusing himself and the reader.

A work of metafiction like *Tristram Shandy* deals with the disparity between art and life, taking this difference into account, instead of keeping up the pretence that fiction presents a picture of reality. In the novel the distance is exhibited through conflicting uses of language and through the characters' various ways of interpreting reality. Toby, for instance, makes a model town that measures up to an empirically correct standard. Walter, on the other hand, employs an *a priori* method, using words or names as his point of departure for grasping reality. Tristram differs from his father and uncle in his awareness that the difference between art and reality cannot be bridged, and he shows this by ridiculing conventional literary practices, and by stressing that fictional time does not correspond to clock-time. Tristram is willing to compromise, to aim at less than perfection in art, recognizing that such a solution is the only possible one.

☆

In the examination of the reader's role in *Tristram Shandy*, a distinction was found to exist between the actual reader outside the novel and the narratee, the reader inside the work to whom the narrator directs his remarks. Through his direct comments, the narrator makes clear his conception of the ideal reader. In the narratee he creates a role which the actual reader may slip into and identify with, and thereby the narrator to some extent ensures the desirable attitude of the reader outside the work.

Much attention is given to the reader because she represents an important part of the narrative situation as a whole, which is what metafiction tries to illuminate. *Tristram Shandy* demonstrates by, for instance, Walter's and Dr. Slop's different conceptions of Yorick's sermon, how communication depends on the reader's preconceptions and background. The narrator's abilities constitute another factor decisive for successful intercourse, which in fiction may take place on an intellectual or an emotional level. In the novel Trim establishes a contact with his audience by appealing to the heart, while Walter and Tristram speak to the intellect.

Tristram proves himself more successful than his father because of his greater awareness of the narrative situation. The relationship between narrator and narratee may differ, depending on which of the two is given most attention and weight. *Tristram Shandy*, however, advocates the importance of an equal balance between narrator and narratee, securing the reader's participation by leaving room for the play of her imagination and forming the narrative out of consideration for her understanding.

The view that the making of the narrative depends equally on the narrator and the narratee discloses a great deal about the novelist's "vision of experience". The author regards the artistic process in terms of a collaboration between narrator and narratee, and *Tristram Shandy* discloses this not only in its direct comments to the reader but by the characters' attempts at communication between themselves. In this way the novelist's task takes on a wider significance; his endeavours to express himself artistically become representative of human intercourse in general. The theme of communication forms an important feature in *Tristram Shandy*, the question remains to be answered whether this pertains to other works of metafiction as well.

☆

As an 18th century writer, Sterne explores the human situation, the interrelation between men rather than the relation between God and man. This may be seen, for instance, from the presentation of the narrator's role. Tristram underlines his autonomy, and because of his detachment his position may be compared to that of a god. But Tristram does not make such a comparison himself, and the most he ventures is to draw a parallel between the narrator's situation and that of a king (cf. p. 255). Maybe the reason is simply that as a child of his time, he subscribes to Pope's opinion that "The proper study of Mankind is Man".

Similarly, the discussions of death in the novel deal with its consequences for human existence here and now. In the chapters where Tristram describes his flight (cf. vol. VII), death is not considered a positive force. To Tristram, death means a stop to the life he cherishes so highly and to his writing. The thought that his art may possess the immortality that is denied himself does not offer itself as a consolation to him. He clings to life, deploring its brevity and praising its joys: "Time wastes too fast: every letter I trace tells me with what rapidity Life follows my pen; the days and hours of it, more precious, my dear *Jenny*! than the rubies about thy neck" (p. 469).

Sterne does not debate the metaphysical aspects of writing to any extent, but he makes up for his lack – if it may be so considered – by his keen awareness of man's earthly life, exploring its meaning in terms of fictional creation.

II. Nabokov's *Ada:*
Metafiction as Aesthetic Bliss

During the first twenty years of his exile from Russia, which he left in 1919, Nabokov sustained himself by composing chess problems, among other odd jobs. In his autobiography, *Speak, Memory,* he describes the tremendous mental effort that went into this kind of work and he compares it to the writing of fiction: " . . . competition in chess problems is not really between White and Black but between the composer and the hypothetical solver (just as in a first-rate work of fiction the real clash is not between the characters but between the author and the world)".[1]

One will indeed find that all of Nabokov's 17 novels to date focus, more or less explicitly, on the author's situation, his artistic and existential problems. Ganin, the protagonist of his first novel, *Mary,* plans an elopement with the wife of another Russian émigré. He mistakes her for his own long-lost love, but has to admit in the end that Mary is just a figment of his imagination. This book, written in Russian, was published in Berlin in 1926. Nearly half a century later, in 1974, Nabokov's latest novel, *Look at the Harlequins!* was published. This is a much more elaborate and sophisticated work of metafiction. The author is described as one of the characters, and the whole book may be regarded as a review of Nabokov's own literary career. Nevertheless, like Ganin, the protagonist/narrator is troubled by an over-active mind. His mental state borders on madness and only through recreating the world in works of fiction can he keep his sanity.

Critics have not failed to acknowledge Nabokov's concern with artistic creation, from the very beginning. Khodaševič, a Russian émigré critic, writes in 1937 about Nabokov, or Sirin, which is the pseudonym he wrote under in the 20's and 30's: "Sirin not only does not mask, does not hide his devices . . . but . . . places them in full view . . . This, it seems to me, is the key to all of Sirin."[2] He further states that in this Nabokov is in line with the Russian Formalist School of literary criticism and its call for the effect of "making it strange" (*ostranenie*).[3]

Nabokov's life and literary career from 1919 onwards fall neatly into three major periods. His Russian penmanship spans the years from 1919 to 1940 when he left France for America. All of his Russian novels are now translated into English. His sojourn in the States lasted roughly another 20 years and saw the publication of his first English novel, *The Real Life of Sebastian Knight*, in 1941, together with *Bend Sinister* (1947), *Lolita* (1955) and *Pnin* (1957). Since 1959 Nabokov has been living in Switzerland, and the novels that date from this period are *Pale Fire* (1962), *Ada or Ardor: A Family Chronicle* (1969), *Transparent Things* (1972) and *Look at the Harlequins!* (1974).

Of all Nabokov's novels, *Ada* bears closest affinity to *Lolita* in its choice of motifs. Both books treat illicit love, and Ada and Lolita make their sexual debut at a shockingly early age. On more essential points the two novels differ decisively. While the whorelet Lolita may at best be described as an average American teenager, Ada at twelve is a rather innocent and highly gifted girl. Humbert Humbert, the protagonist of *Lolita*, understands only too late that his feelings for his stepdaughter are more than mere erotic attraction towards a minor. Ada and Van, who soon realize that they are sister and brother, live through their first ardent summer at the ages of 12 and 14 respectively. They remain life-long lovers – at the end of the novel, Ada is 95 and Van 97 years old, and throughout their relationship they have experienced their love as something unique, as possessing a transcendent quality.

The purpose of this examination is to consider *Ada* as a work of metafiction, subjecting the novel to a textual analysis which will centre on three factors: the conceptions of narrator, narrative and narratee as presented in the book. The main tenor of criticism of *Ada*, as of most of Nabokov's works, is that the novel brilliantly displays the author's technical and verbal skill, but has no general human interest.[4] The present analysis hopes to refute such a view and reveal how the author intends – and manages – to create moments of intensity, of eternity, of poignant art through his masterly detailed descriptions. In this novel the author struggles with "problems of infinity, eternity, identity, and so forth", to use Nabokov's own half-ironic description of his work.[5]

1. Narrators as Lovers

When discussing the concept and role of the narrator in *Ada*, the first problem to be considered is: Who is telling the story? The novel does not yield an unequivocal answer to this question. The book is mostly narrated from the authorial, 3rd person point of view. At the end of the opening chapter, the first intrusive remark occurs. Ada objects to the clumsy repetition "whose hue" in the preceding paragraph: "Hue or who? Awkward. Reword! (marginal note in Ada Veen's late hand)."[6] Ada's comment hints that Van should be regarded as the narrator of at least the foregoing passage, especially as this is a personal reminiscence of his.

On other occasions the roles are reversed: Ada is intended to represent the narrator with Van as the commentator. In chapter 17 the narrative deals with Ada's birthmark, which she thinks stems from her mother, who had hers removed being "in love with a cad who complained it resembled a bedbug ... 'Cad is too strong,' remarked Van. 'I used it fondly.' 'Even so ...' " (p.105). This bit of conversation indicates that one should realize that Van is not the sole narrator. Ada shares in the task.

Very often the reader is left in doubt about the exact identity of the narrator, and he is *meant* to be so. He is given to understand that there are two narrators, Van and Ada, and that they sometimes take turns at the task of telling the story. This is made clear by for instance comments like "Go on from here, Ada, please!" (p. 70) and "now it's really your turn, Van" (p. 71).

But mostly the reader does not know which of the two is telling the story. The narrators' individualities seem to fuse in the joint effort of recording their love story. The narrators are both separate and one, relying "on the mutual correction of common memories" (p. 109). This paradox is also emphasized when Ada objects to Van's description of an intimate scene and he answers: "Sorry, no — if people remembered the same they would not be different people. That's–how–it–went." And Ada: "But we are not 'different'!" (p. 120).

The shift between one and two narrators has its parallel in the use of changing viewpoint. Mostly the 3rd person point of view is applied. The readers know there are two narrators and also in some passages that one of them provides the talking. When Van and Ada speak about themselves in the 3rd person, this adds to the narrative a tone of objectivity. The narrators' detachment from the story is clearly felt.

Van and Ada's aloofness from the proceedings of the past is also disclosed when Van, for instance indicating to his typist the emotionally strong scene of Lucette's suicide, spells out the difficult words (cf. p. 494). Thus the narrators present their past in perspective. This is directly stated at times: "After the passage of about eight decades all this sounds very amusing and silly – but at the time ..." (p.295). Through the use of the 3rd person point of view, the story attains a more general significance.

Sometimes the first person narration occurs (cf. pp. 124-5), and even the first person plural "we" is used at times (cf. p. 338). It appears as if the narrators despite their general detachment cannot help making their separate personalities felt at times. The reader is reminded of the fact that after all the story has two narrators. The occurrence of the first person point of view in the 3rd person narration underlines that the "family chronicle" is the result of a collaboration between two narrators. The use of changing viewpoint indicates that the narrators are paradoxically both "different people" and the same one.

The use of two narrators creates a special effect on the presentation of the narrative. Van and Ada represent two ways of tackling the narrative task, as will be seen from their separate handling of artistic work. Finally their individual approaches merge in their work on the family chronicle.

In his reminiscence of "Nabokov as teacher" Ross Wetzsteon quotes a pet phrase of the author's: "the passion of the scientist and the precision of the artist," adding that this saying "could well stand as an epigraph" on Nabokov's work.[7] This phrase is particularly relevant to *Ada* as an apt description of the two main characters. Ada, the scientist, is passionately devoted to the study of lepidoptera and botany. Van pursues his career as psychiatrist, but he soon understands that all his undertakings indicate that his real calling is that of an artist.

Science and art combine in the relationship between Ada and Van. Ada subtly hints at this when she says: "But we are not 'different'! Think and dream are the same in French. Think of the *douceur*, Van!" (p.120). Ada is here probably meant to represent the thinking aspect of the narrator and Van that of dreaming. That the alliance of the Veens signifies a union between art and science is also stressed when Demon describes a painting by Bosch. The two factors "passionately . . . incestuously . . . meet in an insect, in a thrush, in a thistle . . ." (p. 436).

It is further pointed out how Bosch here "was just enjoying himself by crossbreeding casual fancies just for the fun of the contour and color . . ." (p. 437). Bosch's painting mirrors the novel itself which constitutes a "crossbreeding" of art and science in the union between Van and Ada. In the course of their relationship the lovers undergo a similar development. The two tendencies become manifest and merge in both of them individually, as they themselves blend in the co-operation of Vaniada.

Before they start their life together they are both creative. Ada, the scientist, works directly with natural phenomena breeding butterflies in her larvarium, even mating them "by hand" (p. 57). Her interest in natural science expresses her relation to and concept of reality. It is directly stated that the narrators consider "reality and natural science . . . synonymous" (p. 77) in their chronicle.

Ada's attitude to nature or reality is revealed when she is teaching her sister to draw flowers. She insists that Lucette is "to use for model a live specimen of another orchid" (p. 289) in addition to the one in the botanical atlas. She rejects mechanical reproduction and objects to Lucette's idea of copying by placing a transparent paper over the picture in the book. The flower pictures she makes are "realistic" to the extent that she produces an art close to nature, even based on scientific study and knowledge, though she does not refrain from "crossbreeding" species at times à la Bosch (cf. p. 99).

Instead of breeding and collecting butterflies she likes in later life "to film them in their natural surroundings" (p. 567). This underlines how the general strain of her artistic endeavours is down-to-earth, even of a documentary quality. Science and art overlap in her pictures as in her filming. In her own life she undergoes a development from science to art when she goes in for acting instead of a career as a natural scientist. One interest does not supplant but merges with the other in her maturity. Before Van entered her life, her interest in natural science was at its peak. At the time of their joint narration pure "Natural history was past history" (p. 95).

Van finds Ada's talk about larvae and flowers rather boring and he has no interest in natural science. His "breeding" takes place entirely in his head, in lofty speculations. He writes his first literary production, a novel called *Letters from Terra,* without Ada's assistance and at a time when their relationship was at its lowest ebb. It is based on "vagaries observed by him in mental patients" (p. 338) about the planet Terra. The book "showed no signs of life whatsoever" (p. 338), and it leaves its author with a feeling of emptiness.

Van's art constitutes the opposite of Ada's, with its foundations in her own experiences and sense impressions. It is based on the whims of mentally deranged people and has little or no relation to his own world, Antiterra. Also in Van the scientist joins hands with the artist, but his field of science seems rather close to artistic fantasies. It is a kind of philosophic psychiatry, centring on the problems of time and space.

Van writes several books in between the first, *Letters from Terra,* and the family chronicle, and Ada is mentioned as sharing in at least one of them. Even so, the last of Van's works marks a new stage in his literary career: "all his published works . . . were not epistemic tasks . . . but buoyant and bellicose exercises in literary style. . . . why did he not choose a big playground for a match between Inspiration and Design" (p. 578). Ada "with all her larvae" plays an important part in the development of this last book, of which she is the heroine and co-narrator.

Some attention should be paid to the relationship of Marina and Demon, who act as foils to their children, Ada and Van. The intense affair of their parents does not survive the changes worked by time on their appearance. Looking at an elderly version of Marina, Demon cannot discover any resemblance between her and the youthful image of his memory (p. 251). Van, on the other hand, recognizes *his* Ada despite her changes when they at last move permanently together in their fifties. Ada and Van form a unique relationship, experiencing a supreme happiness transcending the here and now: "for yet another immortal moment they stood embraced . . . enjoying . . . the 'happy-forever' feeling at the end of never-ending fairy tales." (p. 287). In their union Ada's feeling of palpable, poignant reality combines with Van's sense of dimensions. In one incident, Ada, clinging to the moment, insists that "this is reality, this is pure fact – this forest, this moss . . . this cannot be taken away, can it?'' To which Van answers ''it will, it was'' (p. 153), and he wants to move on as he is afraid of being lost in the forest. He has a need of orientation, of making ''sure of our whereabouts and whenabouts'' (p. 154). If their love in their combined artistic effort is to outlast the moment, a perspective of time and place has to be joined with the reproduction of acute sensual impressions.

Van and Ada become the ''unique super-imperial couple'' amongst an innumerable quantity of lovers, both because of the quality of their love *and* the quality of their rendering of it in their narrative. What they aspire towards in *their* art – and Nabokov in *his* – Ada describes as ''the most difficult'': It is the presentation of ''beauty itself as perceived through the there and then'' (p. 71). The problems of time and space will be dealt with in the discussion of the narrative as essential in *Ada*.

In the novel, Van and Ada function both as narrators and as characters. The two roles overlap, and the fictitious nature of both these parts is underlined, for instance in the last chapter: ''By the way, who dies first? Ada. Van. Ada. Vaniada. Nobody.'' (p. 584). The two Veens become in the end indeed Vaniada, which is a name referring to their ''family chronicle''. And ''Nobody'' does not mean that the deaths of the lovers remains ambiguous.[8] Rather it points to the fact that as fictional characters they do not ''die'' in the ordinary sense.

Cross-references between the narrators' world at the moment of reminiscence and that of the characters tend to emphasize that narrators and characters alike are not ''real''. Van at 14 has not acquired the habit of a ''post-coital cigarette'' (p. 120). Finishing the description of the Veens' first sexual union, Van at 90 helps himself to ''a Cannabina cigarette'' (p. 122). In this scene the connection between character and narrator is set in relief by a comparison: ''impatient young passion (brimming like Van's overflowing bath while he is reworking this . . .)'' (p.121). The reader becomes frankly amused when the activities of the young and old Van are placed side by side, and this is the satiric effect the narrative is aiming at. Ada complains – and with some reason – that Van here transforms their ''poetical and unique past into a dirty farce'' (p. 120). When the narrator's 90-year-old self intrudes between the young Veens and the reader, one realizes that Ada and Van's tender encounters are fiction after all.

Besides the characters' fictitiousness, another point is also clear from the Veens' double function as characters and narrators. The ''family chronicle'' about Van and Ada, siblings and lovers, illuminates their second role, that of narrators. The love story is presented as a metaphor of the narrative function. The underlying idea is the obvious parallelism between sexual and verbal communication – a characteristic most works of metafiction seem to share – and the narrator states nonchalantly and en passant that communication constitutes the theme of the novel: ''The novelistic theme of written communications has now really got into its stride'' (p. 287).

The drama of Van and Ada's love is re-enacted in words and transposed to the level of art, and it is this aesthetic level, not the love story *per se,* the novel deals with. As youngsters, the lovers play with each other and with words in intricate contests of scrabble. In old age they are left with the linguistic games. Van, we learn, is at 87 "completely impotent" (p. 575), but despite his physical deterioration, he experiences an "unbelievable intellectual surge, [a] creative explosion" (p. 577). Sexual activity has been replaced by mental activity and expresses symbolically the creation of art.

The relationship between the siblings is remarkable in many ways, not least because of their superior intellects (Ada sports an IQ of above 200). This intellectual standard manifests itself in the fantastically complicated codes they invent for their love letters (p. 161). Despite the difficulties combined with the use of the codes, they put themselves to the task of expressing their feelings in the coded words. Communication accordingly suffers. The lovers have a hard time both writing and reading the disguised messages. The coded letters illustrate the narrators' position in the novel. Their method requires a high level of technical skill and demands a mental effort both of narrator and reader.

The Mascodagama act – Van walking on his hands – provides another illustration of the narrator's task and the skill required of his performance. This trick is directly compared to the work of the narrator: "Van on the stage was performing organically what his figures of speech were to perform later in life – acrobatic wonders that had never been expected from them and which frightened children" (p. 185). The Mascodagama act takes the audience by surprise because of its unexpected, subtle deception. Masked Van performs first on his hands with a false head between his legs, and the audience thinks he is walking normally on his feet because of the disguise. When he next turns over on his feet, the audience is equally deceived, believing him now to be strutting around upside down. Finally, Van unmasks himself, "dancing a jig on his hands" (p. 184).

The Mascodagama trick indicates the deception bound up with the narrator's performance in *Ada.* The novel gives the impression of being "a family chronicle". This one assumes from the title and the elaborate chart of the family tree. In one sense, the title is justifiable: Ada and Van both belong to the Veen family, being sister and brother. One soon realizes that this label is misleading, and the account of the Veen family turns out to be a love story between siblings. However, this too, proves to be a false lead when Van, the narrator, like Van on the stage, unmasks himself, disclosing that the novel deals with the narrator's extraordinary performance, his ability to deceive and to show his deception.

Some pages prior to the Mascodagama incident, Van describes his encounter with a card gambler, Dick, who acts as his foil. Dick hides his tricks. When playing poker, he employs all kinds of small mirrors and lenses. Van outwits him by using some tricks of his own, not failing to show his contempt at the other man's naive deception. On a later occasion Dick informs Van of a new method of marking the cards which he now prefers to the trick with mirrors: "that's the beauty of it, no preparations, no props, nothing!" (p. 177).

Dick's stratagem is comparable to the narrator's practices. The use of foils, for instance, may be seen as a kind of "mirror" device, and in mosts novels the narrator pretends to do without props, trying to hide the fictitiousness of his work. Dick is a scoundrel and can therefore not be "called out" for a duel by Van, who belongs to another class of people. In this way the disparity between the two men is underlined: Van relies on props, a fact of which he makes no secret. As in the final stunt of the Mascodagama act, Van reveals his tricks. Also like Mascodagama in a special Oxford performance, he parodies himself, as seen for instance in the incident with the coded letters. One may be tempted to ask whether there is nothing more to *Ada* than the circus tricks of the narrator; his masked game, so to speak. As will be shown in the discussion of the narrative, the metaphor of the Mascodagama act is not exhausted. It is linked with the concepts of fiction and reality in the novel.

2. Narrative as Revealed Deception

The ideas of space and time are important in the concept of the narrative as presented in *Ada,* and both of these aspects concern the relation between fiction and reality in the novel. The problem of space in *Ada* focuses on the constellation of the "sibling planets", Terra and Antiterra. It may be useful to recall that the Mascodagama act involves a threefold deception, and is indeed a case of "standing a metaphor on its head" (p. 184). Dealing with the relation between Terra and Antiterra, the narrator again uses the handwalking trick, but now in a verbal performance.

For the sake of clarity, it may be worthwhile first shortly to consider the three layers of deception, before resorting to the more detailed analysis of the meaning of space in the novel. Thus, in *Ada* Terra and Antiterra figure as two planets, Antiterra being the world of Van and Ada, and Terra is described as a place believed in by a few and rejected by most people as a chimera in the minds of lunatics. Secondly, Terra and Antiterra suggest "reality" and the fictional world respectively. Besides, the two sibling planets metaphorically express the relationship between Van and Ada. Finally, Terra and Antiterra exist as possibilites in the mind, more exactly in the narrator's imagination.

The world of the novel, "our terrible Antiterra" (p. 338), is described as a contrast to "Terra, the Fair", which is presented as a wild notion of deranged minds. But many people in Antiterra think of it as a heavenly place. The insane, such as Aqua, Van's formal mother, report that it is a world of "alabaster buildings one hundred stories high ... giant flying sharks ... magic-music boxes talking and singing, drowning the terror of thought" (p. 21). Our western society of the mid-twentieth century is easily detected in this "Eden".

Politically, also Terra differs from Antiterra. The main contrast which the Antiterraneans find "sidesplitting to imagine" (p. 17), concerns the position of Russia on Terra as a country situated on the other hemisphere. On Antiterra Russia is an American province somewhere north of the U.S. The two worlds do not correspond completely in time either: "a gap of up to a hundred years one way or another existed between the two earths" (p. 18). In a filmed version of Van's book about Terra, the year 1940 Terranean time corresponds roughly to 1890 on Antiterra.

One puzzling feature of Antiterra, which explains what it actually represents vis-à-vis Terra, is the so-called Lettrocalamity. This disaster is not described except for its results: the banning of telephones, tape-recorders, motors and similar implements (cf. p. 147). The use of magnetism is forbidden and even the word is considered obscene.

Probably, "Lettro" is meant to suggest a pun on "electro" and "letters", to the effect that the modern era, ushered in by the utilization of magnetism and electricity, was a calamity for letters or literature. In contrast to the people of Terra, the Antiterraneans are for instance forced to fall back on letters or the written word instead of communication via telephone. Marina has just explained to Van that formerly telephones were in use at Ardis Manor, when a servant comes up with a letter from her husband (p. 82). On Antiterra they do not have music from magic "boxes" or loudspeakers to blunt their senses and ability to think.

The "Lettrocalamity" results for one thing in stimulating the imagination of the Antiterraneans and dreams of Terra flourish to a greater extent than before the ban. Terra itself, the "heaven" of technical wonders, appears as a sterile world and a place, ironically enough, the Antiterraneans are believed to inhabit after death.

Apparently, then, Antiterra represents the world of fiction, Van's and Ada's habitat and a slightly distorted version of the readers' "Terra". To explain why Russian language and culture have such a prominent place on the American Antiterra, it is tempting to refer to the background of the author in whose mind reminiscences of Russia certainly blend with those from his American years. The time gap of some fifty to a hundred years between the two earths seems plausible when one bears in mind that the novel was written in the middle of the twentieth century while the events in the book take place from the 1880's onwards. So far the relation between the planets appears logical enough.

However, the reader's sense of reality becomes confused when one recognizes that Terra represents the normal 20th century westernized society and this from the point of view of Antiterra is considered a wild whim. Which is the real world? Antiterra despite its anachronisms comes alive and seems plausible enough. Terra with its "flying sharks" and "drowning . . . of thought" appears nightmarish and unreal, though after all this world is presented as an all too credible picture of the readers' "Terra".

In this way the constellation Terra/Antiterra serves for one thing to underline the correspondence between fiction and the "real" world, and secondly, to underline the ambiguity of the concept of reality. The fictitious world may have a claim on reality within its own terms.

The confusion about reality and fiction which the novel creates has its counterpart in *Ada* itself. The film based on Van's *Letters from Terra* re-kindles the belief in the existence of Terra and people question the reality of their own Demonia or Antiterra: "Demonian reality dwindled to a casual illusion . . . Our world *was*, in fact, mid-twentieth-century . . . Terra" (p. 582). The readers of *Ada* respond in the same way as the film spectators: The earth with its "flying sharks" appears illusory described from the point of view of Antiterra, and they recognize the Antiterra of *Ada* as more real.

When discussing above the second layer of deception in the Terra/Antiterra constellation, the sibling planets were referred to as a metaphor of the relationship between Van and Ada. The correspondence between the planets has to be viewed in the light of the Veen union to be fully understood.

On Antiterra, theories about the two earths centre on the question of their identity which some reject and others confirm. The "believers" find the slight dissimilarities that do exist unimportant and they assert that

> two chess games with identical openings and identical end moves might ramify in an infinite number of variations, on *one* board and in *two* brains, at any middle stage of their irrevocably converging development. (p. 19)

This comparison presents the deceptions of *Ada* in a nutshell. The description of the planets also pertains to Van and Ada, who, with the same set of parents, have "identical openings" and whose loves eventually merge. The reference to the "variations" that occur within "two brains", suggests that Terra and Antiterra as well as Van and Ada are identical. Though differences in act or appearance may occur, these belong to the surface and do not concern their essence. Lastly, the "*one* board" indicates that the story of the planets and of the two Veens has its origin in the narrator's mind – as will be discussed later.

The connection between the planets and the human siblings may be seen, for instance, in Van's parentage. Van and Ada share Demon and Marina as their parents, but Van feels closer to his official mother, the insane Aqua: "it would have been so much more plausible, esthetically . . . if she were really my mother." (p. 30). Spiritually, he is the son of Aqua, whose belief in Terra he also nourishes. With Demon as his father, the planets Terra/Antiterra meet in Van, as Demonia is another name for Antiterra.

The two worlds also merge in the family chronicle, the Veens' joint narrative task. In the constellation Terra/Antiterra, Van represents mainly Terra and Ada Antiterra. The letters Ada writes to Van out of the agony of rejected love are set up as a contrast to Van's "Terranean" letters: "Ada's letters breathed, writhed, lived; Van's *Letters from Terra*, 'a philosophical novel,' showed no sign of life whatsoever" (p. 338).

At fourteen, Van is tormented by the ideas of Terra and the endless space he senses outside Antiterra:

> His nights . . . were now haunted not so much by the agony of his desire for Ada, as by that meaningless space overhead, underhead, everywhere, the demon counterpart of divine time, tingling about him and through him, as it was to retingle – with a little more meaning fortunately - in the last nights of a life, which I do not regret, my love. (pp. 73–4)

His philosophical speculations, metaphorically presented as interminable space, lead to a void without Ada. The union of the lovers results in the family novel which becomes a book about Terra and Antiterra, Van and Ada, philosophical speculations and sensual love.

But more than anything else, the novel deals with the relation between fiction and reality, the two worlds between which the narrators move. Van states that he feels the two of them are like "secret agents in an alien country". To which Ada replies: "Spies from Terra?" (p. 264). As narrators of a fictitious world, they are indeed spies from the "real" world. This comparison also implies that through their supreme happiness they become uniquely different from their ordinary surroundings, and further it may suggest that in the fictitious Antiterra, in the confusions of illusion and reality, their relationship stands out as the only reality.

Finally, we have to penetrate the last layer of deception (which is the narrative itself) by considering how the ideas of Terra and Antiterra are presented as notions within the narrator's mind. Van is one of the few people on Antiterra who takes the ideas of Terra seriously and guesses its true nature. His concept of Terra differs from that of the other "believers". He sees this planet as situated not in "outer [but in] inner space" (p. 339), and he accepts "the existence of Terra . . . as a state of mind" (p. 264).

Terra is the domain of dreams and lofty philosophical speculations. Van's unfinished dissertation bears the title: "Terra: Eremitic Reality or Collective Dream?" (p. 182). Since the thesis is not finished, this means perhaps that Van is open to and rejects none of the possibilities: Terra is both dream or fiction *and* reality and the same pertains to Antiterra, its sibling planet.

In the Mascodagama act Van is "overcoming gravity" (p. 185). He repeats the trick with his narrative where he conquers "gravity" by wrenching himself loose from the conventional ideas about Terra and Antiterra, reality and fiction. Gravity is essentially also a magnetic power, the use of which is forbidden on Antiterra, where people believe that the Government keeps the identity of the two planets a secret (cf. p. 582). This may imply that the Lettrocalamity has the positive result of rekindling literary culture, but also the true relation between fiction and reality.

Van is able to free himself from "gravity" and to stand the accepted, usual conventions on their heads. He does not attack the problem of mimesis in the usual way by undertaking a mere act of imitation. Van tackles the problem from the outside, as it were, by dealing with the relation between fiction and reality as such, making mimesis the subject of his narrative.[9]

His "overcoming gravity" results in "a richly colored nether world that he had been the first to discover" (p. 185). This "nether world" indicates on the one hand Antiterra, Van's and Ada's domain, which he discovers afresh when he looks at it from a new angle. The phrase also refers to the book itself: *Ada*, it is stated, means "hell" in Russian. The novel is indeed rich and colourful despite the fact that it deals with the philosophical problem of the artist's handling of the relation between fiction and reality.

The Mascodagama performance gives Van enormous satisfaction because he manages to overcome the absurd task of expressing "something, which *until* expressed had only a twilight being (or even none at all – nothing but the illusion of the backward shadow of its imminent expression)" (p. 184). Here Van reveals the innermost, the real deception of fiction: His narrative is after all nothing but artifice, engendered in the mind.

The problem of space in *Ada* is presented in the relation between the sibling planets, and to "overcome gravity" means, roughly speaking, to understand the connection between fiction and reality. In the Mascodagama act, which metaphorically expresses the narrator's performance in creating the novel, "overcoming gravity" is compared to and mentioned as "a triumph . . . over the ardis of time" (p. 185). "Ardis", the narrator explains, is a Greek word, meaning "the point of an arrow" or "arrowhead", and may be intended as a pun on "ardour". "Ardis Hall" is the name of the Veen manor, the setting of Van's and Ada's first amorous summers. "The ardis of time" in the novel refers to moments of intense experience, for instance the physical embrace of the lovers.

The instants of happiness are felt as palpably real to Ada and Van:

> It would not be sufficient to say that in his love-making with Ada he discovered . . . the agony of supreme 'reality'. Reality, better say, lost the quotes it wore like claws . . . The new naked reality . . . lasted a moment, but could be repeated as often as he and she were physically able to make love. (pp. 219–20)

The reality of "the ardis of time", moments of ardour, is transitory and limited to the duration of the lovemaking: "The direction of Time, the ardis of Time, oneway Time, here is something that looks useful to me one moment, but dwindles the next to the level of an illusion obscurely related to the mysteries of growth and gravitation'' (p. 538). To triumph ''over the ardis of time'' means, then, to grasp a reality outside the intensity of acute sensual experience.

When the narrators in old age consider the development of their love, their memories work differently; Ada sees the relationship in terms of ''an extremely gradual and diffuse growth'' while Van selects ''specific episodes branded forever with abrupt and poignant . . . physical thrills'' (p. 110). The novel is a combination of both methods of reminiscence, which correspond to the different conceptions of time.

The ardis of time has its counterpart in ''the texture of time''. This is a title of one of Van's works and presented in Part IV of *Ada* (pp. 535 ff.). Here Van goes against the usual notion of time as ''passing'' or ''lapsing''. To him, time is duration. Nabokov explains that in *Ada* texture ''is precisely in everyday life . . . that we can concentrate on the 'feeling' of time and palpate its very texture.''[10]

But ''texture'' of time is intimately bound up with the ''ardis'' of time as illustrated by Van's experience during the time he receives Ada's ardent love letters. Their number of five grows in Van's memory, when he looks back, to at least fifty:

> No doubt the singular multiplication of those letters in retrospect could be explained by each of them casting an excruciating shadow . . . over several months of his life, and tapering to a point only when . . . the next message began to dawn. But many years later, when working on his *Texture of Time,* Van found in that phenomenon additional proof of real time's being connected with the interval between events, not with their 'passage' (p. 337)

The moment when the letter arrived constitutes an ''ardis'' of time, but the interval between the letters are felt as ''texture''. The moments between the arrival of the letters are experienced as equally real as the time of the actual reception of them. This is because the acuteness of the outstanding moment – when the letters arrive – multiplies in the time span in between events, just as the letters become fifty in his memory.

Important in Van's theory is the concept of past and present time. The past becomes a reservoir of impressions or ''an accumulation of sensa'' (p. 544). The family chronicle of Van and Ada calls forth both the ''textures'' of the past and the moments of ''ardis'' of time.[11] According to Van's theory, the present is considered as the most immediate time span one is aware of. In the present, the ''textures'' of the past may be recalled.

To Van, the future appears as non-existent and illusory because ''our hopes can no more bring it into existence than our regrets change the Past'' (p. 560). The texture of time is a *now*-feeling which the narrators may experience at the moment of recreating the past and which is imparted to the reader at his

4

moment of perusing the novel. It seems logical that the narrator should repudiate the future as the narrative comes alive only at the moments of creation and reading.

When the narrator speaks of his triumph "over the ardis of time", this implies that he does not succumb to the fictional world and its concepts of reality. He has liberated himself from the lovers' point of view, who see the moments of intense experience as the only real moments. The narrator points out that another way of experiencing the reality of time consists of grasping the texture of it in between the instants of intense happiness.

The narrator's experience and concept of time as texture versus the characters' ardis of time underlines the ambiguity of time's reality as presented in fiction. The moments of Van's and Ada's love together, their ardis of time, are a precondition and a necessity for the experience of the texture of time, but they are not real to the narrator and the reader before recaptured in fiction. [12]

The problems of time and space in *Ada* are essential aspects of the narrative. In the book the narrator tries to express the relation between fiction and reality through his presentation of the ideas of space and time. Space is mentioned in the narrative as "the demon counterpart of divine time" (p. 73). Van has earlier attacked these problems separately: His *Letters from Terra* deals with his idea of space, and he tackles the problem of time in the book *Texture of Time*. In *Ada* his separate efforts merge. The novel becomes "Space-Time" (p. 562), a "cross-breeding" between the chief factors a narrator has to come to terms with in his work.

In this discussion of the concept of the narrative, some attention must be given to the literary allusions in *Ada*, which serve to underline the fictitiousness of the book. From the opening sentence, which is a slight distortion of the first line of Tolstoy's *Anna Karenina*, references to the works of the other writers abound. [13] To give just one example: Bored Van looks out of the window at "a larch plantation, borrowed, Ada contended, from Mansfield Park" (p. 231). This allusion is used as a mere embellishment to the general theme of stressing the illusory reality of the novel.

More important are the examples of "a play within the play," works of art, such as literature and photography produced by some of the characters, and serving as a foil to the novel itself. These works share with the family novel its choice of motif; the Veen siblings.

The governess, Mlle Larivière, writes a story called *La Rivière de Diamants*. The mere overlapping between the title and the author's name indicates that her work is meant to be understood as a parody. The connection to the Veens seems remote. The story deals with a false diamond necklace, and in the family chronicle a genuine necklace, which Van presents to Ada, recurs as a leitmotif. Van breaks the necklace when he learns that Ada is deceiving him, and the work on their novel is described as the threading of beads "in the torn necklace" (p. 109).

The governess points out that in her story "every detail is realistic" (p. 87). But hers is a pure surface realism, an attempt to reproduce "the drama of the petty bourgeois" (p. 87). She fails, however, because she stupidly overlooks the most important detail of all; and consequently "the story lacked 'realism' *within its own terms*" (p. 87). Mlle Larivière is too shortsighted to discover the drama that goes on under her very nose. She has no suspicion whatever of the Veen incest, which could have supplied her with a thrilling theme indeed.

The life of the siblings is remotely reflected in Mlle Larivière's fantastic, implausible story, *Les Enfants Maudits*, whose English title reads *The Young and the Doomed*. Cross-references occur between the characters in this novel and the Veens. Marina reads aloud from the film script of this story about the heroine's lovers while Ada is surrounded by two of *her* paramours. The products of the "novelist" Mlle Larivière afford a contrast to the family chronicle because of its conventional and superficial "realism" Eventually the governess has great success as a writer – another indication of the quality of her work.

Kim, one of the servants of Ardis Hall, presents his version of the family chronicle in the form of snapshots in a photo album. The pictures primarily exhibit Van and Ada in compromising situations. This is intended as another parallel to *Ada* and even the family tree is represented in the album in the form of photos of the family portraits from the Ardis gallery.

Nothing is lacking from Kim's album, not even Van's first impressions of Ardis Hall, but there is an important difference: "The first item in the evil series had projected one of Van's initial impressions of Ardis Manor at an angle that differed from that of his own recollection" (p. 398). Kim has watched the lovers from a very special angle. Through his photos the love story turns into pornography. His photographic account has the same standing as the drawings produced by mad people: This is implied when Ada looks at the pictures through "a magnifying glass (used by Van for deciphering certain details of his lunatics' drawings)" (p. 400).

As a revenge on Kim for his peeping, Van has him blinded, which underlines the photographer's mental blindness to the actual events. Also, the whole incident with Kim's album suggests that reproductive art, whether photography or literature, fails to give a true picture of the proceedings of life. Like "realistic" art, Kim's photo album in one way supplies the most accurate copy of the past, but its claims on a realistic rendering are highly disputable. It misrepresents the love story, changing it into "*odious stills*" (p. 500).

Actually, Kim's album provides Van with the idea of giving *his* version of the Ardis romance: "Art my *foute*. This is the hearse of *ars*, a toilet roll . . . I will either horsewhip his eyes out or redeem our childhood by making a book of it: *Ardis*, a family chronicle" (p. 406). Where Mlle Larivière is too fanciful in her rendering of the Veen story, Kim proves too accurate. Still, both produce distortions of "the ardors of Ardis".

51

Also other external observers of the Veens' love affair feel inspired to express themselves artistically. Van's and Ada's relationship becomes the subject of popular ballads and stories: Ada informs Van: "a veritable legend was growing around you and me while we played and made love . . . 'All of which,' said Van, 'only means that our situation is desperate' " (pp. 408-409). It is suggested in the same passage that especially the aspect of incest attracts the public at large and makes the Veen affair so popular and so widely known: "Eccentric police officers grew enamored with the glamour of incest" (p. 409).

Van's remark that their situation was desperate may be interpreted in two ways: Their relationship is too generally known to be kept a secret from their parents for long. It also suggests that their situation as narrators is hopeless. As proved by the many ballads celebrating their affair, their public at large will only too easily misunderstand their novel as a story about incest and a purely romantic affair. The narrators' intention with their work will not be comprehended or appreciated: They want to present, through the love story of the siblings, the artist's struggle to communicate the ambiguous relation between fiction and reality.

3. Narratee as Intimate Intruder

Apparently the narratee does not play a prominent part in *Ada*. The book, focusing on the narrator's role, deals with the theme of communication, and the work seems to pay much attention to the narrator's skilful handling of words and to care ostensibly less for the reader's comprehension of the final result. Does the novel stress the projector's part and neglect that of the recipient? By way of approaching this problem, it may be worthwhile first to find out who fills the role of the narratee.

The last picture in Kim's album shows the whole staff of Ardis Manor plus an unknown tweed-clad gentleman, who has joined the servants, mistaking them for a group of tourists like himself, inspecting an old castle. The picture is called "Kim's apotheosis of Ardis" (p. 406). This indicates that the romance of Van and Ada undergoes a kind of apotheosis in the minds of the witnesses of their drama, including Kim, one of the recreators of it, and the gentleman, a casual passer-by.

This unknown spectator represents the narratee who, like the gentleman, has a place within the book itself, forming a part of the narrative. Ada, trying to damp Van's suspicions about another lover, swears that this man "was, and has always remained, a complete stranger" (p. 408). In the story he ranks as a mere on-looker. He is not invited to active participation in the narrative, like Sterne's narratee in *Tristram Shandy*.

When, in the course of the story, the narrator addresses the "reader", it is in an off-hand kind of way, as for instance, after the description of the complicated code of the love letters: "the description of our lovers' code . . . with a little more attention and a little less antipathy, the simplest-minded reader will, one trusts, understand . . ." (p. 161). The *our* should indicate that a contact exists, though remote, between narrator and narratee. The comment is inserted primarily to ward off criticism of the difficult, preceding passage. The narrator seems to say that if the reader does not understand, he himself is to blame.

However, in addition to the part of the narratee being represented by more or less remote "readers," the novel provides a set of more intimate holders of that role, i.e. the narrators themselves. Ada and Van share the narrative task, recalling the past and recording the recollections to each other: "Thus they had to rely on oral tradition, on the mutual correction of common memories. . . . Calendar dates were debated, sequences sifted and shifted, sentimental notes compared, hesitations and resolutions passionately analyzed" (p. 109). At first hand, they address their narration to each other. This the novel discloses by the many intruding remarks, especially "in Ada's hand" and by direct mentioning of names. At times, the narrator speaks to a "rereader": "The modest narrator has to remind the rereader of all this . . ." (p. 19). In this case, it is probably Ada who serves as the "reader" and the "rereader" corresponds to the more remote narratee, embodied in the strange gentleman.

Van and Ada as narrators are primarily interested in the response of each other. A successful co-operation exists between them when they share the narrative task and they become for each other the ideal narratee. In whom else could they hope to reach such a degree of understanding and complete communication working both ways from narrator to narratee and vice versa? When Van prefers fiction to drama, it is because "For him the written word existed only in its abstract purity, in its unrepeatable appeal to an equally ideal mind" (p. 425). To Van, Ada possesses this ideal mind. The novel, then, deals with communication, apparently between unique lovers, but actually between an ideal set of narrators and equally supreme narratees.

The "rereader", the more distant narratee, functions as a foil to the ideal ones. This can be seen, for instance, from Van's comment on Ada's description of one of her larvae: "Lovely stuff! said Van, but *even* I did not quite assimilate it, when I was young. So let us not bore the boor who flips through a book and thinks: 'what a hoaxer, that old V.V.!' " (p. 56). Though he has to admit that as a young man he, too, was not taken in by Ada's scientific talk, Van sees himself as a contrast to the casual, stupid reader.

On other occasions the more learned readers get the better of it: "Questions for study and discussion" follow the description of Van's handwalking and an observation that this deprived him later of the ability to shrug his shoulders: "1.

Did *both* palms leave the ground ... 2. Was Van's adult incapacity to 'shrug' things off only physical ..." (pp. 82–3). Such comments ridicule the scholar's approach to the novel. He is brutally torn away from the idyll of Ardis Forest and transported to his classroom or study, and reminded of the fictitiousness of the work.

The intruding comments generally function by opening the reader's eyes to the deception of the literary work. This is even more the case with the appeals to the "rereader" than with Ada's and Van's comments to each other. These remove *us*, the readers outside the work, just one step from the narrative. We recede still another step with the "rereader" such as "the boor".

The literary critics do not get off scot-free, especially those who, in contrast to the more ideal readers, may find the novel a pornographic work: "For the sake of the scholars who will read *this* forbidden memoir with a secret tingle (they are human) in the secret chasms of libraries (where the chatter, the lays and the fannies of rotting pornographers are piously kept) – its author must add ..." (p. 220). This is a kick at readers who will, like Kim, classify the love story as pornographic.

Similarly, Demon's objections to the incest of his children may allude to the reaction of the public at large: "All right, I have bribed many officials in my wild life but neither you nor I can bribe a whole culture, a whole country" (p. 443). Demon condemns the relationship mostly on moral grounds, and indirectly he points to the narrators' difficulty in getting across their message that the book deals with the "theme of written communications" (p. 287) and is least of all concerned with incest. [14]

The "editor" of *Ada* occupies a rather ambiguous role in the work. He shares with the two protagonists the position of a character, but he is also portrayed as a kind of narrator and as a sort of narratee. Mr. Ronald Oranger plays no prominent part among the characters of the novel. He figures, for instance, as the editor of Ada's translations (cf. p. 577). It may seem questionable to claim for him the position of a narrator, but it can be justified on the basis that the narrative is presented as sifted through him before reaching the reader. How to label him seems less important.

Through his reactions to the manuscript of the family novel, Mr. Oranger reveals himself as self-centred and unintelligent with his extremely malapropos remarks, inserted in square brackets in the text. In one of Ada's passionate love letters to Van, the unresponsive "editor" cannot swallow her phrase "in the long ruin" and coolly inserts: "[sic! 'run' in her blue stocking. Ed.]" (p. 335). Like Kinbote in *Pale Fire* he evinces his self-absorption by intruding with irrelevant, personal remarks: "Van Veen [as also, in his small way, the editor of *Ada*] liked to change his abode ..." (p. 365). The function of the "editor" equals that of the narratee generally, in the novel: The "rereader" serves as a contrast to the more genuine representatives of the narratee, Van and Ada; and the reminders of his presence in the narrative stress the fictitiousness of the work.

Conclusion

The fact that the narrative task is shared by two people, Van and Ada, is essential to the concept of the narrator's role in the novel. The joint narrative performance has its reflection, and is metaphorically expressed in the love story. This tends to stress that the book is concerned with Van and Ada as narrators rather than as lovers. Further, the narrator's real concern, his ability to communicate, is suggested by the double function of Ada and Van as lovers and narrators: the sexual communication of the young people corresponds to the narrators' verbal intercourse.

The Mascodagama act also makes clear that the novel deals with the narrative function, and a picture of the narrator emerges as a juggler whose main characteristics are his brilliancy and the fact that he reveals his tricks. Also in the collaboration of Ada and Van, science and art join hands both as regards the contents and the form of the novel.

The narrative debates the relation between fiction and reality through the narrator's struggle with the ideas of space and time. The fictional world of the characters, Antiterra, is presented as a contrast to the "real", 20th century westernized world of Terra. However, the ambiguity attached to the concepts of reality and fiction is underlined when Antiterra emerges as a world more plausible and alive than the modern nightmare of Terra.

The two sibling planets further represent the relation between Van's philosophical speculations and Ada's sensual awareness. These aspects become happily integrated in the lovers' shared narrative undertaking in the "family chronicle".

Lastly, the two worlds of fiction and reality are seen as possibilities in the narrator's mind. Van's mastery of these problems is suggested by his acrobatic Mascodagama trick where he "overcomes gravity" by dancing on his hands. This means that Van manages to free himself from the conventional attitude to the relation between fiction and reality in his narrative. Van's story focuses on the question of mimesis as such rather than on that of fictional reproduction.

Van's narrative also "overcomes gravity" in its presentation of the time aspect. The intense but momentary experiences of reality are transcended in Van's story about his relationship with Ada. In this way the novel combines the two concepts of time as possessing both transience and duration.

The literary allusions with which the novel abounds hint at the illusory nature of its fictional world. This is also the case with the various alternative renderings of Ada and Van's love story in the novel. Besides, these serve as a contrast to the lovers' own version. Mlle Larivière's story, though aiming at realism, becomes too far-fetched and fantastic. Kim's photos are also misrepresentations even if these snapshots copy accurately enough some of the moments in the siblings' love story. But wrenched from the general context, these pictures reduce the genuine love story to pornography. Lastly, the many popular ballads and stories stress the incestuous aspect of Ada's and Van's relationship. This indicates that the public at large will be unable to grasp the theme of the narrative, the narrator's revelation of his struggle to transcend the fictional conventions of time and place in his account of the love story.

The novel operates with two kinds of narratee. There are the general readers who do not understand too much of the proceedings of the novel and function as passive observers. Van and Ada constitute the ideal readers. In the double function of narrators and narratees, they take an active part in the shaping of the narrative and also evince complete understanding of the narrator's intention.

In *Ada* the creation of art constitutes the highest bliss to the narrators, of equal worth to procreation in life and to existence itself. The fictional world is considered an alternative to, and not a copy of, the human one, equally real within its own terms. Nabokov confesses to having no confidence in Einstein's idea of the universe,[15] but he does believe in his own artistic abilities, and without commitment to any creed or school,[16] he cherishes art as the only alternative in a world of flux, political unrest and suppression, as shown most explicitly in *Bend Sinister*.

Nabokov's *Ada* portrays a dreamland, a fairytale Eden, where elements from Russia and America, the 18th and the 19th centuries combine. Nevertheless, Nabokov's universe comes alive with its beautiful perceptiveness and exactness of observation, providing true aesthetic enjoyment, though one has to unwind layer upon layer of deception to get at his meaning.

Nabokov admits that he writes "mainly for artists, fellow-artists and follow-artists",[17] just as Van seems to limit himself to the narratee of the ideal *mind*. However, if *Ada* is lacking in warmth, this is more than compensated for by its dazzling beauty. And in addition to the aesthetic enjoyment, the book's handling of the questions of time, eternity, and reality should indicate that *Ada,* by focusing on the narrator's situation, deals with problems of "general human interest."

III. John Barth's Metafictional Redemption

One of the stories in John Barth's fifth book *Lost in the Funhouse* (1968) is called "Petition". It is written in the form of a letter to the King of Siam from a man who is a Siamese twin. The petitioner implores the King's help to be parted from his twin brother. His stomach is fastened to his brother's back, and the reason he wants to be separated from his brother is that their personalities differ totally despite the physical union

His brother is an extrovert who takes care of the public side of life, earns and spends the money, tends the housework, pursues the women; but he has no feeling for art, or the spiritual side of life, and pays no attention to the wishes of his brother. *He* has to be a witness and silent participant in whatever his brother undertakes, in his getting drunk, in his adventures with women.

The twin writing the petition is himself somewhat of a teetotaller and shy with women, and he describes himself as a dreamer, a thinker, an observer of life. What is making matters worse is the fact that they now have fallen in love with the same woman, Thalia. It has become unbearable to be present at his brother's sexual excesses with the very woman he himself wants to hold chaste conversations with. Then, the petition-writing twin envisions a life on the stage, dedicated to art, for the three of them. The other brother tries to persuade Thalia to go off with him alone to live in a cottage in the country.

This story may serve as an illustration both of the *theme* Barth is mostly concerned with and his *methods* of expression. Barth uses the Siamese twins, who at the same time are two different people, but united in one person, as a metaphor of the poet's situation. The story deals with the theme of the artist's split personality. One part of his psyche is active and extrovert and wants to partake in life: it is a life-directed urge. At the same time the poet is a dreamer, a brooder who keeps life at a distance the better to understand and describe it. This other part of his personality is dedicated to art, and represents in a way a drive towards death.

Barth's technique and way of expressing the story afford ample illustrations of his humour and his pungent sexual world, and it contains an example of the typical Barthian triangle of two men and a woman. Barth draws frequently on sexual symbolism to illuminate his theme and in the case of "Petition" the author's meaning is further emphasized when the woman the twins pay court to is named "Thalia", which is the name of the Muse of comedy and pastoral poetry.

The theme of the two strains in the artist's psyche or the conflict between art and life may be traced in most of Barth's works and seems to constitute Barth's own dilemma as a novelist. In an interview the author has called attention to the continuity of his work: "More than many writers when I am thinking of what to do next, I do it in terms of what I have done before."[1]

However, Barth at the same time points to the changes in his art, and in another interview he has offered a division of his work "into sets of twos".[2] Barth describes his two first novels, *The Floating Opera* (1956) and *The End of the Road* (1958), as "relatively realistic" while *The Sot-Weed Factor* (1960) and *Giles Goat-Boy; or The Revised New Syllabus* (1966) he finds "relatively fantastical or irrealistical". His most recent works to date, *Lost in the Funhouse* (1968) and *Chimera* (1972), are collections of related short stories.

The theme of the artist's divided psyche finds different treatment in the various works. When Barth considers his two first books to be "relatively realistic", this may be partly due to the contemporary setting of mid-20th century Maryland. In *The Floating Opera* the protagonist, Todd Andrews, appears as a psychologically developed character while in Barth's subsequent books, with the possible exception of *The End of the Road,* there are no attempts at realistic portrayal of the characters, who are meant to be seen as types. The two strains of the artist's psyche are embodied within Todd Andrews, whose apparently existential struggle in fact expresses the artist's difficulties in finding a balance between involvement and detachment in his relation to the objective world.

In *The End of the Road* the two aspects of the artist's personality are projected into separate characters: Joe Morgan is the physically active, the extrovert who stamps his image on the world, preferring to walk where it pleases him and symbolically making his own paths across the lawn. Jacob Horner has a completely different approach to the world, which overwhelms him with its complexity and freezes him into mental and physical immobility. Horner finds a temporary solution in articulation or art: "To turn experience into speech . . . is always a betrayal of experience . . . but only so betrayed can it be dealt with at all . . ."[3]

The pair of Joe and Jacob in *The End of the Road* has a parallel in Ebenezer Cooke and Henry Burlingame in *The Sot-Weed Factor*. They both suffer from "cosmopsis", Jacob Horner's existential disease, which deprives man of any ability to act and move. While Eben, the idealist, at first reacts with introversion and detachment, Henry stamps his own image on the world. A similar couple appears in *Giles Goat-Boy* with the idealistic would-be hero George Giles and the pragmatic "swindler" Harold Bray. This pairing also occurs in some of the stories of *Lost in the Funhouse,* for instance the title story and "Petition", while this motif is not so predominant in *Chimera*.

Barth's method of presentation changes considerably with *The Sot-Weed Factor*, which leaves the contemporary scene for 18th century England and America; and still more so with *Giles Goat-Boy*, with its fantastic setting. Barth says about these two books that they are "novels which imitate the form of the Novel, by an author who imitates the role of Author".[4] With these works Barth abandons any attempt at creating "realistic" fiction, and the metafictional quality of the books is more prominent. An even more deliberate distortion of reality takes place in *Lost in the Funhouse* and *Chimera*, with their fabulous, surrealistic setting.

The following discussion will concentrate on John Barth's longest novels, *The Sot-Weed Factor*, and *Giles Goat-Boy*. They occupy a middle position, in several respects, especially with regard to their form, as they are wedged between the "relatively realistic" first novels and his surrealistic last works. Barth produces from his very first book a self-conscious kind of fiction that deals with the artist's or writer's situation, first and foremost the relationship between art and reality and the poet's difficulties of communication.

The Sot-Weed Factor

1. The Poet as Saviour

Very few critics regard *The Sot-Weed Factor* as a work of metafiction.[5] Tony Tanner points out that in *The Sot-Weed Factor* he finds that "What Burlingame does *in* the book, Barth does *with* the book" and that the characters' problems of identity correspond to the author's problems of form.[6] However, Tanner does not develop this idea in the relatively limited space he devotes to the novel. McConnell also recognizes the metafictional quality of the novel when he states that it is "not so much a book about history or historical characters as about the nature of storytelling ..."[7] Like Tanner, McConnell does not elaborate this point to any extent.

Barth has chosen the omniscient, third person point of view for *The Sot-Weed Factor*. The story is told from the first person point of view in Sterne's

Trisram Shandy, Nabokov's *Ada*, Beckett's trilogy, and in the novel to be discussed next, *Giles Goat-Boy*. The first parts of these analyses concerned the narrator, his role and his conception of himself as presented in the novels. In *The Sot-Weed Factor* there is no self-conscious narrator, but there is the protagonist, Ebenezer Cooke, extremely conscious of his role as Poet Laureate of Maryland. The whole novel may be regarded as a process of self-discovery and self-realization for Eben as a man and as a poet. Instead of exploring the narrator's situation, Barth examines that of the poet-protagonist.

In addition, Barth clearly indicates a relation both between himself as the real author of the novel and its protagonist, Ebenezer Cooke, and between the so-called "Author" of Part IV and Eben. John Barth has entitled his novel *The Sot-Weed Factor* and presents in his book a poet, Ebenezer Cooke, who shares his name with the historical author of a long narrative poem with the same title. The plot of the novel follows largely that of the poem.[8]

The parallelism between the author's role and the protagonist is further emphasized in Part IV whose title reads: "THE AUTHOR APOLOGIZES TO HIS READERS; THE LAUREATE COMPOSES HIS EPITAPH."[9] The "Author" admits that when dealing with Captain John Smith in *The Sot-Weed Factor*, he has taken certain liberties with Clio, the Muse of history. In the novel Eben's relation with Joan is of major importance. She releases the poet in him and after their first meeting he is inspired to write a love poem. A parallel exists between Eben's relationship to Joan and that of the "Author" to his Muse. The "Author" acknowledges that "Clio was already a scarred and craftly trollop when the Author found her" (p. 743), and so is Joan Toast when Eben first meets her.

The epitaph Eben has written for himself is presented almost at the end of the novel and stands as a final inscription not only for the protagonist Ebenezer Cooke, but for the novel itself. The two first lines run: "Here moulds a posing, foppish Actor/Author of THE SOT-WEED FACTOR" (p. 755). The title may refer both to Ebenezer Cooke's poem and to the novel, and when this is made ambiguous, the identity of the "Author" of the novel and the protagonist, Eben, blur.

Eben has been mentioned as the protagonist of *The Sot-Weed Factor*, the character with whom the "Author" identifies and through whom he expresses his concerns with his role. Henry Burlingame has been given nearly equal importance, and Henry and Eben represent two aspects of the Poet's personality or two kinds of poets.

In the novel Benjamin Bragg, the bookseller, wants to know what kind of poet Eben is, the better to accommodate him in his choice of notebook:

> would you have 'em think you a man . . . in love with the world? A Geoffrey Chaucer? A Will Shakespeare? Or . . . a Stoical fellow, that . . . hath his eye fixed always on the Everlasting Beauties of the Spirit: a Plato, I mean, or a Don John Donne? (p. 109)

Eben does not know; he feels himself as "much a Stoic as an Epicurean" (p. 109). Eben has, though, great affinities with "a Plato" at this stage.

Eben's uncertainty about what role he should play as a poet, reflects his confused views about existence in general. In his discussion with Bertrand about gambling he brings his servant to the point of distraction by asserting on the one hand: "the gambler is a pessimistic atheist ... To wager is to allow the sovereignty of chance in all events, which is as much as to say, God hath no hand in things." And in the next breath Eben holds: "Who says Yea to Luck, in short, had as well say Yea to God, and conversely" (p. 210). Eben here vacillates between a materialistic world view, and a belief in God which he eventually embraces.

What kind of poet you are depends to some extent upon your religious or philosophic outlook. Eben asserts later that *"A poet is born, not made"* (p. 381), thereby disclosing a belief in the poet's calling as something given him from a source outside himself. Henry Burlingame scoffs at this idea, particularly as he has himself, disguised as Lord Baltimore, appointed Eben Poet Laureate of Maryland before he had "penned a proper verse" (p. 381). Henry avows a mechanistic, materialistic outlook: "Here we sit upon a blind rock hurtling through a vacuum, racing to the grave ... do we seek our soul, what we find is a piece of that same black Cosmos whence we sprang and through which we fall" (p. 345).

Eben and Henry are presented as illustrating contrasting types of poets or various aspects of the poet's psyche. This has its basis in different philosophies or ideas about what is behind existence. In the discussion of the narrative, this point will be considered more closely. Here I will first discuss Henry Burlingame, his outlook and attitudes and the roles he plays.

Eben says to Henry Burlingame: "Thou'rt a Virgil worth a better Dante" (p. 165). This reference suggests that Henry's moral outlook and standards belong to a pre-Christian world. Henry serves as a guide and mentor to Eben, but eventually the roles are reversed; Eben undergoes a development and becomes Henry's teacher.

Alan Holder shows how Burlingame is not concerned with questions of good or evil in the ferocious contest between warring parties in Maryland: His chief concern is action. Henry's sole aim, according to himself, is to match Coode's ceaseless energy in staging a plot.[10] Holder further contends that this seems Barth's sole intention with his novel as well:[11] The author's intention corresponds to that of Henry Burlingame. This discussion hopes to show that Burlingame stands for just one aspect of the poet's psyche, and that Barth has another aim with his novel than constructing a marvellous plot.

Henry is indeed "a plotting Coode" (p. 162). With his extraordinary mental abilities he has great understanding and also concern for the world: "he loves the world, and comprehends it at first glance ... yet his love is flavored with contempt, from the selfsame cause, which leads him to make game of what he loves'' (p. 415). Like his half-brother, Charley Mattassin, Henry has little reverence for God's creation; he despises it and wishes to manipulate it and to think up alternatives. Henry has not quite reached the stage of Charley, whose reaction to the world is expressed by a derisive laugh. Charley has given in to his "dark angel", i.e. the belief that the world is meaningless, while Henry is still contending with this thought according to Ebenezer (p. 422).

Henry's plotting is presented as a consequence of his rootlessness and lack of values. Indeed to play puppet master and to manipulate his surroundings, becomes his credo in life. Existence has no value *per se*, only the act of creation has meaning:

> One must needs make and seize his soul, and then cleave fast to't . . . one must choose his gods and devils on the run, quill his own name upon the universe and declare, ''Tis *I*, and the world stands suc-a-way!' One must *assert, assert, assert*, or go screaming mad. What other course remains? 'One other,' Ebenezer said with a blush. ''Tis the one I flee . . .' (p. 345)

Henry gives vent to a thought frequently expressed in Barth's work, for instance by Jacob Horner: "Articulation! There, by Joe, was *my* absolute."[12]

Eben indicates that the way *he* has chosen is another solution to the existential dilemma. His identity as Poet and Virgin, he feels, is bestowed upon him from above: " 'Twas the choice made *me*" (p. 60). Eben is mostly concerned with the quality of his poetry, which, he finds, depends on a high moral standard. *What* he writes, has to him more significance than Henry's *how*; the process, the scheming itself has significance to Henry, who watches the result with a shrug.

It is made quite clear in the novel that Henry is an alternative to Eben as Poet Laureate. Henry at one time takes on that identity to mislead his enemies (p. 332). When he poses as Mitchell's son, Henry gives himself the mock title of Laureate: "He calls himself the Laureate of Lubricity, that he says means simple smut" (p. 314).

In this novel Barth uses sexual metaphors to express poetic creativity. When Henry is said to have "learnt old Mother English to her very privates" (p. 384), this refers not only to his kind of vocabulary but to his insatiable sexual appetite. And here again the contrast to Eben has to be stressed. When Eben takes pride in his virginity, which he considers a condition for his status as a poet, Henry sees himself as a lover of totality: "I am . . . the Cosmic Lover!" (p. 497).

Henry's incessant plotting has a parallel in his sexual vitality. While Eben nourishes a constant love for Joan Toast, Henry functions as a "Husband to all Creation" (p. 497). Burlingame's fierce sexual activity results from his lack of identity. He is constantly on the go, trying out various roles and relationships. Henry Burlingame figures at times both as Lord Baltimore and as his opponent John Coode. He plays with such dexterity that Eben for one is quite at a loss about Henry's true identity and his intentions. Henry reminds him: "your true and constant Burlingame lives only in your fancy, as doth the pointed order of the world. In fact you see a Heraclitean flux" (p. 330).

The question of Henry's identity is bound up with his procreative capability. He has to prove to his stern father, the Indian chief Chicamec, that he possesses this ability before he is accepted among the Indians and can plead the cause of civilization. The eggplant recipe gives the solution to Henry's dilemma, which is not impotency as has been alleged,[13] but insufficiently developed genitalia. Henry's sexual activities know no retention: "I have sown my seed in men and women, in a dozen sorts of beasts, in . . . trees and . . . flowers" (p. 328). This is because he is excluded from normal intercourse with the woman he loves.

Eventually, after the discovery of the eggplant recipe, Henry fathers a child by Anna Cooke and is accepted by his father. When Henry Burlingame at last finds his identity, his endeavours take on a decisive course; he joins forces with Eben in rescuing Maryland from the chaos of racial wars. The story of Henry's sexuality expresses metaphorically the dilemma of the poet who without basic identity and belief cannot produce work of enduring quality.

Henry embodies the poet or narrator in his function of creating fictitious tales and characters. He possesses a resourceful imagination that never goes dry. But apart from his creativity, Henry is a void, he has no identity, no self. The emphasis is on the aspect of play and pastime, and consequently in the role of narrator or poet Henry figures as a mere entertainer whose work has no lasting value and no message.

Ebenezer Cooke represents an alternative to Henry Burlingame, in nearly every respect; for instance as regards the latter's philosophy, his plotting and his sexuality. Henry is a pessimistic atheist while Eben thinks his calling as a poet is given him from God, whose representative on earth is Lord Baltimore, Proprietary of Maryland. Thus he greatly approves of Father Smith's remark about God as "the Supremest Lord Proprietary of All" (p. 353). He has a firm belief in authority, order and justice.

Eben nourishes a clear conception of the poet's role. When Henry sees his task as that of an intriguing entertainer, Eben has a strong belief in the didactic function of the poet. Lord Baltimore has made him Poet Laureate that he may create a Maryland in song that will "lure the finest families of England to settle there; 'twould spur the inhabitants to industry and virtue, to keep the picture true as I paint it" (p. 76). Eben discovers that the Maryland of his imagination does not correspond at all to the Maryland of reality and he decides that instead of a panegyric, he will describe in detail the treatment he was given. His intention, however, with his poetry has not changed: "Thus might others be instructed by my loss" (p. 458). The poet should, according to Eben, teach and instruct mankind through his verse.

However, before Eben's appointment as Poet Laureate fills his life with a purpose, his existence is not unlike Henry Burlingame's. When they were children, Eben's and his sister Anna's favourite pastime was play-acting. They assumed the identities of various men and women and played wordgames. As a young man, Eben has great difficulties in choosing a career because every profession represents a possibility to him. He may easily imagine himself in the role of every man on earth: "He admired equally the sanguine, the phlegmatic, the choleric" (p. 11). When Eben preserves his virginity it is due to a lack of commitment; "he was no person at all" (p. 45).

Eben's situation bears both affinity to and is different from Henry Burlingame's. At this point, Eben like Henry lacks identity and purpose, but whereas Henry commits himself versus life and acts out one role after the other, Eben's play takes place in his imagination. Eben and Henry as representatives of the poet are both assuming various roles, just as the poet will identify himself with the various characters he creates. But Eben's roles and his poetry in general spring solely from his imagination while Henry is steeped in life and it is difficult to see through the disguises he assumes.

Eben's conception of the poet's function undergoes a development in the course of the novel. He thinks that being a poet does not depend on your own choice; it is a God-inspired role, and at first he even asserts that the poet is like a god. He tells his servant: "But the mask of the valet masks a varlet, while the poet's masks a god!" (p. 214). And he goes on to explain how the poet acts as a seer and prophet who knows men's hearts and the springs of good and evil. The irony in this statement lies in the discrepancy between Eben's ideal of the poet and his deplorable situation at the time.

Eben likes to imagine himself in the role of a god. Early in his career, during his time as a clerk in the London office, Eben plays relentless providence to an ant which happens to cross his account book; he closes his eyes and shakes his ink-filled quill whenever the ant treads on certain numbers: "Although his role of *Deus civi Natura* precluded mercy, his sentiments were unequivocally on the side of the ant" (p. 43). The ant expires and Eben weeps, but he sticks to his role without interfering, even if he is hard put to it.

Also on another occasion Eben plays god. He describes to Bertrand, his valet, how *he* imagines the ideal state should be: "In my town . . . a poet shall be their god, and a poet their king, and poets all their councillors: 'twill be a *poetocracy*!" (pp. 285–6). This wishful thinking on the part of Eben is actually fulfilled when he saves a negro, "Drakepecker", who forthwith worships him like a god and obeys his every command. But after this experience Eben finds that "godding it" is too hard work: "If we reach our golden cities, my own shall be republican, not theocratic, nor have I any wish to be its ruler. That much Drakepecker hath taught me" (p. 291). The poet as a remote god is a role that does not fit Eben, mostly because he cannot keep the proper distance from the world: as in the incident with the ant he becomes involved despite his original resolve.

The part Eben wishes to play as Poet Laureate, especially in the beginning, as discussed above, does not exactly correspond with his real role. Eben plays Adam to his sister's Eve when they are children and Henry, their tutor, enacts the third part of this Biblical triangle. When Eben forfeits his estate out of ignorance, Henry compares him to the fallen Adam turned out of Eden, but he tells Henry to his face: "If I am Adam, I am Eveless, and Adam Eveless is immortal and unfallen. . . . . If knowledge be sin and death . . . there stands a Faustus of the flesh – a very Lucifer!" (pp. 402–3). Ebenezer, adhering to his state as " Poet and Virgin", disparages the carnal aspect of existence which Henry represents. Eben considers worldly experience dangerous to the immortality he seeks through his poetry. The role of the poet is irreconcilable to secular experience and knowledge: To create the immortal works of the spirit needs a virgin poet, an Adam before the Fall.

However, Eben also holds another conception of his role as poet. He exclaims after receiving his commission as Poet Laureate to Maryland: " 'Sweet land! . . . Pregnant with song! Thy deliverer approacheth!' There was a conceit worth saving, he reflected: the word *deliverer,* for instance, with its twin suggestions of midwife and saviour" (p. 94). But it is not by means of the moralizing poetry that Eben plans to write that he will be able to "deliver" Maryland. The practical side of his role has more weight than Eben imagines. By actively engaging himself with the people and the affairs of Maryland, he becomes its "saviour".

Eben is repeatedly referred to as a Christ figure. In the following, we will first consider some of the Christ parallels and then the symbolic function of Eben's relation to Joan Toast.

The last part of Eben's journey to his estate, Malden, has obvious parallels to the Passion. Christ was sent to the world as its redeemer; Eben goes to Malden as *"redemptioner"*, i.e. as an indentured servant on the same estate he has inherited from his father; he plans to "expiate . . . his folly by undoing the cooper William Smith" (p. 439). Further, like Christ in the Garden of Geth semane (cf. St. Matt. xxvi, 38) he feels "sick unto death" (p. 439) and he talks about his "final hours on earth" (p. 440). Lastly, Eben has himself agreed to be indentured instead of the scoundrel Tayloe: "Turn Tayloe free, and bond me in his stead" (p. 448). This refers to the biblical incident where Barabbas, the robber, is discharged instead of Jesus, who is sacrificed to save mankind.

The poet as saviour and redeemer of the world is allegorically represented by Ebenezer's relation to Joan Toast; it is pointed out that she is the "very sign and emblem" (p. 468) of the world from which Eben at first feels so aloof. What makes Eben a poet is not Lord Baltimore's commission; the title "Poet Laureate" only gives a certain purpose to Eben's poetry. It fills him with a distinct vocation, which is that of redeemer of the New World. But Joan is the one who makes Eben a poet. Before he met her, he tried to write poetry, "but abandoned the effort each time for want of anything to write about" (p. 28). After Joan has left him in his chambers, still a virgin, he feels brimful of inspiration and writes a love song. He boasts to his friends on this occasion that Joan has "played all innocently the midwife's part" (p. 95) in bringing forth the "fetus" of his true self, Poet and Virgin.

The Christ allegory is also used in connection with Joan. While Eben eventually behaves like a Christ figure in his relation to Joan, the opposite is the case with a Captain Mitchell, who appears in a story Joan/Susan relates about herself. Mr. Mitchell and his wife give Joan opium and she imagines herself to be *"the bride o' Christ"* (p. 305) and Mitchell, Christ himself. He kills the fetus he has fathered and is largely responsible for Joan's ruin. Obviously, Captain Mitchell figures as an "antichrist", which Joan also calls him, while Eben is to be regarded as her true saviour. Thus at one point Joan/Susan says to Eben: "Christ! Christ! ... Ye will refuse me" (p. 309).

Eben at last "saves" Joan restoring her self-respect, first by formally making her his wife and then by agreeing to their sexual union: "I shall sacrifice my essence to save your self-respect!" (p. 319). Eben, finally, fully accepts Joan, and he does indeed "redeem" her before the eyes of the world restoring Joan's, i.e. the world's, belief in herself and faith in life. A noble task for a poet.

The allegorical meaning of Eben's relation to Joan Toast becomes clearer when the role played by Eben's sister, Anna, is also taken into consideration. Eben's relation with these women demonstrates the two strains in the Barthian poet that we discussed earlier, a longing towards the world, on the one hand, and towards art on the other. Eben feels drawn both towards Anna and towards Joan.

Anna represents the spiritual side of existence, with whom Eben cultivates a Platonic relationship: This is Eben as "poet and virgin" with high ideas of his "calling" , but no real knowledge of his situation and possibilities. When, in the course of the story, Eben betrays Joan and flees from her, he remembers that he has first pledged himself to Anna. His first and only responsibility is to his art: "What business hath a poet with the business of the world? ... I am a poet and no creature else; I shall feel conscience only for my art, and there's an end on't!" (p. 474).

However, Eben does not stick to his "manifesto" . His conscience over-masters him, and he takes full responsibility for Joan, seeing that he also has a share in her undoing. Joan's cause significantly fuses with that of civilization, metaphorically expressed by her possession of the eggplant recipe. Eben admits his guilt, both in relation to Joan's fate and in contributing to the general human misery, and he considers himself a representative of and spokesman for suffering humanity.

Another "credo" of the poet finds expression in Eben's words: "But 'tis not the English case I plead: 'tis the case of humankind, of Civilization *versus* the Abyss of salvagery" (p. 662). The word "versus" indicates that Eben speaks for the whole of mankind, both "civilization" and "salvagery". This will be discussed later; suffice it here to stress the connection to Eben's relationship with his two women.

In the end he does not reject Joan and accept Anna, or, expressed in other words: he does not discard life for art. He manages to achieve a balance; Anna and Joan, art and life, do not stand in opposition; their various roles eventually blur. In a dream Eben sees the beautiful face of his sister Anna take on the features of Joan's face, which again changes into Anna's and so forth. This synthesis, for instance, is further indicated by the fact that both of the women bear a child; the child of Joan, the London whore, is born in wedlock while the child of the "spiritual" Anna is illegitimate.

Eben's great work in the novel, rescuing Maryland from civil war, demands that he engage himself with his entire personality. This calls for his compassion and his commitment, but then it is made clear that only a man of Eben's innocence and idealistic faith in his role could be fit for the task. Henry Burlingame, for instance, possesses the knowledge and love of the world plus the energy to act; all of these qualities Eben at first lacks. But Henry has no belief in his own value, nor in the value of anything else. In *The Sot-Weed Factor*, then, Barth seems to advocate a conception of the poet as redeemer and saviour, simultaneously pointing out that this means that the poet must find a balance between the two opposing strains of his personality.

2. Reconciliation Through Narrative

Henry Burlingame relates to Eben his experience with the two rivals, Henry More and Isaac Newton, during his time at Cambridge. The former is described as a neo-Platonist and anti-materialistic philosopher, and Descartes' affirmation of God's real existence fascinates him. Newton, however, disagrees fundamentally with Descartes and Henry More:

> But his loathing for Descartes ... hath its origin in a difference betwixt their temperaments. Descartes ... is a great hand for twisting the cosmos to fit his theory. Newton, on the other hand, is a patient and brilliant experimenter, with a sacred regard for the facts of nature. (p. 23)

The opposition between Descartes and Henry More, on the one hand, and Newton, on the other, has its parallel in the difference between Ebenezer Cooke and Henry Burlingame. These characters represent two opposing philosophical views, the difference between which has its origins in "the ancient quarrel" between nominalists and realists, which will be considered later at greater length. Henry and Eben stand for various attitudes to life, which again are reflected in contrasting conceptions of poetry.

The difference between the two makes itself explicitly felt in a discussion about virtue, more especially that of virginity. Eben distinguishes between "plain" and "significant" virtues. The former are not ends in themselves but serve as guides through life and are therefore practical and social. The "significant" virtues possess value in themselves only; they are "forms of ceremony" and "mysterious or poetic" (p. 157). Eben finds that his virginity belongs to the class of significant virtues, thereby expressing what he cherishes most.

The two views on virtue in reality indicate two conceptions of what poetry should be like; a distinction seems to exist between *"Instrumental"* and *"terminal"* (p. 156) literature; either a socially oriented literature with a didactic touch, or a poetic-religious literature with no value beyond itself. Barth leans towards the latter conception. He states, for instance, in an interview that "I'm not very responsible in the Social Problems way, I guess".[14] *The Sot-Weed Factor* shows that he has not entirely shed that kind of responsibility, as the novel in one sense may be described as a presentation of the different views of poetry described above.

The battle between Isaac Newton and Henry More ends with reconciliation in Henry Burlingame's story; they move into the same lodgings, deciding to "couple the splendors of the physical world to the glories of the ideal" (p. 24). This is an apt description of the novel itself. The book as a whole ends in this kind of synthesis, and Eben and Henry eventually fight for the same cause.

The various conceptions of literature in *The Sot-Weed Factor* focus on two issues that will be discussed next: First, the question of mimesis, or the extent to which art should imitate reality; and secondly, the question of value, whether literature possesses value in itself without regard to the reader's response or to its practical use.

Henry Burlingame's attitude to reality is that of a man accepting the world in its totality, but at the same time having no deeper regard for it. His stance as a "Cosmic Lover" manifests itself in shocking and grotesquely funny ways at times, for instance when Henry tells Eben about his love of "Portia", who turns out to be a sow. Burlingame holds that his disposition, his love of the entire world, marks the true poet: "Ye say that women are oft the stuff o' poetry, but in fact 'tis the great wide world the poet sings of: God's whole creation is his mistress, and he hath for her this selfsame love and boundless curiosity" (p. 327).

When Henry presents a sample of his poetry, Eben finds it as tasteless as Henry's "cosmic love" that embraces even a pig:

> *"Let me taste of thy Tears,*
> *And the Wax of thine Ears;*
> *Let me drink of thy Body's own Wine –"*
> "Eh! 'Sheart! Have done ere you gag me!" Ebenezer cried. *"Thy body's own wine!* Ne'er have I heard such verses!" (p. 327)

Henry indeed goes to the extreme in his process of prying into "every plain and secret part" (p. 326) of his beloved or of the world and then rendering his impression in poetry.

In "the Wax of thine Ear" and the like phrases the poet discloses a remarkable sense of realistic detail ... However, the strictly mimetic approach to poetry that Barth here ridicules may have such crude effects as Burlingame's short poem. To turn the world into poetry without distinction of any kind produces at best a comic kind of verse without any claim of artistic merit. In an interview, Barth points out how it is impossible to create a hundred percent true imitation of reality in fiction. Instead he prefers to emphasize the gap between reality and fiction.[15]

Compared with Henry, Eben approaches reality in his fiction in a directly opposite way. When as a boy he studies geography and history, he refuses to accept the world of the geographical and historical facts as the final version (p. 8). He holds the worlds which originate in his imagination as real as God's creation.

Eben greatly favours play-acting as a child, but these games, "like the facts of life and the facts of history and geography" (p. 270), are equally real or unreal to him. It is emphasized that he considers both life and the world of play "from the *storyteller's* point of view . . . never could he really embrace either" (pp. 270–1). Eben does not recognize any division between life and fiction. The world of poetry represents an addition to and not a copy of life. The question of mimesis has at first no relevance in Eben's case. In his verse he does not want to create a reflection of the world, but produces an alternative to it.

When Ebenezer Cooke in his inexperience sets out to fulfil his role as "poet and virgin", Burlingame very appropriately asks: "But what on earth hath a virgin to sing of?" (p. 121). Ebenezer meekly confesses that he has written one poem "on the subject of my innocence" (p. 121). Still, Henry wonders what apart from his innocence Eben may write of, since life itself lies outside the scope of Eben's knowledge. In fact Eben has problems with what to choose for his subject matter until he meets Joan. The poem Eben composes, inspired by his love for her, abounds in references to classical literature and centres on his own chastity; his beloved Joan is just mentioned.

Ebenezer does not use the actual woman of flesh and blood as a source for his poem. He draws on his own ideas and his own learning. McEvoy, Joan's pimp, sees that Eben loves "the vision" and not the girl herself: "Think not ye love Joan Toast, Mr. Cooke: 'tis your *love* ye love, and that's but to say 'tis yourself and not my Joan" (pp. 61–2). The ideal Joan that Eben has conceived in his mind and that he transfers to the girl, has little relation to Joan, the London whore.

Similarly, when Eben decides to write his *Marylandiad* and wants to describe first his voyage to the province, he is not bothered for long by the circumstance that he has not even started his journey yet: "he resolved to write his epic *Marylandiad* in the form of an imaginary voyage, thinking thereby to discover to the reader the delights of the Province with the same freshness and surprise wherewith they would discover themselves to the voyager-poet" (p. 168). This surprise becomes even greater than Eben imagines because of the discrepancy between his verse and the Maryland he eventually meets with. Also on board the ship which takes him across the Atlantic, Eben is in for a surprise when the food falls markedly short of the "Delight/As met our Sea-sharp'd Appetites" (p. 211) in his epic.

But again he does not act upon his discoveries: "All this, however, was mere disillusionment, the fault ... merely of Ebenezer's own naïveté or, as he himself felt mildly ... of the nature of Reality, which had failed to measure up to his expectations" (p. 212). For yet some time Eben cleaves to the ideas of his imagination, expressing these in his poetry, and paying no attention to life as it unfolds around him.

That Ebenezer here pursues a blind alley that leads nowhere but to destruction and death, the novel emphasizes in several ways. Joan in the disguise of Susan, "a swine-maiden" (p. 301), tells Eben a story which shows the danger of choosing the ideal for the real world. Humphrey, the protagonist of the story, marries Susan because of her likeness to his beloved, Elizabeth, who has just died. Susan feels that her husband does not love *her*, but her likeness to the diseased Elizabeth. She forces him to choose between the dead Elizabeth and her living self: "And choose he did, though not a word be said of't; for next morn he was too ill to rise, and died not four days after" (p. 303). To reach for the ideal means death, because it lies beyond mortal man to attain it.

This story serves as a warning to Ebenezer. Like Humphrey, he has a choice to make between the ideal Joan of his imagination and Joan/Susan, pox-ridden but alive. Eben at this stage rejects Joan, which in fact means that he still prefers his ideal, imaginary world to life. Shortly after this encounter with Joan/Susan, he signs away his proprietorship of Malden, his estate, out of blind idealism and ignorance: " 'twas not rum, wrongheadedness, or the rage o' the mob that brought ye low, but simple pride and innocence, such as have ruined many a noble wight before" (p. 435), Eben is told when the truth dawns on him.

Eben's innocence and idealism land him where he least expects; as a servant on his own estate. No-one receives him as the Poet Laureate of Maryland. He tries, nevertheless, to cultivate his ideals of "Justice, Truth, and Beauty" (p. 387) in his poetry. But his first literary attempts are not successful while his mock-epic "The Sot-Weed Factor" is read and praised and outlasts the death of its author.

Both Henry and Ebenezer fail in their approaches to the question of mimesis in poetry. While Eben soars too high above the ground in the upper spheres of philosophy and idealism, Henry is too closely involved in the sordid realities of life. The novel advocates a reconciliation between the two ways of regarding reality. After the devastating experience at his estate, Ebenezer realizes both the values and the short-comings of his former attempts:

> What moral doth the story hold? . . . is't that
> what the world lacks we must ourselves supply?
> My brave assault on Maryland – this knight-errantry
> of Innocence and Art – sure, I see now 'twas an edifice raised not e'en on sand, but
> on the black and vasty zephyrs of the Pit. Wherefore a voice in me cries, 'Down
> with't, then!' while another stands in awe before the enterprise; sees in the vanity
> of't all nobleness allowed to fallen men. 'Tis no mere castle in the air, this second
> voice says, but a temple of the mind, Athene's shrine, where the Intellect seeks
> refuge from Furies more terrific than e'er beset Orestes – (p. 629)

This outburst about his two inner voices discloses Eben's awareness of the two strains in his personality. He recognizes the limitations of his lofty "Marylandiad", a poem from the "virgin" era of his life.

The solution to the mimetic problem in literature, which *The Sot-Weed Factor* arrives at, is closely connected with the general view of reality in the novel. One incident concerning Eben's sister serves to illustrate the basic conception of existence in the book. Anna, after marrying an Indian, turns all savage and becomes a dirty, dumb squaw; to keep the balance between cultivation and savagery, her husband turns into the perfect English gentleman. The process is reversed when Anna later becomes a civilized woman and her husband goes Indian again.

The Sot-Weed Factor presents a cosmology where the chaotic forces are kept in check by order and civilization, and where outlet of energy is balanced by repression and control. This view is further underlined by the many triangles, sexual, racial and political, which the novel abounds in.[16] The triangles in *The Sot-Weed Factor* symbolize the transcendence of opposites into a harmonious whole – which is also the aesthetic credo of the novel.

That this wholeness which Eben reaches in his conception of reality has importance for him as a poet becomes clear from one of his dreams. Eben has twice a dream of twin mountains separated by an abyss. These mountain cones have at least two connotations. The word *twin* indicates the connection between the two mountains, and Eben and his twin-sister Anna. An incident where Eben meets Anna in her status as a squaw indicates the meaning of the mountains. Eben tells Anna: " 'tis as if we were on twin mountaintops, with what an abyss between! We shall span it ere we leave this cabin" (p. 654). Anna, the temporary savage, and Eben, the civilized gentleman, here represent the life/art dichotomy that Eben eventually will "span". Secondly, the reference is to Parnassus and the poets trying to climb to the top (cf. ch. xxxii of Part II).

In this dream Parnassus consists of two cones. Eben lands on one of the tops, and at first he wonders whether he has got to the right one, which should then be Parnassus. He thinks there is only one kind of Parnassus and one kind of poetry, the "virgin" one. But a poet who has reached the top earlier tells Eben: "Sometimes I think 'tis one, sometimes the other. . . . What doth it matter?" (p. 455). This underlines Eben's limitations, both existentially, when pursuing the life of a virgin, and as regards his ideas of poetry.[17]

Eben manages to attain a synthetic view of life whereby both parts of existence are taken into consideration. And it is at this point in his development that he possesses the insight through which he performs the heroic work of the poet that he originally intended. His first *Marylandiad* represents one extreme in its portrayal of reality; the inhabitants of the province become semi-gods in this poem. "The Sot-Weed Factor" that Eben writes afterwards, contains a more balanced approach to reality. The poem does not soar to the lofty heights of the spirit, nor does it aim at a "true" picture of life with all its sordid details. "The Sot-Weed Factor" is a mock-epic, caricaturing the people of Maryland and concluding with a curse on this province *"Where no Man's Faithful, nor a Woman chast!"* (p. 462).

The second issue of this discussion concerns the question of the value of literature. Also on this point Eben and Henry disagree. In a debate with Henry Burlingame (disguised as Peter Sayer), Ebenezer contends for the inherent *merit* of a poem which exists regardless of its creator and whether it finds readers or not. Henry stresses the importance of the poem to create *Interest*. He finds that the value of a poem depends on the reader's range of human experience, of which he himself possesses far more than Eben, and he accordingly tells his friend that Eben's poem has greater significance to him than to the poet himself (p. 123). This dispute whether the poem has inherent value or not, Henry holds to be "an ancient one" (p. 137), and by this he refers to the discussion in antiquity concerning universals: According to the realists, universals exist prior to things and independent of physical experience. This theory was supported by Plato and opposed by the nominalists who hold that universals have no real being but exist *post res* or after things.[18]

The debate concerning the merit versus the interest of a poem discloses that Eben sympathizes with Plato while Henry leans towards nominalism. The poem that gives rise to the quarrel between them shows how Eben has a disregard for human beings: "the message of the whole was simply that we folk were too absurd to do credit to a Sublime Intelligence" (p. 124). Thus Eben holds poetry to have value *per se*, and he ranks it above human beings.

When Eben receives his commission from Lord Baltimore alias Henry Burlingame, he gives a speech on the value of poetry versus the actual incidents it describes. People and historical events that would otherwise be forgotten attain immortality in poetry. Ebenezer asserts that the greatness of a prince lies "not in [his] deeds . . . but in their telling" (p. 74). In poetry "bright grow brighter" (p. 74), and the factual world does not count, but is presented in an ennobled state in verse. When Lord Baltimore asks Eben to "make me this Maryland, that neither time nor intrigue can rob me of'' (p. 92), this suits Eben very well. The worth of poetry depends on its ability to idealize the world.

Ebenezer Cooke discards all pecuniary considerations. He has no eye on material gain with his writing. The incident where Eben maltreats Ben Bragg's account book stresses symbolically his disregard for the world of business in connection with poetry. He intends to use this book as notebook for his poetry compositions. He rips out the used pages, and he wants to blot out the book's categories of debit and credit by gluing in his commission as Poet Laureate instead. For Eben the value of poetry has nothing to do with material qualities.

In Eben's opinion poetry should guide and enrich man in his needs: This view Eben embraces at the outset of his journey, and it is thoroughly ridiculed in the episode where Eben has dirtied himself. Waking up in a stable, he starts to look for means of getting rid of the dirt. At last he finds that his only solution is to look towards literature for help. He tears out some unused pages of his notebook reflecting on the cleansing effect of poetry: "the unused sheets were songs unborn, which yet had power, as it were *in utero*, to cleanse and ennoble him who would in time deliver them" (pp. 174–5). This satiric incident is the only example in the novel where poetry possesses a "purifying" effect. In the course of the story, Ebenezer Cooke changes his evaluation of poetry. As will be discussed later, he discards the idea that poetry has value first and foremost as an instrument of purification and idealization.

Before considering Eben's ultimate view as regards the value of poetry, the discussion will turn to Henry Burlingame's ideas in this connection. His emphasis on the capacity of a poem to appeal to the reader's interest, leads to a disregard of the ethic and aesthetic qualities a poem may possess. Henry's slight evaluation of poetry has its foundation in his general attitude to life. Henry Burlingame changes his personality incessantly and this corresponds to his idea of the world as having no order, no constancy (p. 330).

This view also pertains to moral questions. Henry's tutoring of Eben aims at teaching him that Lord Baltimore is not all good and Cooke all bad (cf. pp. 485 ff.), but the danger attached to this kind of lesson is that Eben will find nothing good or nothing bad; the flux of the world becomes total, also in a moral sense. Eben rightly doubts his friend's good intentions at times, believing him to be on the side of evil.

Henry does not particularly cherish anything as good or evil, or of greater and lesser worth. This relates also to his regard of poetry: "we set no such criterion as significance" (p. 386), Henry informs Eben when they have the contest in composing Hudibrastic poetry. What counts with Henry is not the meaning of poetry, but merely the effect it may have on the readers: "I could have writ my own *Principia* of the flesh! ... to cause whate'er reaction I pleased" (p. 331). Poetry has worth only to the extent that the poet may use it for his own intended effect.

Eben does not go along with Henry Burlingame's disregard of value and order. He may at times give in to Henry's sophistication in proving the world a flux, and then he exclaims: "I know of naught immutable and sure!" (p. 128). But on the whole he finds meaning and purpose where Henry dismisses the case with his characteristic shrug. Eben eventually sees his role as the saviour of "humankind". Accordingly, he finds the value of poetry in its capacity to arrest the flux or the chaos by creating order and meaning.

Eben's esteem of poetry or the word may be seen from an episode where Henry deplores his state as an orphan. Henry has no knowledge of his forefathers and his past. His only feeling of identity and belonging stems from his name, Henry Burlingame the Third, which he cherishes as his most precious possession. Ebenezer agrees, stressing the value of the name further by exclaiming: " 'Tis your name that links you with your forebears; thou'rt not wholly *ex nihilo* after all! 'Tis a kind of clue to the riddle!'" (p. 131). The name or the word, and in larger contexts the narrative, the tale, is a means of salvation; it imposes order on a chaotic world.

This point is further emphasized by the role the various journals and "privy" histories play in the novel. Henry Burlingame learns with the assistance of Ebenezer that in Maryland two manuscripts exist which may contain the secret of his family and his descent. One is "Captain John Smith's Secret Historie of the Voiage up the Bay of Chesapeake" in which a certain Burlingame figures prominently as one of Smith's party; and the second manuscript is this same Burlingame's "Privie Journall" of his experiences on Smith's expedition.

Because of the scarcity of writing material in Maryland, both Smith's and Burlingame's accounts contain, on the reversed side, writings of a more official nature: On the *verso* of Smith's "Historie", the Journal of the 1691 Assembly in Maryland has been written, while the *verso* of Burlingame's "Journall" has "Coode's record of confiscations and prosecutions during his brief tenure of office" (p. 729).

Both the official journals and those that concern Henry function in the same way in the novel. The official papers have been smuggled away by the party that opposes Lord Baltimore's authority in the province. The Assembly Journal "was exceedingly valuable to the cause of order and justice in Maryland" (p. 265). The manuscript functions as a kind of national identity. It provides a record of the proceedings of the past that may serve as a guiding-line to the chaotic conditions of the present. The Journal contains evidence against Coode, Lord Baltimore's opponent, and the whole of Maryland may be lost in war and racial strife if the Journal is not found.

The "Journall" that holds the clue to Burlingame's past functions in the same way. It supplies Henry with a private history. This manuscript also helps to establish peace and order in the province, because it contains the eggplant recipe with the help of which Henry may prove his procreative ability and be accepted as the son of the Indian chief. Henry must gain the favour of the Indians to save Maryland from civil war.

Both the incidents concerning Henry's identity and those concerning the Assembly Journal suggest where the significance of literature lies. The value of literature comes from its capacity to create order and meaning in a chaotic world. This view represents a reconciliation between Eben's and Henry's attitudes; Eben's view that literature should ennoble the world; and Henry's, that literature has value only as far as it appeals to the audience. In the last instance it is Ebenezer Cooke, Poet Laureate of Maryland, who procures the missing parts of the "Privie Journall" and becomes the saviour of the province and "humankind".

As for the question of the truth of fiction, the novel emphasizes that this is an irrelevant problem. The value of fiction does not depend on its "truth". Thus to save Anna's honour in the eyes of the world, and especially in her father's, Eben makes up a tale that the child Anna and he bring up, belongs to Joan, who died in childbed, while actually it is Anna's own boy fathered by Henry: "This fiction, once established, had a marked effect on Ebenezer and his sister" (p.749). Anna gets over her shame of bearing a child out of wedlock and lives happily with Ebenezer.

The tale about the parentage of Anna's child "once established" has greater consequences than the truth. In this case, as with the replaced "Journalls", literature creates meaning and order of the sordid facts of life. Besides, Eben's nonchalant handling of "the truth" has its parallel in the free use Barth makes of the historical sources of the novel. [19]

This brings us back to the discussion of mimesis. Ebenezer attains a balance in his poetry as regards the question of mimesis. This is because he arrives at a view of reality which reconciles the opposing forces of life. Also as to the problem of value in literature adherence to the truth, or mimesis, becomes less important. Literature has value as far as it manages to create meaning and order, and this again depends on its ability to incorporate the antithetical elements of existence without suppressing any of them.

Finally, this discussion will briefly look into the relation between Eben's poem, "The Sot-Weed Factor", and Barth's novel of the same title. In his last stage as a poet, Eben adopts the same mock-epic style in his poem as John Barth in his novel: *The Sot-Weed Factor* satirizes the people and conditions of colonial Maryland as well as the traditional epic genre. In addition, the novel parodies the 18th century language and other literary forms besides the epic. [20] The fact that the novel mirrors the poem, leaves a hint about the essential quality of the book. Like the poem, Barth's novel does not intend to present a realistic picture of the 18th century: *The Sot-Weed Factor* discusses the nature of storytelling, especially the ethical/religious and aesthetic problems this entails for the narrator.

3. The Capricious Reader

The narratee plays a rather modest part in *The Sot-Weed Factor*. A remark Barth makes in an interview strengthens the impression one gets from the novel about the reader's role: "I enjoy the freedom to follow purely aesthetic leanings ... Obviously, I'd like a large distribution and as large a readership as possible, but such thoughts don't begin to enter until I've finished a book".[21] Not till the fourth and last part of *The Sot-Weed Factor* does the author address the reader explicitly. This part functions as a kind of coda to the main proceedings of the novel which on the whole terminate by the end of the third part.

But John Barth is a writer of greater moral concern than, for instance, Nabokov, despite his aesthetic manifesto and has a religious dimension not found in the works of the older novelist. Ebenezer Cooke, the author's spokesman, has a message to convey, but he does not allow consideration of the audience to change his writing to any large degree.

In the first three parts of *The Sot-Weed Factor*, more or less indirect references to an audience do exist and the impression is conveyed that the readers on the whole misunderstand the author's meaning. After having written his masterpiece, the poem "The Sot-Weed Factor", Ebenezer thinks that this epic will not make the public favourably disposed towards its author:

> ... he affixed his full title – *Ebenezer Cooke, Gentleman, Poet & Laureat of the Province of Maryland* – in full recognition that with the poem's publication, should he ever send it to a printer, he would forfeit any chance of receiving that title in fact.
> Publication, however, did not especially interest him at the moment. (p. 462)

Ironically enough, the poem is well received, and thus the audience's reactions are contrary to the poet's expectations.

That an audience cannot be trusted in its evaluation of art is further emphasized in Part IV, which lists more accurately the reactions to Ebenezer's publications, particularly to "The Sot-Weed Factor":

> ... its net effect was precisely what Baltimore had hoped to gain from a *Marylandiad*, and precisely the reverse of its author's intention. Maryland, in part because of the well-known poem, acquired in the early eighteenth century a reputation for graciousness and refinement ... and a number of excellent families were induced to settle there. (pp. 754–755)

The author intends to describe the barbarous conditions of Maryland so that future settlers may be warned off.

Especially the first three parts of the novel reveal a low opinion of the reader's ability to grasp the point, while in the fourth part the "author" assumes a confidential air when addressing the reader, taking mutual understanding between author and reader for granted. This may by due to the fact that in the last part the author steps forth *qua* author and speaks to the readers directly, above the heads of characters such as Ebenezer. This can be seen from the subtitle to this part: "THE AUTHOR APOLOGIZES TO HIS READERS" (p. 741), and from the fact that the author speaks to the readers as "we".

Nevertheless, the impression prevails that the author of *The Sot-Weed Factor*, just like the author of the poem of the same title, does not really care about the reader. He is not primarily writing to educate his audience. In the novel, the author displays, on the one hand, a strong belief in the inherent power of the Word to create order and meaning. Thus, he lets a poet become the saviour of "humankind". But, at the same time, Barth is sceptical about the reader's ability to grasp the message, which the public reception of Eben's poem, "The Sot-Weed Factor", exemplifies. The author's ambivalent attitude towards the Word becomes an issue of greater significance in *Giles Goat-Boy*.

4. Conclusion – *The Sot-Weed Factor*

In contrast to the other novels under consideration in this study, *The Sot-Weed Factor* is written from the third person point of view. Instead of focusing on the narrator, the discussion deals with the protagonist of the novel and his concerns. Ebenezer Cooke, in his role as a poet, faces problems similar to those of the first person narrator in the other novels. Besides, Barth stresses the similarities between the author and the poet-protagonist in his book.

Eben and his friend Henry embody opposite aspects of a poet's personality or represent two kinds of poets. The difference between Eben and Henry has its roots in contrasting philosophical views. Eben believes in the poet's mission as God-sent – an idea which Henry with his materialistic atheism rejects.

The difference between Eben and Henry manifests itself in what they regard as their roles in the world. Henry involves himself completely in the affairs of his surroundings, which he manipulates to his heart's delight for no other purpose than the pleasure he takes in plotting and stirring up action. His activity has no ultimate purpose. In contrast to Henry, Eben keeps himself aloof from the world. He imagines the ideal poet to be a remote god or a prelapsarian Adam and holds that poetry has a didactic function.

The novel moves towards a reconciliation between the two extremes represented by Eben and Henry. In the first two parts of the novel, Eben is without a real identity. To play the role of the true poet, i.e. to become the redeemer of the world, he has to take an active part in the affairs of life. At the same time, however, Eben has a need for his idealism and belief in his calling, to rescue "humankind".

Eben's and Henry's standing as poets is expressed in terms of their relations with the opposite sex. Eben eventually abandons his state of virgin poet, dedicated to art, and attains a more real identity as an artist when he commits himself to Joan. Henry's numberless affairs with women suggest his immense creative resources. He has, however, to find his real identity before he can produce something of value – symbolically expressed through his fathering a child.

Finally, the two strains in the poet's personality balance each other as can be seen from Eben's example. He manages to reconcile his dedication to art – which will ultimately terminate in death – with his commitment to life.

☆

In the discussion of the narrative, Eben and Henry were found to hold different views, particularly concerning the question of mimesis in art and the value of poetry.

As regards mimesis, Henry observes an accurate rendering of reality in his poetic attempts, while Eben is too remote from the actual world in his poetry. He regards the poetic flights of his imagination, not as imitations of, but as alternatives to the existing world.

Eben believes that poetry has inherent merit and is valuable because of the idealized version it presents of the world and this has an ennobling effect on the readers. Henry regards the ethic and aesthetic qualities of a poem as unimportant; poetry has value only as far as it may create interest with the readers.

On both these issues, Henry and Eben represent the extremes in their views, and the novel indicates a reconciliation of their opposite opinions. Eben's only successful poem, "The Sot-Weed Factor", is neither a too accurate nor a too remote reflection of reality, being a satiric exposure of Maryland. The incidents with the various official journals and private "histories" demonstrate that the value of literature depends both on its inherent qualities and on its ability to create meaning in a chaotic world.

☆

The novel does not attach great significance to the narratee, as he is only directly addressed in the fourth part. This ties in with the author's view when he says that only towards the end of the novel does he think of the reader. In the last part the narrator discloses his confidence in the reader through his use of "we".

The first three parts form a contrast to the last one: The reader is not directly spoken to, and, because of the unexpected reception of Eben's poem, the readers' opinions are not esteemed very highly.

Giles Goat-Boy

Giles Goat-Boy is a work deeply related to *The Sot-Weed Factor*, but it appears structurally more complicated because of its various allegorical levels. One could roughly divide the existing criticism on the novel into two groups; mythological and symbolic-allegorical criticism. The first category examines the relation between the novel and studies of the mythic hero.

Campbell Tatham and David Morrell show how Barth applies the twenty-two stages of the hero as explained in Lord Raglan's book *The Hero. A Study in Tradition, Myth and Drama*, when describing the goat-boy's development.[22] Raymond Olderman discusses the novel on the basis of Joseph Campbell's *The Hero with a Thousand Faces*. He finds that George follows the pattern of Campbell's "monomyth"; departure, initiation and return.[23]

John Barth explains that he did not read either Raglan or Campbell till critics pointed out the influence of these works in *The Sot-Weed Factor*, and then he consciously used the pattern in his next novel: "*Goat-Boy* is not the orchestration of any particular myth of a wandering hero; it embodies elements which can be abstracted from almost all of them. And it consciously follows that pattern, of course, in a satiric fashion".[24]

John Tilton's article on *Giles Goat-Boy* is a valuable contribution to the symbolic-allegorical criticism. He sets out to examine "first, the Hero Myth, centering on Giles, Bray, and Anastasia ... second, the Founder's Hill Myth, embracing Stoker and Lucius Rexford and exploring the myth of the devil; and third, the Boundary Dispute Myth, involving the rivalry between East and West ..."[25] Tilton here lists the three major allegorical levels in the novel. He finds that the message of the novel is that "Passage" and "Failure", good and evil "are not strict opposites but polarities, together forming a unity in the harmony of opposites".[26]

Several critics have commented on the political historical allegory of the novel – which corresponds to Tilton's third category: The global East-West consolidations after World War II are presented in terms of opposing campuses within a university (i.e. universe).[27] As for metafictional criticism, no full-length, systematic study exists to my knowledge:[28] Possibly, this aspect may constitute the fourth allegorical level, representing, in the story about the goat-boy, the origin and nature of fiction.

1. The Heroic Narrator

Before reaching the narrator's own story in *Giles Goat-Boy*, the reader is first presented with the Editor-in-Chief and four sub-editors in "Publisher's Disclaimer"[29] and then with a "J.B." in his "Cover-Letter to the Editors and Publisher" (pp. xvii-xxxi). This letter explains "J.B." 's role in the composition and production of the ensuing narrative: His unfinished manuscript for a novel called *The Seeker* is "mixed up" with the typescript to *The Revised New Syllabus*, which is left on his desk by Stoker Giles, the goat-boy's son.

In the cover-letter, "J.B." describes his contribution to the novel as fairly inferior; he functions more in the line of an editor than a novelist. Stoker Giles also insists on having played a minor part in the production of the novel: It is the huge computer WESCAC that has produced the manuscript partly from stories that Stoker Giles has compiled from the goat-boy's first followers, partly from material the computer has stored from the goat-boy's own lecture notes and conferences (p. xxvii).

In this novel the distance between the author and the narrative is emphasized through the introduction of the various contributors: Editor-in-Chief, board of editors, "J.B.", Stoker Giles, WESCAC, and lastly the narrator, George, the goat-boy, who tells the story from the first person point of view. Morrell explains that the many stages between the readers and "the original" is used by Barth to demonstrate how "reality comes to us filtered and truth distorted".[30]

Another effect of this insisting on the distance between the actual author, John Barth, and the narrator, George, the goat-boy, is that the fictitiousness of the narrative is emphasized. This is further underlined by Stoker Giles's claim that WESCAC is the originator of the manuscript to *Giles Goat-Boy*. The computer has indeed fathered George in more ways than one; not only has it mysteriously "impregnated" George's mother; it has produced the story about George. And George, what more is he than a fictitious character in a novel? The story of George's life actually represents allegorically the story of the novel's genesis and development.

In his next book, *Lost in the Funhouse,* Barth expresses the idea of the narrator representing the narrative still more explicitly. For instance in the preface, Barth explains how the story called "Autobiography" is actually the story telling its own story: "The title 'Autobiography' means 'self-composition': the antecedent of the first-person pronoun is not I, but the story, speaking of itself."[31]

When one considers "J.B." 's role as displayed in the "Cover-Letter", it is obvious that this is a device Barth uses to explain the author's relation to the narrative. "J.B.", introduced to the readers as the author, comes closest to the actual author, John Barth. "J.B." has been given his initials, and he has also other affinities with John Barth, who had, for instance, already written his first long novel, *The Sot-Weed Factor*, when starting on *Giles Goat-Boy*; "J.B." admits of just having finished a novel of 800 pages.

The relatedness between "J.B." and the characters in *Giles Goat-Boy* is hinted at in the "Cover-Letter". "J.B." 's manuscript, *The Seeker*, where the main character is actually "J.B." himself, is "mixed in" with Stoker Giles's manuscript. This means that "J.B." 's or the author's conception and descriptions of himself go into the finished novel.

In addition, the features "J.B." means to bestow on his autobiographical hero are shared out to some of the main characters in *Giles Goat-Boy*. From "J.B." 's original protagonist in *The Seeker*, George inherits his crippled foot, Eierkopf his scientific inclinations, Dr Sear his cancer, and Greene his twisted vision (p. xxii). Thus, the author's relation to the narrative has been brought into focus by emphasizing the affinity both between John Barth and "J.B." and between "J.B." 's autobiographical hero and the characters of *Giles Goat-Boy*.

One should mark that it is only during the talk with Stoker Giles that "J.B." gets the idea of developing his original protagonist into several other characters. Stoker Giles guides him towards seeing the world as he does. He inspires him with his vision and places the box containing the story of George, the goat-boy, on his desk. He then disappears – it is hinted to another world from which he came.

Though Barth describes the whole of Stoker Giles's visit in an ironic way, he wants to make clear that what makes "J.B." a poet is this "visitation" from outside, and what turns *The Seeker* into a work of art, or a "real" novel, is its admixture with this tale bestowed upon its author from "above" so to speak. Despite the satiric treatment of "J.B." 's situation as a kind of self-irony on the novelist's aspirations, the impression prevails that Barth wants to advocate the idea of the inspired poet.

The protagonist of *The Seeker* is described as a man

enchanted with . . . everything that *is the case* – because he saw its arbitrariness but couldn't understand or accept its finality. He would deal with reality like a book, a novel that he didn't write and wasn't a character in . . . But in truth, of course, he *wasn't* finally a spectator at all; he couldn't stay 'out of it' . . . (p. xxiii).

Stoker Giles condemns "J.B." 's way of regarding the world as wrong, and "J.B." admits this to be true, and he sees the reason for it; the hero of *The Seeker* like himself has no grip on the world. All his roles, all his functions, are just masks; "a procession of hoaxes perhaps impressive for a time but ultimately ruinous" (p. xxiii).

"J.B." as "author" does put on various masks, but no final identity exists behind these masks. To demonstrate what is wrong with "J.B." and his writing, Stoker Giles makes him look at his manuscript of *The Seeker* through a lens; "J.B." just sees his own eye reflected and magnified. This incident discloses "J.B." 's existential position and his situation as a novelist. His writing is just a reproduction of himself: He lacks identity, which means that in his writing he has no message to convey.

"J.B." acknowledges the difference between himself and Stoker Giles, the visitor from the "other world" who wants him to take on responsibility for the manuscript about the goat-boy:

> his authenticity lies not in what he says but in his manner and bearing, his every gesture, the whole embodiment of his personality. And in this salient respect (which I dwell upon because of its relevance to the manuscript he left me) Mr. Stoker Giles was effective indeed. (p. xxiv)

Stoker Giles possesses an identity, which is what "J.B." lacks, and he brings a message he desperately wants to communicate.

Like his own protagonist in *The Seeker*, "J.B." has also found his way into the narrative about George, in the disguise of Harold Bray: The novel underlines the affinity between "J.B." and John Barth, as well as the relation between the latter and Harold Bray, who is the representative of the author. Further, like "J.B.", Harold Bray is without a proper identity, being everything and nothing. Lastly, the difference between "J.B." and Stoker has its parallel in the tension between Harold Bray and George, the goat-boy. These points will be considered at greater length in the following discussion about Harold Bray's function in the novel.

Harold Bray's role in *Giles Goat-Boy* has given rise to much critical speculation. Tanner points to the obvious likeness between him and Henry Burlingame in *The Sot-Weed Factor* – they even share the same initials.[32] Tilton sees Bray as a representative of "organized religion and the established church"[33] while Beverly Gross is one of the few suggesting that likeness exists between this character and the "author" in Barth's works.[34] Regarded in this light, the character of Harold Bray becomes much less mysterious, and as will hopefully be shown, this is a view which has support in the text.

Harold Bray's first appearance in the novel comes at the end of a theatre performance of *Taliped Decanus,* i.e. *Oedipus Rex*. He descends on the stage as a *deus ex machina* and reveals, after removing his mask, "a round, black-mustachioed countenance" (p. 314). Bray's features are modelled on those of John Barth himself (cf. the photo on the cover of the Doubleday edition) and in addition, he is labelled a "Minor poet" (p. 314). The reference to *deus ex machina* gives a concrete indication of the author's role. He is in complete command of his characters, operating them from behind the stage as a god, but also intruding like a John Barth into the world of the narrative, revealing the fictitiousness of his work.

Eierkopf, the scientist in *Giles Goat-Boy*, draws attention to this last-mentioned characteristic of Bray when he explains Bray's character to George: "the curious thing is that he's posing without disguise" (p. 330). Eierkopf further describes him as "a gross impostor" (p. 328) who plays many roles but is just one single man, and he is omniscient, all of which features may mark the author. Near the end of the novel, Bray even changes into all the characters of the novel, one after the other.

Despite the fact that Bray mingles freely with the characters in the novel, he is of another kind compared with them. He operates in their world but is not *of* their world. Eierkorpf talks of his mysterious origin, and in addition, nobody has seen him undertake the normal physical activities, such as eating and drinking. Because he is of another species, as indeed the author is distinguished from his fictional characters, Bray cannot "mate" with Anastasia in the end, however much he wants to (p. 668).

Bray possesses one rather puzzling feature. When he is driven away from the "university" by George, his appearance bears resemblance to that of a machine that gives out both humming and clicking noises, a terrible smell and at the "mating" occasion, a green fluid. The intention may have been to suggest an author at work with tape-recorder, typewriter, computer or other technical facilities. Besides, Barth divides his work into "reels" instead of "chapters" and attaches a "Posttape" to the ending. In this way, the author becomes a machine-like, unfeeling being, remote from the world of the characters. Also, Barth uses this aspect of the author's work to add to the fabulous atmosphere that surrounds Bray.

Harold Bray's allegorical role as the author gets a further dimension in Bray's relation to George, the first person narrator in the story about the goat-boy. From Bray's first appearance till he vanishes at the end of volume two, a furious battle goes on between him and George. Both claim to be the "Grand Tutor" or the Messiah who has come to save mankind. Bray has actually secured for himself the authority to "certify" people, i.e. to hand out certification cards as a token that they are saved. George considers Bray's aspirations as prophet and saviour to be false. When Bray assigns a task for George on his way to salvation, George resents this, and he refuses to acknowledge Bray's authority over him or anyone else and vehemently protests: "You're an impostor!" (p. 379).

In the course of the struggle, Bray and George literally don each other's masks: Bray poses as George to ensure his success with Anastasia, among other things; and George feels himself obliged on two occasions to put on Bray's mask. This signifies an interchange of identity between Bray and George and underlines the relatedness between author and narrator. The author may find it difficult at times not to identify with the narrator-protagonist. To maintain a distance to the characters all the time and not get involved is an impossibility.

When Bray, also in keeping with the author's role, withdraws "mysteriously" from the world of the characters at the end of the second volume, George comments in the "Posttape": "his nature and origin were extraordinary and mysterious as my own" (p. 703). He further points out that though the two of them are opponents, they are also necessary to each other and in the end "undifferentiable". This should indicate that the narrator-protagonist depends on the author for his fictional existence, and their identities overlap at times.

When George twice wears Bray's mask, this suggests that the narrator-protagonist puts himself in the author's place, claiming to be his own creator, acknowledging no authority but his own. George aspires to the position of Grand Tutor or Saviour-Hero. He possesses a belief in his own role which also convinces his old teacher Max, who at first is rather sceptical about what he sees as George's self-instituted authority.

But George puts all objections aside: "the Grand Tutor defines Himself ineluctably and exclusively in the Grand-Tutoriality of His deeds. There was no cause, I strongly felt, to *worry* about myself: if I was indeed Grand Tutor then I would choose infallibly the Grand-Tutorial thing –" (p. 207). George here gives vent to a view about the designation of the narrator-hero similar to that expressed by Ebenezer Cooke in *The Sot-Weed Factor* about the poet's role: a poet is born, not made. In the same way, George asserts that his power as "Grand Tutor" or saviour is given him by birth, and it accordingly infuriates him that an impostor like Bray should claim authority over him or assign him tasks.

The battle between Bray and George may be interpreted as an indication of their divergent conceptions of the narrator's role· George holds it to be a calling and the narrator to be divinely inspired. Bray represents the view that the narrator, and the narrative he gives expression to, signify neither more nor less than what the author chooses to make of them. The author, though admittedly a fake and an impostor, is more of a "Grand Tutor" or Saviour than the narrator he has created. Thus, the essential problem may be formulated like this: To what extent does the narrator and accordingly also the narrative possess ethical or "saving" qualities independent of and despite the author's fallibility?

In *Giles Goat-Boy*, the contest between Bray and George concerns just this question. George thinks that one way to save mankind would be to short-circuit WESCAC. Bray discourages the idea: "Don't be silly, George ... do you really think it's worthwhile to take WESCAC so seriously? It's only a symbol" (p. 636). Bray not only flaunts his own fictional nature, making no secret of being an impostor, but he also functions as a means to stress the unreality of the entire narrative, in which George becomes no more than a fictional character.

Bray disclaims George time and again as "Grand Tutor". On one occasion when George wrongly thinks he will give him an official certification of the role to which he aspires, Bray instead publicly strikes the kneeling George and bans him from the community. However, George refuses to give in to Bray. He defines his task as saviour-hero to conquer Bray, the false "Grand Tutor", that mankind may be saved by himself, the true "Messiah": "Bray had been appointed ... to pretend to Grand-Tutorhood himself, in order that I might drive him out at last ... in proof of my authenticity'' (p. 511). George succeeds in his expulsion of Bray. Whether he also manages to "save" mankind will be considered in another connection.

From the battle between George and Bray about who is the real "Grand Tutor'', it is obvious that Barth wants to discuss first the relationship between author and narrator and secondly the question of authenticity: The author is clearly an "impostor" creating a fictitious world, and a fictional hero. But the narrator may nevertheless convey a message of true value to the readers.

In the course of the novel, George undergoes a development in three stages. First, he asserts the importance of differentiation: one should clearly distinguish between east and west, good and evil, etc. He then jumps to the other extreme when the bad effects of his first policy make themselves felt: all divisions must be erased, the whole of the universe should embrace. This results in a collapse of the entire community.

Finally, George arrives at a conception that incorporates both the former stages. This could be formulated as "difference in unity"; east remains the opposite of west, evil of good, but both elements are necessary parts of totality. This is the message George achieves and that he finds may save mankind.

George conceives his message in a highly symbolic incident. During his third and last passage through WESCAC, which he undertakes together with Anastasia, he fathers her child. As in *The Sot-Weed Factor*, Barth employs sexual symbolism to suggest the narrator's creativity.

The protagonist, in the role of a poet or a narrator, has to represent the whole of existence to become a "saviour" of mankind. George considers himself a spokesman for humanity, and he discovers in his individual development stages similar to those in the history of the world (p. 255).

The artist-saviour is also representative in the way that he experiences on a more conscious level what each man undergoes individually: "what everyone went through for himself ... Grand Tutors went through on the level of the whole student body: 'Every college needs a man now and then to go to the bottom of things' '' (p. 262).[35] George becomes representative because he tries to grasp the essence of existence.

George's message does not only proffer a solution to man's ethical problems. It also concerns the aesthetic aspect of the novel. George arrives at an integrated vision of the world; despite its conflicts and oppositions, he manages to see the universe as "difference in unity". He draws a similar conclusion about his relationship to Harold Bray: "As for Bray ... all that could be said was that he was my adversary, as necessary to me as Failure is to Passage. I.e., not only contrary and interdependent, but finally undifferentiable" (p. 703).

The novel advocates a synthesis of Bray's attitude, the poet as trickster and skilled technician, and George's, the poet with a burning message of salvation.

Barth has expressed similar thoughts about art in an essay: "I'm inclined to prefer the kind of art that not many people can *do*: the kind that requires

expertise and artistry as well as bright aesthetic ideas and/or inspiration".[36]
This ideal Barth has set out to fulfil in *Giles Goat-Boy* as well as in his other
work, and not only that; he also reveals the process of attaining his goal,
making it the very theme of his novels.

2. Auto-Narrative

In the discussion of the narrator in *Giles Goat-Boy* it was mentioned that the
novel may also be interpreted as a fiction describing its own genesis. The tale
about George, the goat-boy, may be regarded as an allegory about the origin
and development of a fictional work. The following discussion will first try to
show the extent to which this hypothesis finds support in the text and then deal
briefly with questions concerning the value and function of literature, as
expressed in the novel.

As was mentioned earlier, the computer WESCAC has fathered George,
and it has produced the manuscript containing the story of George's life. When
George tries to find out about his origin, Max tells him that he was found in a
booklift (p. 66) in the computer's "belly". Max also directly speaks of him as a
kind of book, though a rather uncommon one: " you got a momma and poppa
someplace . . . it's like you were found in a rare-book vault, you know, that
nobody but an old grand chancellor and his viziers had got the keys to "
(p. 68).

When George for the first time realizes that he differs from the goats and
escapes from the world of the goat pen, he enters a door which leads into the
stacks of a library, i.e. "the Livestock Branch of the Library" (p. 44). So when
George becomes conscious of his situation as different from that of animals,
the world of books becomes his domain.

The world of *Giles Goat-Boy* seems indeed a "literary" one. Barth manages
to stuff his novel with all kinds of "bookish" references. The chancellor,
Lucius Rexford, once campaigned on a pledge "to break up the reference-book
monopoly" (p. 139), and Ira Hector, another important man of the goat-boy
society, owns a reference-book firm (p. 142).

But in this novel most of the literary allusions concern George himself.
George's first contact with literature comes when a lady, who actually turns
out to be his mother, reads the story of "The Three Brothers Gruff" and their
meeting with the Troll under the bridge. This has an immense impact on
George. He identifies with the billy-goats, feeling that "the story named no
breeds, but I was sure in my heart that this initial Gruff (to my mind, the real
hero) was of the same species as myself" (p. 19). This refers to the fact that

86

George at this stage behaves like and lives among goats and is a kind of billy-goat himself.

However, George belongs to the same species as Mister Gruff not only because both of them are presented as half man and half beast: Both also figure as fictional characters in a story, which is further underlined when George's mother reminds him "it was 'just a story' " (p. 19) to calm his agitation. George identifies to such an extent with the contents of this tale that he actually devours the pages as his mother finishes reading them. This means that George becomes one with the story: The present narrative incorporates this older piece of fiction.

It is significant that George begins with one of the oldest kinds of stories, a fairytale from folk-literature, and it is also important that this is transmitted to him orally. In the course of the novel, George lives through the whole history of literature, absorbing and identifying with more complex literary forms. Thus, George symbolically represents the novel entitled *Giles Goat-Boy*, which is based on previous narratives.

T. S. Eliot gives expression to a similar idea about literature when he argues in an essay that art partly builds on former achievements and that the artist is born into a tradition.[37] Barth illustrates this idea by portraying quite literally how George devours items of former fiction and at the same time narrates his own story.

The first reading George undertakes consists of "ancient narratives" (p. 23), which have titles like *Tales of the Trustees* and *The Founder-Saga* in keeping with the university motif of the novel. Again George's dependence on past literature is stressed: His mother's "grandfather ... had once been a professor of Antique Narrative ... inasmuch as the books I devoured were all from his collection, my speech came to be flavored with the seasons of older time" (p. 22). George adopts the style of former literature, but what really interests him is "the hero's performance" (pp. 79–80) in the old stories of adventure.

Further, George has the typical Barthian hero's disregard of facts, and his preferences give a good description of the novel in which he figures as the protagonist. Max points out to George that his life follows the same pattern as the lives of the heroes in the stories he admires so much: "I had, he confirmed, met nearly all the prerequisites of herohood ... the mystery of my parentage ... the irregularity of my birth ... these and other details corresponded to what Max had found true of scores of hero-histories" (pp. 108–109).

Among the literary heroes he has in mind Max mentions among others Virgil's Aeneas, Dante in *Divina Commedia* and Christ (pp. 110–111). In the course of the novel George attends a performance of *Oedipus Rex* and between him and the protagonist parallels abound; George has a limp, he near-rapes his mother and tries to kill his father (WESCAC), and he is on a quest to find his true identity.

The many references to literature and the parallels between George's life story and that of other literary heroes underline the fictitiousness of the novel. By absorbing previous literature and presenting a pattern of the hero recognizable in a great many stories, the present narrative may be seen as the quintessence of narrative art in general. The story of George's life presents the genesis of the novel itself, though not in a strictly chronological manner. Also, George's story enacts the history of literature from old fairy-tales to computerized fiction.

George's quest for the truth about his own identity represents allegorically an inquiry into the value and meaning of fiction. The other characters in George's world also try to find meaning in their existence. They arrive at various solutions. Stoker holds that "the Answer's *power!*" (p. 180). Dr Sear finds that "Beauty in fact was as close to being the Answer as anything he knew" (p. 191). Peter Greene does not bother about the answer *per se* as much as the circumstance that "a fellow's got a right to whichever Answer strikes him best" (pp. 217–218), giving vent to the typical American liberalism. These are all limited approaches, presenting a partial solution.

The universe in which George operates is marked by a deep-going dichotomy: Stoker has his counterpart in the Chancellor, Eierkopf in Croaker, Greene in Leonid, EASCAC in WESCAC, George in Bray, etc. Max, the Jew who is George's teacher and guide, represents the Old Testament way of thinking; an "eye-for-an-eye" kind of philosophy, and has a strong moral sense of right and wrong. George very soon discovers that his own experience of the world does not always correspond to Max's teaching: When Max denounces Stoker, he feels that "in a way beyond my describing there was something *right* in Stoker's attitude" (p. 211).

As was discussed previously, George eventually manages to attain a view of the world whereby he sees it as a whole and at the same time preserves a sense of its diversity. This is the answer George arrives at, which differs from the solution of all the other characters because of its coherence and completeness.

Accordingly, the function of literature is to find a pattern in the chaos of opposites, to impart a sense of meaning to an apparently meaningless world. A "Grand Tutor" or poet is great because of his capacity to embrace the entirety of the world. Consequently, the value of a work of art depends on the extent to which it manages to present "the difference in unity" ethically, by presenting an "Answer" to man's quest for meaning, and aesthetically, by pointing to the ideal narrative as being both technically brilliant and visionary.

3. The Single-Minded Reader

The narratee in *Giles Goat-Boy* plays a more considerable role than in *The Sot-Weed Factor*. Barth seems to be concerned not only with conveying the importance of his message, but also with the way in which people receive this message.

One of the few direct addresses to the reader is found on the very first page in the "Publisher's Disclaimer", which as a whole is meant to prepare the reader for the narrative proper. The Editor-in-Chief asks that "The reader must begin this book with an act of faith and end it with an act of charity" (p. ix). He claims further that the reader could trust his preface as the only piece of reliable information while the rest of the book should be taken with a pinch of salt. The Editor here introduces one of the central concerns in the novel through his address to the reader, i.e. the question of fictional authenticity.

Formerly we discussed how the "author" in the disguise of Harold Bray enters the world of the narrative as one of the characters. Also the reader finds his way into the novel in the form of an insignificant young girl. In a rather perplexing episode George, fleeing his pursuers, asks this girl to tell him the way. She is sitting behind an information desk, reading a large book which turns out to be the novel itself. This reader has even reached the same point in the novel as we, the readers outside the novel. George speaks of her as:

> Mild, undistinguished creature, never seen before or since . . . in your moment of my time you did enounce, clearly as from a written text, your modest information! Simple answer to a simple question, but lacking which this tale were truncate as the Scroll, an endless fragment!
> "*— less fragment*", I thought I heard her murmur . . . I paused and frowned . . .
> (p. 666).

The girl's words, echoing parts of the narrative, puzzle George, who only sees her as another minor character in his world. The actual author as well as the actual reader, operate on a level outside the narrative and George's consciousness. The reader, however bleak and unpretentious, is like the girl, vital to the narrative: George's flight and thus the narrative itself would have suffered an abrupt termination without the co-operation from the girl. And in the same way the narrative needs a reader to come alive. When the reading stops, the world of the novel comes to a temporary end as well.

Barth cares a great deal about the readers' reactions to the novel. But this is shown rather indirectly. Very rarely does he try to enlist the reader's sympathy through direct appeals to a narratee. In the "Publisher's Disclaimer", four editors speak their minds about the novel. They are asked by the Editor-in-Chief to give their reasons why they think the book should be published or not. In these widely differing reactions, Barth anticipates and satirizes the readers' varying attitudes to his work.

Two concerns are at the basis of the four statements; the editors react to the novel either out of moral considerations or they regard it from an economic point of view. Editors B and C belong to the latter category. They evaluate the manuscript mainly from a pecuniary viewpoint. Editor C says outright that he is voting against publication because the book will not yield a profit, and he finds the manuscript without the moral or aesthetical values that would justify publication despite bad sales.

Editor B does not particularly like the style of this kind of literature. He finds it nevertheless not unlikely that the book may sell at a later date when the penniless followers of its author become influential and establish themselves in society. Editor B recommends therefore that the novel be published.

Editor A rejects the manuscript as unfit for publication on moral grounds. He finds it "a bad book, a wicked book" (p. xi) and wonders whether the Editor-in-Chief would "permit his own daughter to be taught by such a man", i.e. its author.

From the comments of some of the other editors, it is clear that A reacts so violently against the manuscript for highly personal reasons: His own daughter was seduced and then abandoned by a man not unlike the goat-boy. To a great extent the editors' liking or disliking of the manuscript stems from personal rather than professional reasons. The editors must be seen as representative readers who are voicing personal opinions without paying sufficient heed to the author's intentions with his novel.

Editor D reacts completely differently from A. The manuscript has made such an impact on him that he resigns his post. The message of the book has shaken him to the very roots of his being so that he assumes the same kind of attitude as does George at the end of his life. He finds that any act on his part has no effect; whatever he does, it amounts to the same. The world will not change either way. "Publish the *Revised New Syllabus* or reject it; call it art or artifice, fiction, fact, or fraud: it doesn't care, its author doesn't care, and neither any longer do I" (p. xvi). So it is the same to Editor D whether the manuscript is published or not.

George displays a similar indifference to the work which, he claims in the "Posttape", Anastasia has nagged him into undertaking. Without her pressure, George would not have made his recordings into WESCAC, to produce the tapes that will make up the main material for the very manuscript Editor D is asked to consider. George sees that the story of his life will not help anyone to reach the truth he has attained. He finds that every individual has to experience the truth for himself. Man cannot be taught the truth by help of words, because any verbal presentation of the truth is a distortion, a lie.

This is the message Editor D has grasped to the extent that he exclaims: "My judgment is not upon the book but upon myself" (p. xvi). Editor D finds the publication of books futile, just as George asserts that his words of advice to his students "convey nothing" (p. 699). Unlike George, Editor D has not attained the "Answer" to his existence and whether he gets started on his spiritual quest the novel does not say anything about.

One may draw the conclusion from Editor D's example that, contrary to George's assumption about the futility of trying to teach the truth, at least one of his readers has understood that much from the story of his life. It need not disconcert us that George only expresses these thoughts about the futility of communication in the "Posttape", while the rest of the narrative shows how George arrives at an "Answer" to his spiritual quest that may be summed up as "diversity in unity".

"J.B." in his "Postscript to the Posttape" points to the discrepancy between the George of the narrative and the George of the "Posttape", he asserts that the latter does not stem from George at all but has been attached to the manuscript through fraud or by chance. To "J.B.", George's "Answer" is obviously the essence of the novel and not his assumption, expressed in the "Posttape", that truth or his "Answer" cannot be taught, which Editor D singles out as the meaning of the novel.

I do not doubt that "diversity in unity" is an answer or a truth that John Barth wants to convey through *Giles Goat-Boy*, particularly because *The Sot-Weed Factor* also contains a similar message. But in addition, George's existential quest expresses metaphorically the author's artistic concern. What the "Answer" means on this level, and what Barth tries to effectuate, is a combination of brilliancy of form and profundity of message: *Giles Goat-Boy* discusses the genesis and growth of the narrative, besides telling the story about George.

However, the author's concern is not only with the *formulation* but also with the *reception* of the message of the novel. This is underlined through the responses of the editors in the "Publisher's Disclaimer" and of "J.B." in the "Postscript to the Posttape", which all display various reactions to the main narrative.

The problem of fictional authenticity, i.e. whether the narrative conveys a message or truth, is a central theme in the goat-boy story, but it is also made a crucial point in the pre- and postscripts. As mentioned above, the Editor-in-Chief advises the readers to scepticism; two other editors (B and C) are not at all effected by the message of the novel while A rejects it on moral grounds. Only Editor D and "J.B." take the book seriously, but they do not agree about its truth.

The reading girl as an image of the narratee as well as the reactions of the editors and "J.B." illustrate quite clearly that the author is aware of his dependence on the reader and interests himself a great deal in the reader's responses to his writing. But he too nourishes few illusions about the ability of his words to convey his intentions, partly because of the readers' limitations and personal biases.

4. Conclusion – *Giles Goat-Boy*

The many layers in the form of "Publisher's Disclaimer" and "Cover Letter" which the reader is confronted with before reaching the main story widen the distance between the actual author and the narrator-protagonist, George, and add to his fictitiousness.

"J.B.", the writer of the "Cover Letter", is presented as partly responsible for the narrative because his manuscript, *The Seeker*, has been mixed up with the goat-boy's story. "*J.B.*", who has great affinities with John Barth, figures as the representative of the author and explains the relation between the author and the fictional characters. The features of "J.B." 's autobiographical hero have been distributed among the characters of the main story, indicating the author's identification with his characters.

In addition, "J.B." in his meeting with Stoker Giles introduces the central conflict of the main story. "J.B." is described as a man lacking identity who plays many roles without being committed to any of them. Stoker Giles, on the other hand, thinks himself in possession of a message that will save the world and whose first task is to inspire "J.B.". The difference between these two prefigures the opposition between Harold Bray and George, the goat-boy.

Like "J.B.", Harold Bray, whose likeness to John Barth is stressed, functions as a representative of the author and reveals the author-character relationship. Bray's function as author overlaps with the narrator's role; Bray is described as partly omniscient and has no identity of his own, but is constantly playing new parts. He intrudes into the story and identifies with some of the characters, but his banishment and machine-like appearance in the end underline that an author after all belongs to another world than his characters.

The difference between Harold Bray, as the author, and the characters becomes still more explicit in his struggle with George, the first person narrator. George and Bray both claim to be the "Grand Tutor" or the saving Messiah. This means that they both assert their authenticity: Bray alleges the author's supremacy over the characters: George as well as the others depend on him for their fictional identity. In this sense, Bray is the "Grand Tutor".

As for the saving business, Bray admits that he is an impostor who gulls people: Bray reveals here a central characteristic of the author who deceives his readers by adopting roles when creating his characters. Also, Bray discloses his scepticism of his own worth *qua* author.

George refuses to acknowledge Bray's or anyone else's authority over himself. He demands to be recognized as a hero, divinely inspired to save the world with his message. This means that the narrator-protagonist may possess truly genuine qualities despite the author's scepticism about his own role as well as that of his characters.

George's message, which may be formulated as "difference in unity", implies that he manages to achieve a view of existence as a whole, despite its opposing forces and strife. However, George's message concerns not only his status as saving hero, but also his role as narrator. George manages to see Harold Bray as the necessary opponent to himself, which suggests that the ideal narrator should combine Bray's craftmanship and George's commitment.

The discussion of the narrative centred on two propositions; George's story as an allegory about the origin and development of fiction, and the function and value of literature. George may be seen to symbolize a piece of narrative, telling the story of its own genesis. From his "inhuman birth" onwards, when he emerges from the computer, George's "literary" nature is constantly referred to. *Giles Goat-Boy* becomes in a way the quintessence of particularly narrative art: George enacts the traditional role of the hero, and his story incorporates the styles and forms of previous literature.

George's story contains the final solution to his own quest. His message imparts meaning to his chaotic surroundings. This suggests that the function of literature is to give meaning to what is ostensibly meaningless. The value of literature depends on the extent to which its message assumes universal significance. However, visionary answers do not suffice; the ideal work of art must also aspire towards formal brilliance.

Giles Goat-Boy has few references to a narratee. However, the incident with the reading girl who enters the narrative, and on whom the narrator depends for his continuation, shows that Barth is aware of the reader's importance for his story to come alive.

However, Barth satirizes the biased reader by presenting the various reactions of the editors and "J.B." to the main story. Barth is clearly concerned about the reader, but quite disillusioned about his ability to grasp his message.

Conclusion

A conspicuous feature in both of Barth's novels is the relationship between two highly different characters; Henry Burlingame and Ebenezer Cooke in *The Sot-Weed Factor* and Harold Bray and George Giles in *Giles Goat-Boy*. These relationships elucidate a central theme in the two books: the making of the poet. Notions of art and of the creator of art – the poet or the author – vary considerably: Henry and Eben represent adverse types of poets, while Harold Bray and George totally disagree about the status of their roles as author and narrator-protagonist respectively.

In *The Sot-Weed Factor* the fundamentally disparate views on the issue of the poet/narrator's role are traced back to the dispute about the universals in antiquity. While the realists held universals to exist independently of and prior to physical existence, the nominalists claimed that the universals had no independent existence and originated *post res*.

In the two works under consideration this debate is given both a social-existential and a religious dimension: it concerns the poet/narrator's experience of his surroundings and his faith in God's existence. The two novels express, on the one hand, a conception of the poet/narrator as solely dependent on his own experience of the world: this would correspond to the nominalists' idea. On the other hand, the poet/narrator's status is presented as bestowed on him from God and therefore independent of his experiences of the world: this would answer to the realists' view.

Henry Burlingame and Harold Bray embody the nominalist idea. They both take an active part and are well versed in the affairs of the world which they manipulate and deceive. They constantly play new roles, having no identity of their own. Their lack of religious foundation manifests itself in their general disillusion about their own role and their contempt for the world. Henry Burlingame and Harold Bray become the prototype of the poet/narrator who knows all the tricks of his profession, but has no faith in his role and his message.

Ebenezer Cooke and George Giles represent the opposite category, corresponding to the realist concept. At first they both have no contact with the world, of which they nourish the most idealized, preconceived ideas. They also consider themselves as saviours who have been given the mission to deliver the world from its evil. Ebenezer and George may be seen as the kind of poet/narrator who believes himself in possession of a message of divine truth but who lacks the means of bringing it across to the world.

Both novels advocate a synthesis of the two conceptions of the poet/narrator. Eben and George go through an identity crisis by which they finally attain knowledge and acceptance of the world. This is symbolically expressed through their relation to a woman. Eben reaches a balance between involvement with life and dedication to art. George gains a wholistic view of existence recognizing simultaneously its diversity and its unity.

The view of the ideal artist/narrator expressed in the novels is strongly related to the conception of art in the books. However, Barth employs different techniques in his two works to stress the metafictional quality. In *The Sot-*

Weed Factor Henry and Eben have a discussion going on the question of mimesis. Also their respective poems disclose their various approaches to this problem. Henry asserts that literature should render as accurate a picture of reality as possible, leaving in the sordid details. Eben regards poetry as an alternative to existence and aimed at creating an imaginary, idealized world.

In *Giles Goat-Boy* Barth uses allegory to draw attention to the metafictional nature of the novel and its protagonist. George's affinity to a book is pointed out, as well as his relatedness to previous heroes of world literature. Secondly, the novel imitates styles and forms of earlier works. The difference of technique between the novels may be regarded as reflecting Barth's development. In *The Sot-Weed Factor* he abandons the realistic approach of the early novels, the question of mimesis forming a matter of dispute between the main characters. In *Giles Goat-Boy*, where the question of mimesis no longer haunts him, he takes the full step into metafiction, also as regards form.

Both novels express the same view regarding the function and value of literature. In *The Sot-Weed Factor* a synthesis is reached between Henry's and Eben's views. Henry asserts that the value of art depends on its ability to create interest with its readers and that art should be mimetic; Eben holds that art has inherent qualities regardless of its popularity with the reading public and of its correspondence to the world. Eben approaches Henry's ideas in his poem "The Sot-Weed Factor", which has its basis in the factual circumstances in Maryland, but presents its people and customs in a satiric fashion.

In *Giles Goat-Boy*, George's message is not only offering people a solution to their existential problems, it is also a pronouncement on art. Literature should impart meaning by pointing to the pattern of a seemingly chaotic world. However, this aim can only be fulfilled if the narrative combines a distinguished technique with a convincing message.

The narratee plays a less important part in *The Sot-Weed Factor* than in *Giles Goat-Boy*, but the narrator's general attitude to the reader is similar in both novels. The reader is important in the sense that without him the book will not come alive and its message will have absolutely no effect. However, both novels express scepticism concerning the readers' ability to grasp the narrator's intention with his work. Thus, Eben's poem "The Sot-Weed Factor" is interpreted as a paean instead of a denunciation of Maryland. The various reactions of "J.B." and the editors to the story of the goat-boy show that none of them have completely understood the message.

The main introduction to this chapter draws attention to the artist's split personality, exemplified in the image of the Siamese twins, as central in Barth's art. The theme of the two strains in the artist's personality – one directed towards life, the other a drive towards art and indirectly also towards death – is traceable in both *The Sot-Weed Factor* and *Giles Goat-Boy*. The poet – first and foremost exemplified in Eben and George – manages to attain a balance between art and life, technique and message, aesthetical and ethical claims. Thus the triangle of Thalia and the Siamese twins is secured a harmonious life at last, both in *The Sot-Weed Factor*, where this geometrical figure becomes the most significant symbol, and in George's saving message in *Giles Goat-Boy*.

IV. Samuel Beckett's Trilogy:
Circling Disintegration

The general trend in the visual arts after the Second World War has been depicted as a movement where the artist directs his attention towards himself, emphasizing his own individuality. At the same time he tries to escape from this situation by turning towards the technique employed in the artistic creation.[1] This may be taken as an apt description also of Beckett's work, more particularly of the position in which the various narrators in his trilogy find themselves. The relatedness of Beckett's fiction to *avant-garde* painting is not surprising, since he has written and published criticism on contemporary painting and has kept in close contact with modern painters and their work.[2] A comparison between Beckett's art and modern painting directs one's attention to a central issue in his fiction: the artist's concern with his own situation, in both its technical and existential aspects.

Beckett is the kind of writer who puzzles and intrigues his readers, which may explain why his work has attracted an enormous amount of criticism.[3] This examination will discuss Beckett's trilogy from a metafictional point of view. In the last decade criticism concentrating on the formal elements in Beckett has become more prevalent. Michael Robinson says in his book on Beckett that the author makes the writer's "situation the basis of his central work, the trilogy of novels".[4] He points out the metafictional quality of the work in the way the author incorporates earlier fiction "from *Robinson Crusoe* to Proust and Joyce" into his novels and comments on the fictional devices.[5]

Where Robinson mentions the conscious imitation of earlier narratives, H. Porter Abbott discusses the mirror effect within Beckett's fictional universe: the two-part structure in the works themselves, such as for instance in *Molloy*, and the similarity in the situation of the various narrators in works like *Malone Dies* and *Molloy*.[6] Hannah C. Copeland examines the artist's role as presented in Beckett's work, his probing within himself and the agony connected with the act of creation.[7] Dina Sherzer also deals with the narrator-artist's situation, but from a linguistic viewpoint. Analyzing the language in the trilogy, especially the use of the tenses, Sherzer debates the part played by the narrators in the three novels.[8]

Other critics, such as Gerald Bruns and Wolfgang Iser,[9] take up the metafictional aspect but to a lesser extent. My study does not dispute to any large degree the essential points of the discussions of Beckett's trilogy by the critics mentioned above. However, in this discussion the trilogy will be approached from a different angle: by focusing on the three narrative elements, the narrator, the narrative, and the narratee, my hope is to throw new light on and develop further some of the points raised in the earlier criticism.

The three novels in the trilogy, *Molloy, Malone Dies* and *The Unnamable*, may at first seem to have few common characteristics.[10] Usually the same characters and very often the same setting recur from one work to the next in a trilogy. Such expectations on the reader's part are not fulfilled in Beckett's trilogy. The novelist has himself stated the connection between the works: "*Malone* came from *Molloy, The Unnamable* came from *Malone*".[11] The opening sentence of the second paragraph of *Molloy* predicts the writing of the two next novels: "This time, then once more I think, then perhaps a last time, then I think it'll be over, with that world too".[12] Critics have centred on the narrator's situation when trying to establish connections between the three parts. Especially his physical deterioration from one book to the next has been mentioned.[13] Dina Sherzer points to what is essential in the interrelatedness between the individual works. She finds that the trilogy concerns the act of writing, the three novels marking three stages in the works of the narrator.[14] Obviously, the narrator's physical deterioration through the three novels expresses metaphorically the narrator's growing feeling of exhaustion and struggle with his subject.

The following discussion will first deal with the tree novels separately, analyzing in each work the narrator's conception of his own situation and how this again influences the narrative and the relation to the reader. Lastly a comparison will be made between the three works of the trilogy.

Molloy, Part I

1. Puppet on a String:
The Uncommunicative, Suffering Narrator

Molloy falls into two nearly equal parts, and the narrators of these parts, despite similarities of character and features, form two distinct individuals. This discussion will therefore deal with the two parts separately, and the question of the interrelatedness between the parts will be considered in connection with the second part.

At the opening of the novel, Molloy presents himself as a man confined to a room where his main occupation is writing: indeed an accurate description of the writer's position. Apart from his staying in his mother's room and his writing, Molloy appears to be in a state of bewilderment concerning both his own situation and the world at large. He does not know how he got to the room nor what his relation is to the man who gives him money in return for the pages he writes, and he worries about the disappearance of his mother. What all this confusion boils down to is the simple question: *why* do I write? "Yet I don't work for money. For what then? I don't know". (p. 7). Despite his flagging will and the declining ability of a dying man, Molloy continues to write. What then is the impetus behind his writing?

This question occupies Molloy and Moran, the narrator in the second part of the novel, to a greater extent than the narrators in *Malone Dies* and *The Unnamable*. Molloy deals with this problem both in the opening of the novel in the description of the visitor, and later when he mentions the inner voices. Molloy presents himself as being directed by an authority from outside whose will does not always conform to his own wishes: "What I'd like now is to speak of the things that are left, say my good-byes, finish dying. They don't want that. Yes, there is more than one, apparently. But it's always the same one that comes. You'll do that later, he says. Good". (p. 7). Clearly a discrepancy exists between Molloy, first person narrator, and "they" to whom the visitor belongs. They are the ones that prompt Molloy to write and he succumbs apparently to their will.

Besides the external incentives, Molloy refers to a voice within himself. Hannah Copeland links this with the visitor: "The voice, like the strange visitor, harries Molloy. Indeed, it seems to convey the creative imperative itself".[15] The difference remains, however, that Molloy presents "them" as forces outside the narrator while he describes the voice as coming from within.

However, Molloy makes the function of the voice quite clear, and demonstrates its connection to the rest of his narrative, including the visitor:

> And every time I say, I said this, or, I said that, or speak of a voice saying, far away
> inside me, Molloy, and then a fine phrase more or less clear and simple, or find

myself compelled to attribute to others intelligible words, or hear my own voice uttering to others more or less articulate sounds, I am merely complying with the convention that demands you either lie or hold your peace. For what really happened was quite different. And I did not say, Yet a little while, at the rate things are going, etc., but that resembled perhaps what I would have said, if I had been able. In reality I said nothing at all, but I heard a murmur, something gone wrong with the silence . . . And then sometimes there arose within me, confusedly, a kind of consciousness, which I express by saying, I said, etc., or, Don't do it, Molloy, or, Is that your mother's name? said the sergeant, I quote from memory. (pp. 93–4)

Here Molloy describes parts of the creative process. The incentive to write, the voice, comes from within the narrator himself who gives expression to the promptings of the voice by inventing the other speakers or characters in the story. The visitor, like his mother or the policeman, is also a figure that arises from his confused consciousness. The difference between the visitor and the other characters is that he may more easily be connected with the voice. As will be discussed in the analysis of the narrative in *Molloy*, the characters represent aspects of the creative process of the narrative.

The narrator in the first part of *Molloy* pays relatively little attention to the visitor's identity, which is bound up with the question of why he writes. He is far more concerned with his difficulties in expressing himself. Molloy's story amounts to a long, rambling monologue. Nevertheless, in the course of the tale he recounts instances where attempts at communicating with another human being have been made.

Molloy's meeting with his mother discloses the difficulties he experiences when trying to establish contact with his fellow men. What is the exact relation between Molloy and his mother? He describes the two of them as "a couple of old cronies" (p. 17), and besides, he finds that they have the appearance of husband and wife. Molloy's three-fold function of son, friend, and husband indicates the universal meaning of the relationship. The mother-son relation represents the relationship between fellow human beings in general. His attitude towards his mother signifies Molloy's or the narrator's relation to the world at large.

Molloy's motives for seeking his mother seem to stem from a genuine "craving for a fellow" (p. 16). But his description of the visit makes one suspect that his reasons are of a pecuniary nature despite his protesting that "I took her money, but I didn't come for that" (p. 19). On the other hand, his mother has never felt too warmly towards him either, and she has been trying to get rid of him from the time of his conception. The communication between Molloy and his mother has strong farcical overtones. She chatters away in a more or less meaningless and continuous monologue. Molloy, however, does not care to listen. Because she is deaf, Molloy conveys *his* message to *her* by means of a code of knocks, aimed at her skull. Even the meaning of the knocks does not always reach her. She often misunderstands despite Molloy's efforts to teach her.

This meeting between mother and son, seen as representing the relation between the narrator and the world, invites a number of possible interpretations. First of all it demonstrates the lack of communication and the narrator's isolation, speaking to and about himself. This impression is strengthened by the fact that in describing his mother he describes in fact himself, bed-ridden and prattling, confined to his room. In the end his writing makes it impossible for him to escape his own situation. As he is physically unable to get away, so his thoughts and words are concentrated on himself. This situation must be seen as a metaphor of the kind of fiction this work represents, the metafictional novel where the narrator lays bare his own situation *qua* narrator.

The meeting between Molloy and his mother also demonstrates the circular movement of the novel, which opens with the conclusion to Molloy's search. Seeking his mother and ending up with himself in her room shows how the whole search is after all for himself. The circular pattern of this novel is repeated in the other books of the trilogy: The narrator makes an effort to describe characters outside himself, but imperceptibly he becomes the subject of the description.

Molloy's failure to establish a meaningful exchange with another human being is repeated in his encounters with the policeman and later with the official at the police station. He thinks he understands the questions directed to him, but the reactions of the others to his answers prove that he is mistaken: "So it always is when I'm reduced to confabulation, I honestly believe I have answered the question I am asked and in reality I do nothing of the kind" (p. 21).

Molloy tries to find the reason why he has difficulties in communicating with others and why he finds conversation so distressing. This he explains, is because he hears and speaks words that lack meaning. He finds that the words are mere sounds to him:

> And this is perhaps one of the reasons I was so untalkative, I mean this trouble I had in understanding not only what others said to me, but also what I said to them. It is true that in the end . . . we made ourselves understood, but understood with regard to what, I ask of you, and to what purpose? (p. 53)

Again here is an utterance which gives rise to numberless possibilities of interpretation. Why are words without meaning to Molloy? First, Molloy obviously lacks contact with the outer reality that surrounds him and therefore he does not attach the same meaning to the words as others do. Molloy is concerned with his own inner reality, his own experiences as a narrator. Secondly, his inner reality, his own situation, is bound to be different from what others experience. Consequently, the words he has inherited from others may appear as unsuitable tools to deal with reality as he sees it: the words do not correspond to reality as he experiences it. No wonder that Molloy has difficulties in being understood and constantly talks of the pain of conversation.

Molloy's sufferings, i.e. his growing difficulties in walking, figures prominently in the novel: "And now my progress, slow and painful at all times, was more so than ever" (p. 81). Molloy has one stiff leg and in the course of the story he experiences a gradually increasing lameness in the other one. Ursula Dreysse explains the crippling of Molloy's legs as symbolizing his drawing back into himself and his failing contact with the world.[16] But also, since the novel deals with the making of literature, Molloy's painful journey can be taken as a metaphorical description of his difficulties as a narrator. Molloy makes this quite clear when he explains that his legs are just a symptom of what really ails him: "if my progress ... was becoming more and more slow and painful, this was not due solely to my legs, but also to innumerable so-called weak points, having nothing to do with my legs. Unless one is to suppose, gratuitously, that they and my legs were part of the same syndrome" (pp. 87–88). Molloy's painful walking indicates his difficulty as a narrator: he has problems in getting on with his story as well as finding words to express his real meaning.

2. Narrative Journey Through Mental Landscapes

Dina Sherzer remarks that in *Molloy* one sees a narrator at work organizing his narrative and at the same time evaluating what he writes.[17] Obviously, in this kind of narrative the borderline between the narrator and the narrative does not stand out very sharply. In the long opening paragraph the narrator has described his own situation. In the next paragraph he manages slowly to shake himself off, and he tries to become involved with his characters. Incidents from earlier times seem to pass in review before his inner eye. But he finds that the people that pass are "hard to distinguish from yourself. That is discouraging. So I saw A and C going slowly towards each other, unconscious of what they were doing" (p. 8). The narrator does not mention where he is situated in relation to A and C, but by the way he describes them it is clear that he sees them from outside. Some few pages later he visualizes his own position, being perched high on a rock with a good view of his surroundings. Traditionally, this position has often been chosen by the poet to indicate his role as detached observer. Coverdale, for instance, in Hawthorne's *The Blithedale Romance*, finds himself a hermitage in some trees that afford a good view and ample opportunity to study the surrounding landscape and its people.

After A and C have passed, another character appears, or rather C develops into an old man with a stick, who in his turn becomes a gentleman with a stick and with a dog following him in circles. This reminds one of the narrator's movements, as described above. (Later in the Lousse incident, Molloy again uses a dog to throw light on his own situation). The narrator climbs down from his observation rock at last and tries to come into direct contact with this gentleman: "He [the gentleman] is kind, tells me of this and that and other things . . . I believe him, I know it's my only chance . . . What I need now is stories . . . I try my best not to talk about myself" (p. 13). However, the man leaves and the narrator feels free to talk about himself. He starts to portray the old man with the stick, but he is so like himself that when he is describing the man's hat, his talk imperceptibly turns to his own hat and then to his own situation.

In all these initial stories, where the narrator tries to get on with a narrative that does not concern himself, he makes it explicitly clear that the characters are fictive, figuring in a story. This is also the case, but not so easily seen, when the narrator continues with himself as protagonist. The narrator starts an account of his search for his mother, after first having described a former visit to her (cf. part one): "Now that we know where we're going, let's go there" (p. 20). As will be shown, the various incidents of this journey illustrate various aspects of the narrator's situation as drawn up in the first part of this discussion, i.e. the question of why he writes, his difficulties of communication and his suffering. The problems Molloy has to tackle are not so easily seen to be those of the narrator. The metafictional aspect of the various incidents in Molloy's journey tend to be overlooked.

The narrator has not ventured very far on his journey when he finds himself being arrested by a policeman who is dissatisfied with his way of proceeding, more accurately his way of resting. It is no use to point out his infirmity to the policeman: "there are not two laws, one for the healthy, another for the sick, but one only to which all must bow" (p. 21). The following interview with the officer shows that the first person narrator has sinned against public decorum and that the whole incident serves as an ironic comment on what kind of narrator and fiction the public wants. The narrator is expected to get on with his story, and not to stop, demonstrating his own inability: this kind of literature is not acceptable. Anyway, the narrator has learned something from this incident; he understands that by his way of resting he sets a bad example to the public; because "people . . . so need to be encouraged, in their bitter toil, and to have before their eyes manifestations of strength only, of courage and of joy" (p. 26). Indeed, this is an accurate description of the kind of function literature is very often expected to have: the public at large demands that fiction should present successful individuals with whom they can identify.

The narrator is arrested for committing an offence against public decency. The police very soon find other things to hold against him. They discover that he has no papers of identity, "nor any occupation, nor any domicile", that he cannot remember his surname nor his mother's address though he "knew how to get there" (p. 23). The narrator is not set free till these things are settled: his name and his mother's he suddenly admits to be Molloy, and when pressed he decides that his mother lives near the shambles. As a narrator, Molloy has broken the rules of the normal way of telling a story. Instead of providing information for the reader, the narrator has left everything in the dark, such as his own identity and that of his mother, and questions of time and place.[18] When the narrator's identity has finally been established as that of Molloy, he very soon finds himself released to start his journey afresh.

However, Molloy's progress is once more hindered as he becomes trapped by a woman called Lousse. The reference is clearly to Circe, the sorceress Odysseus encounters on his way home from Troy.[19] Lousse does not change Molloy into a pig, but she wants him to take the place of her dog, and Molloy feels when the dog is buried that he attends his own funeral: a part of his identity is buried as well. Like her predecessor, Lousse has great knowledge of herbs and tries to dull Molloy's consciousness with "molys" (p. 57). At times he forgets his mother and his original plan of going to her.

Molloy explains his long stay with Lousse in terms of two opposing drives in himself: "For in me there have always been two fools, among others, one asking nothing better than to stay where he is and the other imagining that life might be slightly less horrible a little further on" (p. 51). These opposing forces are concretely represented in the description of two worlds; Lousse's secluded garden and the outside world: "But I left Lousse at last, one warm airless night . . . Outside in the road the wind was blowing, it was another world" (p. 62–3). Lousse's garden is characterized by its changelessness: "For the garden seemed hardly to change, from day to day, apart from the tiny changes due to the customary cycle of birth, life and death" (p. 55). In this world of material satisfaction and spiritual stupor, Molloy is never quite at ease. He compares himself to "a dead leaf" (p. 55) and, in his vegetative kind of existence, he observes that he "forgot not only who I was, but that I was, forgot to be" (p. 52).

In Lousse's world, Molloy is stripped of his clothes and his hat; his beard is shaved off: all this indicating that Molloy is in danger of losing his identity, or that part of his identity that makes him want to continue his journey as a narrator. Molloy connects the Lousse garden with

the indestructible chaos of timeless things . . . leaning things, forever lapsing and crumbling away . . . Yes a world at an end, in spite of appearances . . . And I too am at an end, when I am there, my eyes close, my sufferings cease and I end, I wither as the living can not. (p. 42)

Lousse's garden represents a world free of material cares, which possesses the appearance of durability because of the perpetual cycle of physical renewal but where individual life is lost. Molloy chooses to leave this garden because it destroys his identity as a narrator and makes him unable to continue his journey to create something of lasting value.

The whole of the Lousse incident shows metaphorically the kind of obstructions the narrator meets with. After all, these stem from himself, because the landscapes through which Molloy moves are mental ones:

> But I preferred to abide by my simple feeling . . . that said, Molloy, your region is vast, you have never left it and you never shall. . . . But now I do not wander any more . . . and yet nothing is changed. And the confines of my room, of my bed, of my body, are as remote from me as were those of my region, in the days of my splendour. (p. 70)

After the pleasant but meaningless stay in Lousse's garden, Molloy, proceeding painfully, reaches the sea. Here his range of vision is expanded and he himself becomes more clear-sighted: "Yes, ranging far wide . . . my good eye saw more clearly and there were even days when the bad one too had to look away. And not only did I see more clearly, but I had less difficulty in saddling with a name the rare things I saw" (p. 80). This quotation makes it clear that the looking away means directing his attention away from himself and it is only then his vision improves. Further, Molloy is here as through the rest of the novel concerned with the process of attaching words to things, i.e. with the occupation of writing.

Molloy describes the sea as "one direction at least in which I could go no further, without first getting wet, then drowned" (p. 73). In this novel, as elsewhere in the trilogy, the sea connotes death (cf. the end of *Malone Dies*). At the seaside or in the perspective of death, Molloy gains a clearer view of himself and his surroundings. However, to remain here means "rotting in peace" (p. 80) and Molloy soon finds that the thought of mother starts bothering him again. To find her town, "you had to go inland" (p. 80), which means that Molloy had to look into himself, his search for mother being after all a search for himself.

Turning inland, Molloy nearly gets lost in the forest which also forms a part of his "region". His progress is hindered both by the growing pain in his legs and by the lack of light in the forest. Molloy is detained by a charcoal-burner who does not understand his question about the whereabouts of his mother's town: "He did not know. He was born in the forest probably and had spent his whole life there" (p. 89). Molloy, who is *not* born there, wants to get out despite what it costs him and he kills the charcoal-burner: "But I could not, stay in the forest . . . physically nothing could have been easier, but I was not purely physical" (pp. 91–2). Molloy is more than a physical thing. There are his prompters, his imperatives, the voice which tells him to go on in the teeth of mental and physical exhaustion.

Lastly, Molloy is stranded on a plain, bordering on the forest and with a view of a town that may be his mother's when the first part of the novel ends. He hears the sound of a gong and this gong reappears in the second part. He is promised help, which he gets when Moran takes over as the narrator in the second part of the book. The story of Molloy ends with the narrator close to his destination, his mother's town. The meeting with mother has already been described in the beginning of the novel. The whole journey from Molloy's observation of A and C to his gaining a view of the "promised land" of his mother's abode, is presented as a metaphorical description of the obstacles the narrator has to overcome if he is to continue his story.

The narrative has come full circle when Molloy ends where he started, in the vicinity of his mother's room. In this way the story line as a whole makes one great circle. Departing from his mother's room, which is now his, Molloy in the end returns to it. But Molloy also undertakes circular movements on a smaller scale: the whole narrative of the journey consists of various incidents; Molloy's experiences at the police station, in Lousse's garden etc., interspersed with passages that more directly describe Molloy's situation, his pain and declining health. From every one of the stories, in which Molloy figures as one of the characters, he returns to discuss his own plight quite openly, abandoning any pretence of getting on with the story of the journey.

In the course of the narrative, Molloy refers repeatedly to his way of proceeding in spirals or circles:

> And having heard . . . that when a man in a forest thinks he is going forward in a straight line, in reality he is going in a circle, I did my best to go in a circle, hoping in this way to go in a straight line . . . . And if I did not go in a rigorously straight line . . . at least I did not go in a circle, and that was something. (pp. 90–1)

As always Molloy is indeed doing his best to contradict himself and confuse the reader. The answer to the question of his moving in circles or in a straight line must be both yes and no: despite his eternally circling about himself, Molloy manages to proceed, getting his story told, after all.

The various incidents in Molloy's journey and his way of progressing in circles, have direct bearing on the meaning of the story as a work of metafiction. Another element of the narrative that has importance in this respect is the significance of sex. In Beckett as in other works of metafiction, sexual activity is used symbolically to throw light on the narrator's creative ability. In contrast to Sterne, Nabokov and Barth, Beckett employs descriptions of sex relatively sparingly and besides the protagonist in for instance *Molloy*, I, displays an enfeebled and perverse sex life.

In the discussion of the narrator's role, Molloy's lameness was seen to express his inability to get on with his story. Likewise, Molloy's impotence and his mild adventures with the opposite sex signal his flagging powers as a creator of fiction. He describes, for instance, his affair with a woman whose name he thinks is Edith. Their experience he finds must be given the name of love because that is what the woman tells him. Molloy is not convinced: "Perhaps after all she put me in her rectum. A matter of complete indifference to me, I needn't tell you. But is it true love, in the rectum? That's what bothers me sometimes. Have I never known true love, after all?" (p. 60). First, the quotation shows how Molloy mixes up sex and anal matters. The meaning of this becomes clearer when seen in the light of another instance where Molloy equates what the anus emits with the words that issue from his mouth (cf. p. 85). Creativity, sexual and verbal, seems equally disgusting to Molloy, and both activities are compared to the anal kind of "production". Indeed, Molloy appears to be quite disillusioned about the worth of his narrative.

The quotation given above further discloses Molloy's inexperience and failure in establishing contact with other human beings. Molloy molds his pattern of behaviour in the sexual act on the conduct of dogs: "It seemed all right to me, for I had seen dogs" (p. 60). As this description comes in the middle of the Lousse incident, it may point to the fact that with her Molloy is reduced to a dog, also with regard to sexual behaviour. But, in addition, his description of his experience with Edith indicates his general failure to estab lish normal human relations, his inability to set up a meaningful communication with people other than himself.

This interpretation is also made plausible by Molloy's referring to "the alleged joys of so-called self-abuse" (p. 62). Molloy feels tormented by the thought that "all my life has been devoid of love" (p. 62). Seen in the light of the symbolic meaning of sex referred to above, what Molloy really fears is that he writes not only about himself but also for himself. His narrative is too much bound up with his own person to be of genuine interest and worth to others. His story may be summed up in his own words: "Molloy, or life without a chambermaid" (p. 62). His solipsism worries Molloy and accordingly when his "mother's image sometimes mingles with" that of the other women in his life, this is a thought "literally unendurable, like being crucified" (p. 62). As discussed above, his search for his mother is after all no more than a search for himself. His attempts at establishing contact with others are vain because what he seeks, in reality, is only himself. Molloy portrays himself as a person who knows that his search will end in himself: *he*, the individual man, is what existence amounts to. The references to crucifixion when describing his sufferings may indicate that Molloy sees himself as the only man able to continue despite his realization of the full horror of a life without meaning outside himself. Seen in this perspective one appreciates the appropriateness of anal symbolism to indicate the value Molloy attaches to the narrative about himself.

3. Narratee: Narrator Talking to Himself

In the discussion of the narrative, it was pointed out that no clear distinction exists between the narrator and the narrative because the narrator talks about himself. The same is true of the relation between the narrator and the narratee. Throughout the story, the narrator frequently turns to a "you". The distance between the narrator and the narratee varies: sometimes "you" is hardly distinguishable from the narrator himself: "And the things that are worth while you do not bother about . . . knowing that all these questions of worth and value have nothing to do with you, who . . . must go on not knowing it, on pain of, I wonder what, yes, I wonder" (p. 48). The narrator is here commenting on his way of writing and seems to be talking to *himself* with his reference to "you". This impression is strengthened as the second person pronoun is almost imperceptibly displaced by the first person pronoun "I" near the end of the quotation.

On another occasion in the narrative, the person spoken to, "you", stands clearly aside from the speaker: "For I no longer know what I am doing . . . I don't deny it, for why deny it, and to whom, to you, to whom nothing is denied?" (p. 48). Though the "you" and "I" stand clearly apart, they seem to be on intimate terms with each other. The different relations between the narrator and the narratee reflect Molloy's general problem as a narrator, as discussed in the part dealing with the narrative: he urgently wishes to get away from his own situation and portray other characters, but even when he at times succeeds in this, these other characters have strong affinities with himself. This is true of the narratee as well.

The close relationship between narrator and narratee becomes more noticeable when the two are mentioned as "we": "I apologise for these details, in a moment we'll go faster, much faster" (p. 67). When his narrative turns towards more or less insignificant, minor matters, Molloy is conscious of the fact that this may bore the reader. But he feels confident in the narratee's goodwill when resorting to the first person plural pronoun.

Nevertheless, despite the use of "you" or "we", the narrator is mainly directing his speech to himself. In the following quotation Molloy keeps up the pretence of a dialogue by asking questions and answering them himself: "The house where Lousse lived. Must I describe it? I don't think so . . . And Lousse? Must I describe her? I suppose so. Let's first bury the dog" (p. 37). As has been pointed out, Molloy has great difficulties in being understood by others. Perhaps his talking to himself is just a consequence of his inability to make himself understood and communicate with others.

Molloy seems to reckon with a limited audience to his narrative, which may well account for the intimacy between narrator and narratee. As Molloy is mostly talking to himself, an utterance like "between you and me" (p. 84) has a comic effect. Perhaps it also brings out the pathetic aspect of Molloy's situation, his total isolation. Molloy needs a "you" to whom he can tell his story. The only "you" he can communicate with is himself.

Molloy, Part II

1. The Undecipherable Narrator

In the second part of *Molloy*, Moran takes over as the narrator. The difference could hardly have been greater between the brisk Jacques Moran of the opening pages of the second part of the novel and the decrepit Molloy in desperate need of help at the end of part one. Edith Kern, using expressions from Nietzsche's aestheticism, finds that Molloy's world corresponds to the Dionysian element in art and Moran's to the Apollonian.[20]

Nearly every critic dealing with *Molloy* has been puzzled by the difference between the two parts and has tried to solve the riddle by tracking down similarities between the two narrators, Moran and Molloy.[21] Dina Sherzer finds that the juxtaposition of the two different parts of *Molloy* makes the particularity of *Molloy*, I, stand out more clearly: Moran tries to present a story while in *Molloy*, I, the story-line is constantly broken by references to the narrator's situation as he writes his narrative.[22] Comparisons between the two parts will be made in the course of the following discussion whenever this seems useful as a clarification of the points under examination.

At the opening of his narrative, Moran makes it quite clear that he is writing a story, just as Molloy does in the beginning of part one. But Moran is not dying; he seems to be in his prime, living with his son and moving freely around in his room. And Moran proves to be quite another kind of narrator than Molloy; more able to get on with his story or report. David Hesla sums up the meaning of the Moran part quite accurately when he says that it is "a parabolic presentation of a certain facet of the task of writing . . ."[23] Another indication that the story deals with the narrator's situation is the repetition of the two first sentences at the end of the novel: "It is midnight. The rain is beating on the windows" (p. 189). And then Moran, according to Federman, "cancels his own fiction"[24] by adding "It was not midnight. It was not raining" (p. 189). When Moran in the same breath first affirms and then negates his own statements, the narrator brings to the readers' attention that his story is after all no more than a fictitious tale. Thus the metafictional quality of the narrative cannot be overlooked. In addition, the beginning and the end of part two show that like Molloy, Moran also moves in circles, coming back to the point he started from.

Like Molloy, Moran first describes his present situation. He is sitting at his desk, writing. Then Moran's actual account begins with a description of how he first got started on his investigation of Molloy and on the report he has to make of this, with which he is presently occupied: "I remember the day I received the order to see about Molloy. It was a Sunday in summer. I was sitting in my little garden, in a wicker chair" (p. 99). This idyll is broken when

Moran receives a visitor, Gaber, who presents Moran with the order from "the chief (one Youdi)" (p. 116) to make a report on Molloy. Moran's peaceful garden makes the reader think of Lousse's garden and Molloy's stay here; apart from external resemblances such as the wicket-gate which marks the entrance to both, Moran's indolence echoes Molloy's state of mind at the time of his stay in the garden. Moran also has ambivalent feelings about leaving, i.e. about starting on the narrator's journey. He leaves at last, but reluctantly.

Moran and Molloy both receive a visitor and even if Gaber, having a name, may seem less mysterious than Molloy's anonymous visitor, these are tools, acting on orders from others. Molloy's visitor represents the embodiment of the force that prompts him to write. The same is true of Moran's visitor: The relations between Youdi, Gaber and Moran are bound up with the incentives behind Moran's narrative, the question of why he writes.

Jan Hokenson shows how Youdi and Gaber connote Yahweh and the Prophet Gabriel, who was sent with a message to Daniel in the Old Testament.[25] The incentive to write is presented as coming from a source outside Moran:

> He wants it to be you, God knows why, said Gaber. I presume he told you why, I said, scenting flattery, for which I had a weakness. He said, replied Gaber, that no one could do it but you . . . He doesn't know what he says, said Gaber. He added, Nor what he does . . . In that case it's hard for me to refuse, I said, knowing perfectly well that in any case it was impossible for me to refuse. Refuse! But we agents often amused ourselves with grumbling among ourselves and giving ourselves the air of free men. (pp. 101–2)

In the first line of the quotation above, the "he" in Moran's answer may refer back to "God" in Gaber's statement, indicating an association between Youdi and "God". This suggests that Moran sets out to write his report on Molloy by divine inspiration. However god-like Youdi may be, Gaber's and Moran's remarks about him indicate that he is an irrational power who orders his messengers about their business without knowing why. Moran has no free choice: He writes because this external power tells him to do so. He suspects, however, that there exists no rationale behind his writing, which he indicates by referring to Youdi, a god-like being, whose motives are as irrational and unclear as his own.

Compared with Molloy, Moran ruminates relatively extensively on the relations between himself and the forces that set him going, in his case Youdi and Gaber. The latter is presented as a witless tool without any comprehension of the message he is supposed to deliver. Moran himself, on the other hand, possesses other qualities, such as an inclination towards "Peeping and prying" (p. 101) on his fellow human being – abilities useful for an agent or narrator. But in his "moments of lucidity" (p. 115), Moran admits that probably Gaber and Youdi do not exist: "regarding myself as solely responsible for my wretched existence'' (p. 116). Moran suspects that the impetus to write stems from himself and he has to search in himself for an answer to the question of why he writes.

Now Moran displays the same qualities that he has ascribed to Youdi and Gaber, which supports his supposition that these two exist only in his imagination. A messenger like Gaber is said to be "undecipherable to all but oneself" (p. 115) and "undecipherable" is indeed how Moran wants to appear towards those with whom he comes into contact, for instance Martha, his son and Father Ambrose. He orders Martha and his son about without explaining his motives. He is careful not to reveal the business of Molloy to anyone. Moran further suspects his fellow men of secret intentions of their own and tries as far as possible to make sure that Martha and his son act as they have been instructed to. Even if Moran doubts Youdi's existence, he acts in the way he thinks his chief wants him to behave. When he finds that his son tries to disobey his explicit command behind his back, he manages not to show anger: "Very good, I said. I went to the door. You leave both your albums at home . . . Not a word of reproach, a simple prophetic present, on the model of those employed by Youdi" (p.117).

Why does Moran behave in this secretive, authoritative way? Moran feels the Molloy affair to be below his dignity: "the affair had seemed unworthy of me" (p. 104). He finds it "banal" (p. 106) and "childishly simple" (p.102). Moran's attitude may reflect on Molloy's wretched position: to make such a lazy bum the subject of a search and a report may indeed not seem worth-while. Moran's attitude also suggests that the writing of the report is in itself a dubious business: to dabble in literature is considered below the dignity of respectable citizens like Moran. Moran is ashamed to admit his preoccupation with Molloy: this indicates the low status of literature or art in the materialistic Western culture of which Moran is a prominent representative at first.

Further, Moran's role as a narrator is presented as a spy business that must be kept secret. This has its explanation in the circumstance that he tries to live up to the usual expectations of a narrator. He may risk that the authenticity of the report will be doubted, if the narrator makes it too obvious to the reader that he is behind it all, and responsible for what is written. The narrator, who is the one that makes it all up, must not be seen. His presence and motives had better remain a secret in order to secure the reader's credulity regarding the story: these principles on which Moran acts are reflected in the way he narrates his story. Moran seldom intrudes his presence into the story to break the line of events with overt comments on his manner and ability of presenting the narrative. When most readers find the last part of *Molloy* much easier to follow, it is precisely because Moran is a much more traditional storyteller than Molloy, observing the usual conventions of narrative art.

So far, this discussion of Moran's incentive to write has dealt with the external forces, Gaber and Youdi, and what Moran's dependence on them may mean. Like Molloy, Moran also experiences an internal voice exhorting him to continue. Molloy realizes that it is the voice, not the visitor or "they", which really prompts him. Moran provides flesh and blood, so to speak, to the exhortations of the voice by portraying the visitor and the other characters. Gaber becomes the visual expression of the incentive to write; the characters he creates represent various other aspects of the process of writing.

In Moran's case it takes some time before the internal incentive, the voice, makes itself felt. Moran sets out at the behest of Youdi, whom he obeys out of fear, afraid of evoking the "thunderbolts which might be fatal" (p. 127) if he diverges in any detail from what he takes to be Youdi's will. At this stage, Moran finds it all-important to comply with the external demands and pre- scriptions as to his narrative. However, he has not ventured very far on his way to "the Molloy country" (p. 141) when he begins to pay less attention to what may satisfy Youdi:

> All is tedious, in this relation that is forced upon me. But I shall conduct it in my own way, up to a point. And if it has not the good fortune to give satisfaction, to my employer, if there are passages that give offence to him and his colleagues, then so much the worse for us all ... And if I submit to this paltry scrivening which is not of my province, it is for reasons very different from those that might be supposed. I am still obeying orders, if you like, but no longer out of fear. ... And the voice I listen to needs no Gaber to make it heard. For it is within me and exhorts me to continue to the end ... (p. 141)

This passage shows quite clearly that Moran's "employer" and "his col- leagues" represent conventional literary taste from which he gradually man- ages to free himself. Moran now wants to listen to his inner voice about how to conduct his "scrivening".

The report turns out quite differently from what was expected in the beginning because the narrator, Moran himself, changes and gradually be- comes identical with Molloy, the object of his search and report. At the point in his development when Moran seems furthest from Youdi – the thought of his being punished by Youdi makes him laugh outright – Gaber visits him once more: "I felt extraordinarily content ... enchanted with my performance. And I said, I shall soon lose consciousness altogether ... But Gaber's arrival put a stop to these frolics" (p. 174). While the voice has exhorted him to fulfil his "calamitous part" (p. 141), which means to search out Molloy, Gaber orders Moran to return home. On his way back, Moran in a way renounces the voice, stating that "It was on the way home I heard it for the first time. I paid no attention to it" (p. 182). This is not quite the case: it was on the way out Moran first heard the voice, but he now seems eager to suppress any knowledge of the voice. He arrives home "as Youdi has commanded" (p. 187), apparently restored to his old self again.

Like Molloy, Moran has to contend with two opposing forces in himself: Youdi and Gaber, representing conventional literary taste, *and* the voice, which admonishes Moran to follow a more original, inwardly inspired course of narration. Moran's narrative changes as he himself changes (this will be discussed later). When in the end he returns to his old self, obedient to Youdi's will, he shows that he is willing to use traditional style and technique. He mentions the idea of being punished by Youdi also while staying in the "Molloy country". During Gaber's second visit, Moran is most anxious to learn what Youdi now thinks of him. Gaber answers: "he said, life is a thing of beauty, Gaber, and a joy for ever" (p.176). This is indeed an ironic remark if taken as a comment on Moran's decrepit state at the time. Youdi's cryptic words form an echo to the first lines in Keats's *Endymion*, which run: "A thing of beauty is a joy for ever:/Its loveliness increases ..." This is Youdi's conception of life as well as of art and accordingly also his idea of what literature should aim at. This was Moran's original attitude as well, but he develops and fails both in life and in art to live up to this idea. But Youdi, Gaber tells Moran, "hasn't changed" (p. 176). In the end Moran follows Youdi's decree: he gives up his search for Molloy and "returns home", becoming the conventional narrator once more.

In contrast to Molloy, Moran is not very much concerned with the problem of communication. Molloy contemplates at length the meaning of words, how his conception of the words differs from that of other people. Moran appears as a man with confidence in his ability to make himself understood. The main part of his "conversation" consists in giving orders and examining those he speaks to. He is nevertheless misunderstood at times, but this he entirely blames on lack of wit in the others: "Put in your little knapsack, the one I gave you for your birthday, your toilet things, one shirt, one pair of socks and seven pairs of drawers. Do you understand? Which shirt, papa? he said. It doesn't matter which shirt, I cried, any shirt!" (pp. 110–111). Moran's relation to his son indicates his conception of the narrator's role. He thinks he expresses himself precisely, but like Molloy he has difficulties in making himself understood. Moran does not see this as his problem. His concern is to give a report or to tell the story: the nature of the message he conveys and the extent to which it has meaning to others do not trouble him at this stage.

Molloy's growing lameness was seen as indicating his increasing difficulties in getting his story told and finding the right words to express himself. As Moran ventures forth in "the Molloy country", the same stiffness and inability to move on overtake him. Moran is now forced to lie down because of his stiff legs and he takes delight in examining the horizontal position: "You explore it as never before and find it possessed of unsuspected delights" (p. 150). He realizes that he will become completely paralyzed and death will be the outcome. Moran, experiencing that life is *not* "a thing of beauty and a joy forever" finds pleasure in describing his wretched situation. But he knows he is travelling down a blind alley that can only terminate in death: he finds it difficult to talk about anything but himself. At this stage Moran doubts if he will be "able to tell" (p. 147) his story. (In the discussion of the narrative, the problem of death in connection with art in *Molloy* II will be considered). Eventually, when he has become the Moran of the beginning of the story, i.e. the conventional narrator, his lameness leaves him: he is no longer probing his inner self, and again it is easier to get his story told.

2. Narrative as Self-Investigation

Molloy, the narrator in the first part of the novel, has difficulty in distancing himself from his narrative. The characters he describes tend to become unmistakably like himself and eventually he abandons the pretence of talking about anyone but himself. Moran begins his "report" or story from quite the opposite point of departure. He receives "the order to see about Molloy" (p. 99). Most unwillingly he undertakes the investigation because he feels himself superior to Molloy and ashamed even to mention his name.

Molloy starts his journey or story without a proper identity, and the first incident at the police-station describes how this question is settled in his case. The story that Moran narrates about his search for Molloy to a large extent concerns the question of his identity. Moran has, in contrast to Molloy, a clear idea of who he is at the opening of his story. After a few lines, he gives his name and the reader very soon gets a clear idea of Moran's personality from his description of his house and garden and his behaviour towards his visitor, Gaber, and towards those with whom he stays, his son and Martha. But the authoritative Moran, insisting on punctuality and decorum, soon undergoes a change. The picture of himself that he draws in the beginning does not correspond to his inner self. It is a conventionalized, false identity.

In the above discussion of Moran as the narrator, it was pointed out that the opening and closing of part two of Molloy underline the metafictional aspect of the narrative: Moran explores his situation as a narrator. This is further stressed in the course of the narrative, where Moran gives hints that Molloy is a character figuring in his story: "Molloy, or Mollose, was no stranger to me .... Perhaps I had invented him, I mean found him ready-made in my head" (p. 120). Molloy seems familiar to Moran because he embodies an aspect of his own psyche, but this he is not quite aware of when he presents him as a character in his story.[26] Moran does not realize clearly that in writing about Molloy, he is in fact writing about himself.

Moran starts out as a narrator with sparse knowledge of himself: "How little one is at one with oneself, good God. I who prided myself on being a sensible man, cold as crystal and free from spurious depth" (p. 121). He presents

114

himself as an extrovert, "turned towards the outer world as towards the lesser evil" (p. 122). The change Moran experiences, becoming the Molloy of his imagination, he describes as "a frenzied collapsing of all that had always protected me from all I was condemned to be" (p. 159). Molloy, who has his beginning as a barely audible syllable in his soul (p. 121), turns out to be a chimera (p. 122). He feels like going through a process of "being dispossessed of self" (p. 160). On the way, Moran is restored to his old self again, but only partly. He admits: "I had a sharper and clearer sense of my identity than ever before" (p. 182). The narrative, describing the quest for Molloy, is in reality a search for the narrator's self of which he has gained a deeper understanding at the end of the story.

The change Moran undergoes is revealed in his altered way of narration. The pedantry of his usual self comes out when he starts to tackle the Molloy affair: "My concern at first was only with its immediate vexations and the preparations they demanded of me. The kernel of the affair I continued to shirk" (p. 105). At home in his house and garden, Moran lives only on the surface, and he crams the descriptions of his household and his preparations for leaving with rather insignificant details.

Moran places more emphasis on the peripheral than on the essential aspects of his concerns. But where as in earlier cases he knows at least where he is going and "with what purpose" (p. 106), the present affair turns out differently. He admits that this time he adheres to "the fatal pleasure principle" (p. 106) in such decisions as what means of transport to choose. Moran describes his departure from his son as "the unheard of sight" because he leaves "without knowing where he was going" (p. 133) or how long the expedition will take and without having made proper preparations.

In the discussion of the narrator, the journey into "Molloy country" was seen to mean an approach towards paralysis and death, implying perhaps the futility and the emptiness of the search for the self. But even before the search Moran refers to himself as a man much occupied with death, paying frequent visits to the graveyard, where he has already put up his tomb. He wants to engrave his name and birth date: "Then all it would have wanted was the date of my death. They would not let me. Sometimes I smiled, as if I were dead already" (p. 145). This may mean that Moran even before his search is drawn towards death. But rather, it points to the emptiness of his garden existence, however "crammed ... full of futile anxious life" (p. 131).

After receiving the order about Molloy, Moran is dissatisfied with his stay in the garden: Men, God and animals alike disgust him. To underline the vegetative kind of existence he leads, Moran is indirectly compared with the dog Zulu whose behaviour he imitates — another parallel to Molloy in Lousse's garden. The garden life, despite its regulations and order, Moran describes as "the outer turmoil's veil" (p. 119), which he has to pierce. It becomes to him an "illusory" (p. 119) world because it *seems* alive, with "the noise of things"

(p. 119) bursting around him. But staying there would mean continuing on the treadmill of life with the spiritual scope of a "Zulu". It would further mean that his story would circle the surface of existence without penetrating to deeper meanings.

In the woods Moran is accosted by a man who resembles him. When he murders this visitor, Moran kills his old self. Molloy commits a similar act when doing away with the "dirty old brute" (p. 89) of a charcoal-burner. The narrator's old self is felt to be a hindrance to his progress with his story. He has to shake off his external identity to be able to continue his explorations in a meaningful manner. Moran's growing paralysis and pain suggest that it is a devastating experience despite his nonchalant, cool manner of description. After the killing, Moran compares himself to "the plant that springs from the ejaculations of the hanged and shrieks when plucked" (p. 167). Moran's shriek, the story he voices, reveals the narrator's desperation, despite his apparent indifference and the irony of his tale.

The narrator's journey is a lonely experience. No wonder that Moran hesitates to leave "the absurd comforts" (p. 142) of his home and established self. He feels "too old to lose all this, and begin again" (p. 142) on another story. The Molloy country or Ballyba appears as a meagre strip of land with few inhabitants (p. 144). Moran travels through "icy . . . muddy solitudes" (p. 180) and describes his experience as a ' long anguish of vagrancy and freedom" (p. 142).

Writing about his search for Molloy, Moran becomes identical with the object of his report. He describes himself as a changed man. Molloy's mere appearance leads to his being brought to the police-station. On his way home Moran likewise is arrested; he is stopped by a farmer who is very suspicious of him. Moran admits that as always he has difficulty in answering questions about what he is doing (p. 185), which suggests that the narrator's employment is in itself questionable and particularly the way Moran now carries it out, exploring the narrator's situation *qua* narrator. Moran, true to his vocation, manages to deceive the farmer: he avoids giving a direct answer and instead invents all kinds of stories which elaborate on the narrator's position in a metaphorical manner: indeed the method Beckett employs in his novel.

Though Moran returns to his point of departure, the writing desk in his home, the experience of narration has left its mark on the teller: Moran points out the changes wrought by his absence in his house and garden where all is cold and dead. His old self took comfort in watching the dance of the bees, an image of "the dances of the people of the West, frivolous and meaningless" (p. 182). This image links up with his existence in the garden. Moran's life there represents the comfortable, but empty material life of Western culture. Earlier Moran has found joy in watching this kind of life: "it would always be a noble thing to contemplate" (p. 182). On his way back Moran hopes to indulge in this joy again. But the bees are dead because neglected during the winter.

The frivolous "dance" of modern civilization will never again become the sole object of contemplation nor narration for Moran. He has become aware of the inner voice, which uses a different kind of language than the one "Moran had been taught when he was little" (p. 188).

In the discussion of the narrator's conception of the narrative, Moran's relation to the opposite sex is of significance. Like Molloy, Moran cannot be said to have a very active love life. With Molloy this is due to growing impotence. When Moran's narrative does not contain any descriptions of his adventures with women, this must be ascribed to the narrator's limitations: Moran pays attention to what he considers the liking of his employer:

> I have never had to deal with a woman. I regret it. I don't think Youdi had much interest in them. That reminds me of the old joke about the female soul. Question, Have women a soul? Answer, Yes. Question, Why? Answer, In order that they may be damned. (p. 147)

Youdi, who in the novel represents the embodiment of general public taste and evaluation of art, apparently disapproves of stories where the narrator's "dealings" with women figure prominently.

The quotation in the preceding paragraph shows Moran's contempt for women. His unfavourable opinion of them reveals his disgust with sex, which signifies his general inability to establish meaningful contact with others. He writes of and for himself. This is further underlined by the fact that Moran, who does not describe any heterosexual experience, refers to instances of "self-abuse".

The same tendency to mix the anal and the oral orifices may be found in Moran's as well as in Molloy's story: Moran instructs his son about the use of the thermometer: "You know which mouth to put it in? ... I inclined his young mind towards that most fruitful of dispositions, horror of the body and its functions" (p. 126). These types of references recur in Moran's story, and they indicate not only his disgust with the bodily functions: Moran links anal matters with verbal production and he thereby transfers the abhorrence with particular bodily functions to the field of language. He shows his loathing of his own narrative through anal imagery. His references to "Turdy" underline his self-disgust and his aversion towards his narrative. On one occasion he describes how he will sweep away his story of Molloy and Youdi "with a great disgusted sweep" (p. 173) and then how he himself will disappear as a "turd waiting for the flush" (p. 174). Earlier in the narrative he talks about himself as "Jacques Moran, ostensibly at home in Turdy" (p. 154) and his journey, the narrator's progression, he describes as a "pilgrimage ... To the Turdy Madonna" (p. 186). Moran voices quite as explicity as Molloy his dislike and low opinion of his own narrative.

3. The Neglected Narratee

Moran addresses himself less frequently to the reader than Molloy. However, when he does speak to the reader, his approach to the narratee shows strong affinities with Molloy's manner. In the discussion of the narrative, Moran's lack of contact with the opposite sex was interpreted as indicating his general failure to communicate with others. He moves in circles also in the sense that his writing always returns to himself. Sometimes a clear distinction exists between the "you" to whom the narrator speaks, and the "I". Mostly, however, the narrator speaks to himself.

In a passage where Moran discusses the various functions of messengers like Gaber and agents like himself, he directs his speech to himself. In the beginning of the passage he talks of the role of "We agents" and then he continues by describing how Gaber does not understand what he reads: "it was not as we would have reflected on them, you and I" (p. 114). Most likely "you and I" refers to "We agents" which means in fact himself, because he expresses the opinion elsewhere that he is probably the sole agent in Youdi's employment. When in the course of his journey towards greater self-realization Moran introduces his confidences with phrases like "to keep nothing from you" (p. 115), one suspects that it is to his own self he opens up.

On a few occasions, Moran displays more openly how "you" functions as the audience to the stories he narrates: "Oh the stories I could tell you if I were easy. What a rabble in my head, what a gallery of moribunds. Murphy, Watt, Yerk, Mercier and all the others. I would never have believed that – yes, I believe it willingly. Stories, stories" (147). But "I" is quickly substituted for "you", indicating yet again that Moran functions as his own audience.

A few pages from the end of the story, Moran jokingly talks of how his reading public trusts him as a narrator: "And if I were to tell you . . . you would not believe me. And this is not the moment to jeopardise my credit. Sometimes you would think I was writing for the public" (p. 181). Throughout the story, Moran has done little else than "jeopardising" his credit with the reader by flaunting the fictional aspects of his "report". Also it is clear that Moran, despite his fear of "Youdi", does not pay overmuch attention to the likes and dislikes of the general public. The role of the narratee is mostly played by himself.

4. Conclusion – *Molloy*

A comparison between the two parts of *Molloy* will reveal that the two narrators both deal with the question of why they write or the incentive to their story-telling. Both of them refer to an internal impetus, "the voice", as well as to external prompters: the visitor and "they" in Molloy's case while Moran talks of Youdi and Gaber.

In Molloy the voice is the most prominent and often referred to while he describes the visitor only a couple of times and has some references to "they". Molloy makes it clear that the mysterious visitor represents the embodiment of the voice. In the creation and conducting of his story, Molloy predominantly adheres to his inner directives. This results in a story strongly divergent from conventional narrative.

Moran is more concerned with the external incentives, Youdi and Gaber, and at first he pays attention only to their directions. These are also presented as embodiments of the voice, but they emerge more clearly as spokesmen of conventional, literary taste than does Molloy's visitor. In the first part of the story, Moran acts in accordance with their command. In the more usual manner of the narrator, he functions as a "spy", hiding his own individuality and "reporting" on his characters' personalities. Moran manages fairly well to present a consistent story. However, in the course of the narrative he turns his back on conventional narrative technique and acts more in accordance with what he describes as the command of the inner voice. Moran no longer disguises the fact that his main concern is with himself, and the story is frequently interrupted by comments on his own situation. At the end of the story, Moran again becomes the conventional narrator though more conscious of his own position than when he first set out to tell the story.

Another question pertaining to the narrator's role in *Molloy* concerns the problem of communication. Molloy deals at great length with his difficulties in making himself understood, describing various incidents with his mother and with a policeman. Moran does not recognize that he has the same problem but ascribes the occasions when he is misunderstood entirely to his audience's dumbness. Moran's sole concern is to tell his story: it is no problem of his, it seems, whether his message comes across to the readers or not.

Molloy dwells extensively on his growing lameness, which expresses metaphorically the narrator's difficulty in getting on with his story. At the beginning and the end of the Moran part, the narrator appears to be in excellent health. As he advances into "the Molloy country", however, Moran has trouble with his legs, i.e. difficulty in getting his story told. As he directs his attention inwards, he becomes more and more concerned about himself. His tale develops into one long, rambling monologue to the detriment of significant narrative aspects like plot and portrayal of character and setting. This is the way Molloy presents *his* story and which Moran tends to take over in parts of his narrative.

In the discussion of the narrative, the various incidents in the two parts represent metaphorically aspects of the narrator's situation. Molloy tries at first to get a story going about characters other than himself, but he ends up describing his search for his mother, a creature much like himself. Moran gets an order to write about Molloy, but he eventually describes his own journey, which is also a quest for identity. Molloy starts his story without revealing, for instance, the names of characters or places. Moran, in a more conventional manner, establishes his identity at the opening of his narrative. But this is just an external mask and in the course of the story he changes, revealing Molloy–like qualities.

Both narratives describe how an existence of material comfort and spiritual vacuum is an allurement to the narrators: the garden world signifies the temptation of the narrators to give way to the claims of Western decadence both by employing conventional narrative technique and by resorting to superficial descriptions lacking in deeper meaning. The narratives are further alike in the sense that they come full circle in the end, as the protagonist-narrators return to the beginning. But while Molloy has only a temporary stay in the garden world in the middle of the story, Moran starts out and returns to the garden. His narrative follows more closely the rules of traditional story-telling, but his experience in "the Molloy country" has made him aware of the limitations of his former way of narration.

Sexual symbolism is employed in both narratives to elucidate the narrator-protagonists' situations. Molloy's impotence and Moran's inhibition signify, on the one hand, their incapacity to communicate with the outside world, and, on the other, their growing inability to create stories. Moran refrains from descriptions of heterosexual love, deferring to what he considers the demands of general convention, represented by Youdi. In addition, the narratives in both parts of *Molloy* use anal imagery about "the art of fiction", suggesting the narrators' loathing for their own product and accordingly also for their own roles. Their disgust hints at the despair with which they regard their own situations: their art circles around itself, displaying the narrators' situations and techniques. Both Molloy and Moran exhibit a solipsism from which there appears to be no escape.

Throughout the novel no clear distinction exists between the narrator and the narratee. The distance between the teller of the tale and the listener varies. Sometimes the "you" appears as an individual outside the speaker, but mostly the narrator seems to address himself, despite the use of the second personal pronoun. References to the narratee are less frequent in Moran's narrative than in Molloy's. Moran adheres to a technique of narration where the narrator refrains from direct remarks to the reader. The question of the narratee in *Molloy* discloses the narrator's general problem of isolation: he speaks to himself, having no other audience.

Malone Dies

1. The Obtuse Narrator

The narrator of *Malone Dies* is bedridden like Molloy, but his physical and mental deterioration is more advanced and his thoughts revolve around death much more than in the case of Molloy. The narrator does not deal with the question of *why* he writes or the incentive behind his story, to the same extent as Molloy and Moran. His exhaustion makes him less able to resist and question the state of things. He submits to his fate as a narrator with greater resignation.

The narrator tries fairly early in the narrative to describe his situation and find reasons to explain it:

> Present state. This room seems to be mine. I can find no other explanation to my being left in it. All this time. Unless it be at the behest of one of the powers that be. That is hardly likely. Why should the powers have changed in their attitude towards me? . . . Perhaps I came in for the room on the death of whoever was in it before me. I enquire no further in any case.[27]

This is one of the few times that the narrator refers to powers outside himself as being responsible for his fate, and here he seems to have a rather vague idea of these external forces, even suggesting that they are indifferent to him. What befalls him cannot be ascribed to *their* interference at least. After this observation, the narrator says that he will refrain from seeking the *cause* of his condition.

The narrator does not know why he exists in his present situation, why he goes on writing. He merely ascertains that he feels compelled to continue. He describes this feeling of compulsion by saying that he is born grave, he does not like to play or to invent, i.e. to write. But every time he tried to give up playing "The grown-ups pursued me, the just, caught me, beat me, hounded me back into the ground, the game, the jollity. . . . And gravely I struggled to be grave no more, to live, to invent" (p. 23). The narrator describes his situation and does not say who he means by "the grown-ups". Hannah Copeland shows how the narrator expresses his feeling of compulsion by comparing Macmann, the representative of the narrator, to the statue of Memnon. Despite its stony rigidity, this colossus had to give forth a musical sound when the first rays of the morning sun struck it. Copeland further directs attention to the divine quality of the compulsive force because "(Aurora was a goddess) and, consequently, not to be resisted".[28] But again, as in the first part of the trilogy, the other references to the external incentives of the narrator are just hinted at, and not personified like Youdi or the mysterious visitors in the first part of the trilogy.

The narrator also refers to a visitor, a woman, who tends to his needs. But she disappears, and he is left with a hand which brings him food and takes away his chamber-pot. His commerce with the outside world has been reduced to the pure maintenance of his bodily needs. Despite his few references to "the powers" the narrator describes himself as dependent on his own resources for his mental sustenance and production. The narrator has tried to direct his attention away from himself, but he does not succeed: "But it was not long before I found myself alone, in the dark" (pp.8–9). It is towards this inner darkness the narrator turns. He is half blind and deaf and his senses "are trained full on me, me. Dark and silent and stale, I am no prey for them" (p. 14). And he likewise describes his thoughts as being turned towards his inner darkness. From this darkness his stories seem to come whether he wants it or not: "I know those little phrases that seem so innocuous and, once you let them in, pollute the whole of speech. *Nothing is more real than nothing.* They rise up out of the pit and know no rest until they drag you down into its dark" (p. 21).

As a parallel to the inner darkness, the narrator talks of the single noise that he hears. Formerly he was capable of distinguishing the various sounds, but now the "noises of nature, of mankind and even my own, were all jumbled together in one and the same unbridled gibberish" (p. 35). The narrator has to start from the single noise. He must sort this out in order to create a story of meaning. Talking about Proust's impressionism, Beckett has expressed similar ideas: "By his impressionism I mean his non-logical statement of phenomena in the order and exactitude of their perpreption, before they have been distorted into intelligibility in order to be forced into a chain of cause and effect".[29] In *Malone Dies* the narrator describes this process of creation from sense impressions to intelligible words, but with the difference that Beckett's narrator has his senses directed inwards towards himself.

In *Molloy* both the narrators reveal their failing ability to communicate with others. This problem also concerns the narrator in *Malone Dies,* but the difference remains that instead of talking about and describing himself in various situations, he tells stories of other characters with problems similar to his own. He first talks of the Saposcats, a family described as unusually dumb and impotent. Their lack of wit makes itself felt in their use for language:

> They had no conversation properly speaking. They made use of the spoken word in much the same way as the guard of a train makes use of his flags . . . And their son once signalled, they wondered sadly if it was not the mark of superior minds to fail miserably at the written paper and cover themselves with ridicule at the viva voce. (p. 17)

By describing the clumsiness of the Saposcats with regard to writing and speaking, the narrator voices his frustration at his own performance. Like them he has no proper conversation, in his solitude. After the first passages about this family, the narrator states that "I wonder if I am not talking yet again about myself" (p. 17).

The narrator's feeling of having to draw on himself for inspiration and for objects to write about is further disclosed in his descriptions of Sapo, the son in the family. The beauty of nature makes no impression on this boy. His senses appear too blunt to distinguish one bird from another and one flower from the next. He finds, like the narrator, that all the various sounds of the world "have merged into a single noise" (p. 35). Ursula Dreysse sees the Sapo story as a kind of parody on the traditional Bildungsroman.[30] In addition, Sapo and his family are used to portray the narrator's limitations, the narrator making continual comparisons between himself and Sapo: "I write about myself with the same pencil and in the same exercise-book as about him" (p. 36).

The narrator speaks of the stories he tells in terms of his progeny: "And if I tell of me and of that other who is my little one, it is as always for want for love" (p. 54). His stories, his fiction, become substitutes for life. The narrator makes up his tales about Sapo and the rest in order to have someone to keep him company and to share his feelings: he talks of making "a little creature, to hold in my arms" (p. 54), a creature he will make in his own image "no matter what I say" (p. 54). Despite his efforts to make stories where he himself does not figure as the protagonist, these tales are nevertheless all about him. They do not, however, provide the narrator with any lasting satisfaction: "And seeing what a poor thing I have made, or how like myself, I shall eat it. Then be alone for a long time, unhappy" (p. 54). His stories do not afford a real substitute for his own life, because they are about himself, and this is the reason why story-telling does not yield much pleasure in his case.

In *Molloy* the narrators experience a process of growing lameness, and their physical disability is paralleled by their growing difficulties in getting on with their stories. In the second part of the trilogy the narrator has come closer to death and his bodily disintegration expresses metaphorically the development of his fiction.

When dying, the narrator experiences a feeling of expansion: "But this sensation of dilation is hard to resist" (p. 62). He explains further how his feet feel far away from his head "for that is where I am fled" (p. 63). He describes how his body falls apart, limb from limb, so to speak, while his mind seems to expand because of his inability to concentrate on the here and now. This process has its parallel in his writing: "But my fingers too write in other latitudes ... so that the subject falls far from the verb and the object lands somewhere in the void" (p. 63). His bodily deterioration indicates the disintegration of his narrative.

The narrator portrays the fading world around him; the floor, for instance, seems to him to grow white and give forth a hollow sound when struck. When he portrays his room, he actually portrays the inside of his head. A fragmentation of his body and mental faculties is taking place: "I see at the confines of this restless gloom a gleam and shimmering as of bones'' (p. 52). Michael Robinson finds that the approximation between the room and the narrator's head indicates that "everything he describes is to be located somewhere in this ratiocinating dome. And now that his body has entirely deserted him it is in this crumbling silence alone that he can live ..."[31]

The narrator describes what goes on in his head as a "streaming and emptying away as through a sluice ... until finally nothing remained, either of Malone or of the other" (p. 52). Every story will terminate with the "death" of the narrator and the characters he describes; their lives are over when the story ends. But in *Malone Dies* the narrator feels the fictional process itself like a dying, a dwindling away of both himself and his "little creature".

At the same time, the narrator repeatedly talks of his "death" as a birth: he mentions the process of dying as "the various phases of this deliverance" (p. 52). And as with the dying, the narrator makes no distinction between what is happening to himself or to his characters in his story; it is his birth as well as theirs: "I am being given ..... birth to into death, such is my impression. The feet are clear already, of the great cunt of existence ... My head will be the last to die ... My story ended I'll be living yet" (p. 113). The narrator may be indicating here that he will go on living after the story has been told. But more likely he is hinting at the immortality of art, saying that he will continue to "live" in his fiction.

2. Narrative in Grey

The narrative of *Malone Dies* appears more disjointed than that of the first part of *Molloy*, and according to Dina Sherzer this can be ascribed to the fact that Molloy tells just one story, about the quest for his mother, while the narrator in the other book recounts a series of different stories.[32] But in *Malone Dies*, the narrator fairly early gives the plan of the narrative. This he wants to divide into five parts: "Present state, three stories, inventory, there. An occasional interlude is to be feared" (pp. 10–11). On the whole, the narrator sticks to this outline. By supplying this plan at the outset, he provides the reader with a guide-line through his otherwise disconnected narrative. Secondly, through the plan the narrator discloses part of the narrative process, in this way flaunting the metafictional aspect of his novel.

In the stories, the narrator reveals his own situation, though he does not figure as the protagonist. The first stories Malone recounts concern the Sapo-scats, and the boy Sapo's visits to the Lamberts. Sapo and Mrs Lambert both represent characters reflecting the narrator's flagging ability to keep going.

Mrs Lambert suffers from a disease and seems to be dying. Probably because death will soon overtake her, she has very little time for anything, and she asks questions voicing the hopelessness behind the narrator's struggle: "At the same time angry unanswerable questions, such as, What's the use? fell from her lips" (p. 30). Like the narrator she has difficulty in seeing the point in continuing her sufferings.

Sapo's place in the Lamberts' kitchen is by the window where he spends his time just hanging around, even forgetting to drink his bowl of milk. Malone's bed is placed by the window and he eats his soup "one time out of two" (p. 13). The outward resemblance between Sapo's situation and that of the narrator underlines the mental inertia that plagues them both. Sapo shows no under-standing or awareness of the life that goes on around him. He wanders about like one who is already dead. It is only the "voice" that keeps him going: "And when he halted it was not the better to think . . . but simply because the voice had ceased that told him to go on. Then with his pale eyes he stared down at the earth, blind to its beauty, and to its utility" (p. 34). Sapo takes his directives from a voice. If the voice goes silent, he will remain motionless, and his wanderings will come to an end.

Symbolism in the narrative of *Malone Dies* centres on the relation between life and death. Malone looks upon his coming death as a birth into life, signifying that the narrator lives in his narratives: art is immortal. The paradox of the dying narrator creating living art is suggested in the symbolism of the various stories of the novel. Malone points to the absurdity of the situation when he says that he hopes his present story "should have living for its theme" (p. 26) and then in fact describes his own dying, which he camouflages by the stories he tells.

The tale of Big Lambert has obvious parallels with Malone's situation. This man is old, but still able to carry out his favourite occupation, the sticking of pigs: "His great days then fell in December and January . . . the principal event of which is unquestionably the Saviour's birth, in a stable" (p. 28). His own pig has to part with its life on Christmas Eve, and Big Lambert does not have the same success in breeding pigs as in dispatching them. But his most unbearable characteristic is his tendency to describe in detail to his family the killing of the pigs he has done away with. Then he goes silent till the killing season starts again.

Lambert's story reflects ironically Malone's occupation. The narrator also brings about the death of others, i.e. the characters that enter and leave his story; shortly before Moll dies, Malone remarks: "Moll. I'm going to kill her" (p. 93). Like Lambert he enjoys describing the procedure of his own death and that of his characters. And Big Lambert's record of the dying pig forms an ironic parallel to the narrative of the declining Malone: "For all pigs are alike . . . struggle, squeal, bleed, squeal, struggle, bleed, squeal and faint away" (p. 29). This listing is echoed later in the narrative when Malone gives "the programme" for the end of this story: "Visit, various remarks, Macmann continued, agony recalled, Macmann continued, the mixture of Macmann and agony as long as possible" (p. 98). The paradox of the narrator's situation is also underlined by the fact that Big Lambert's killing season reaches its height at Christmas, when the Saviour is born; the narrator "saves" his characters from sinking into oblivion by telling their stories, at the same time as he finishes them off when the story is done.

Big Lambert's killing does not restrict itself to pigs. He possesses a mule, which he bought at the slaughter-house, because he says "I thought I might screw six months out of him . . . and I screwed two years" (p. 41). In this way Lambert again serves as a parallel to the narrator, who manages to squeeze stories out of himself despite his rapid approach towards death. When the mule has expired, Lambert sees to it that its grave is deep enough: "For he knew how the dead and buried tend, contrary to what one might expect, to rise to the surface" (p. 41). This hinting at the resurrection of the dead suggests that even if the narrator kills off his characters, they nevertheless continue to live in the narrative.

Sapo, who watches the burial of the mule, reveals another ambiguous aspect of the narrator's situation: "He felt better. The end of a life is always vivifying" (p. 40). Not only the audience, the readers, but also the one who gives utterance to the events, the narrator, experiences a renewal through the narrative. According to Deirdre Bair, the writing of *Malone Dies* had a cathartic effect on Beckett.[33]

In *Malone Dies* the narrator occupies a middle position between life and death, which is expressed symbolically through the greyness that colours the narrator and his surroundings: the light sparkling outside his window is reflected less brilliantly in his room: "So that here all bathes . . . in a kind of leaden light" (p. 49). He says of himself that he seems to "emit grey", and he talks of his own light as being distinguished from "the light of the outer world" (p. 49). Perhaps this greyness suggests, as the narrator says in the beginning of the novel, that his stories "will be almost lifeless, like the teller" (p. 8). As discussed above, the room that the narrator lives in is his own head: the greyness may indicate that his gaze is directed inwards towards himself, and he describes a stale, dying world. He is unaware of the beauty of the external world with its "wild many-coloured flowers" (p. 34).

The grey, inner world of Malone, the world of his "head", is opposed to the external world of physical, sensual experience. Malone wonders whether his skull is a vacuum, and he compares it to a cage, the abode of his soul: "that soul denied in vain, vigilant, anxious, turning in its cage as in a lantern, in the night without haven or craft or matter or understanding" (p. 50). This passage where the soul is compared to a bird in a cage links up with the story of Polly, the pink and grey parrot which refuses to be taught more than the three words "Nihil in intellectu" (p. 46). The bird, as a symbol for Malone's soul, expresses his scepticism of his intellectual, inward-directed probing. He experiences indeed his head as a vacuum and his search results in nothingness.

The motif of the greyness of Malone's inner world recurs in Polly's grey plumage, in the grey bodies at the end of the novel, and in the grey hen which Sapo observes in the Lambert kitchen. The dark kitchen suggests Malone's room, or his head. It is a dead world where "the dark had triumphed" (p. 31) and where silence "would one day triumph too" (p. 31). Sapo takes refuge in this place for long stretches of time before he drags himself away. This suggests the narrator's preoccupation with his inner self, where everything is dead except for the voice. It is this inner world the narrator explores. This is further stressed by the grey hen's visits to the kitchen. The bird, like the narrator, repeatedly plunges into this forbidden territory even if it gets scared when chased out into the daylight where it really belongs.

As discussed above, the parts of the narrative dealing with Sapo and the Lamberts focus on the narrator's waning powers, and the symbolism of these stories reflects the narrator's paradoxical situation in relation to the life-death complex. The last part of the novel centres on Macmann, who takes over from Sapo: "For Sapo – no, I can't call him that any more ... So then for, let me see, for Macmann" (pp. 57–8). With Macmann tendencies are futher developed that first appeared in Sapo, representing the narrator's inability to progress. In addition, the aspect of the narrator's suffering comes more to the fore in the descriptions of Macmann.

When Macmann is first introduced in the novel, he is seated on a bench where he remains inert because he finds no reason to move. Macmann at last gets up from the bench only to place himself prostrate on the ground in the position of one crucified: "The idea of punishment came to his mind ... impressed by the posture of the body" (p. 68). He does not know what he is being punished for. As his name indicates he is the Son of Man, and he feels like Christ atoning for the sins of the world. This portrayal of Macmann adds an interesting perspective to the narrator's role. He is presented as a scapegoat subjected to punishment and suffering on behalf of mankind.

As representative of the narrator Macmann experiences the agony of his kind of life because he realizes the pointlessness of continuation. He distinguishes himself by remaining an outsider to life around him (p. 72). With great irony an incident is described where Macmann, operating as a street cleaner, carefully distributes the muck along the sidewalk instead of sweeping it away, earning disgust for his pains: "And yet he had done his honest best to give satisfaction, taking as his model his more experienced colleagues" (p. 73). This is a fling at conventional literary taste, which turns with disgust from books like the one under discussion.

The narrator's suffering, like Macmann's, stems from his lack of contact with the surrounding world. He lives in and for himself, and he makes a careful exhibition of the muck, the pain of his kind of existence, instead of sweeping it away in the manner of his more knowledgeable "colleagues".

In these first episodes, Macmann mostly functions as the exponent of the narrator. Malone then finds that "it is perhaps not inappropriate to wish Macmann . . . a general paralysis" (p. 74). This indicates that Macmann goes through a kind of death and he wakes up again in a heaven-like place: "Macmann came to again . . . in a kind of asylum" (p. 85). This place bears the name of the House of Saint John of God, inhabited by throngs of people dressed in white. The man in charge resembles the Messiah; Macmann is told that his worries are over: "Fear nothing, you are among friends. Friends! Well, well. Take no thought for anything, it is we shall think and act for you, from now forward" (p. 85). Macmann's "death" means a change of roles. Before his passage into heavenly inactivity, he represents the narrator. When this part is over, his role in the narrative becomes more passive; instead of acting, he is acted on, like a character set in motion by the narrator.

In the last part of the novel, Moll and then Lemuel represent the narrator. In Moll's relation to Macmann she clearly occupies the narrator's function. First of all, Macmann is totally dependent on her for his sustenance and she sees to his bodily needs: "For it had been decreed, by those in authority, that one hundred and sixty-six was Moll's, she having applied for him, formally. She brought him food" (p. 86). Here the same vagueness attaches to "those in authority" as to the voice and Youdi in *Molloy*. Moll goes about her business with Macmann in keeping with the rules, and she knows things and guides her protégé: "She informed Macmann, when he did something, if that thing was permitted or not, and similarly, when he remained inert, whether or not he was entitled to" (p. 87). As a further parallel to *Molloy*, it is left unclear whether the incentive to the narrator's operations comes from external sources or from within: "For when it came to the regulations Moll was inflexible and their voice was stronger than the voice of love, in her heart, whenever they made themselves heard there simultaneously" (p. 96). Here Moll seems to be propelled in her operations by an internal impetus.

Moll's function as the narrator is also indicated when she introduces Macmann to the world of letters: "He then made unquestionable progress in the use of the spoken word and learnt . . . the yesses, noes, mores and enoughs that keep love alive" (p. 89). He also learns to read because of "the inflammatory letters" which Moll writes to him. The love relation between the two results in communication on the verbal level, and for Moll, writing becomes the substitute for the actual experience of life; "Moll, despairing no doubt of giving vent to her feelings by the normal channels, addressed [her declarations of love] three or four times a week to Macmann" (p. 91). Like Malone, the narrator she represents, Moll is too old and decrepit to get much pleasure out of mere physical contact and makes up for this by her writing.

Another parallel between the narrator and Moll may be found in their apprehension that death will terminate their preoccupations. Moll writes to Macmann: "For we shall soon die, you and I, that is obvious. That it may be at the same moment exactly is all I ask'' (p. 90). These words are echoed some few pages later by the narrator, who discusses his writing and the narrative of Macmann: "That all may be wiped out at the same instant is all I ask, for the moment'' (p. 98). The narrator fears that he will die before he has finished his story of Macmann, and he expresses this through Moll's anxiety that one of the two lovers should not outlive the other.

The parodic love affair between Moll and Macmann has still another dimension in the relation between the narrator and his characters. It exhibits the origin and development of the Word. Moll needs to break out of her isolation and to have someone to communicate with; Macmann learns to speak and to read, and eventually he becomes the representative of the narrator. The significance of this is revealed through Christian symbolism. Moll possesses just one tooth in her mouth with the symbol of the cross engraved on it. Her two ear-rings are formed in the shape of crucifixes and Moll explains to Macmann: "they are the thieves, Christ is in my mouth'' (p. 93). The reference to the biblical incident suggests the possibility of salvation and eternal life through belief in Christ or the Word: the Christ, significantly placed in Moll's mouth, represents the Word. According to the Gospel of Saint John, the Word became incarnated in Christ and the Word like Christ has eternal life.[34]

Moll, representing the narrator, carries on the divine task of possessing and communicating the Word. Shortly before she dies the tooth with the cross falls out and is stored "in a safe place'' (p. 95). During the period of Moll's decline and death, Macmann starts writing poems. Both of these circumstances indicate that the Word lives on regardless of the death of the individual narrator.

The parodic element in this allegory cannot be overlooked, as one is compelled to compare Moll to the original bearer of the Word and she is portrayed as extraordinarily ugly and weak. Malone uses the dying Moll to indicate his own feelings of inadequacy. But in this story of Moll, the positive element of the narrator's part weighs most heavily on the scales. The saving power of the word or the narrative is at least hinted at and so is the continued existence of the narrator in his work. That Malone finds consolation in this possibility is indicated when he refers to the story of the thieves: "For why be discouraged, one of the thieves was saved'' (p. 84).

When Moll dies, Lemuel takes over her task as Macmann's keeper. This means that from now on he functions as the representative of the narrator.[35] Lemuel proves to be Moll's direct opposite exhibiting quite another aspect of the narrator. Moll manages to make Macmann comfortable and even develop his verbal abilities; he learns to speak and write and becomes a recognizable human being. Lemuel does not seem to care for Macmann at all, he wants to have as little as possible to do with him and the other "prisoners'' under his charge:

> When Macmann, more and more disturbed by his situation apparently and what is more now capable of isolating and expressing well enough to be understood a little

of the little that passed through his mind, when Macmann I say asked a question it was seldom he got an immediate answer. (p. 95)

Lemuel stands for the kind of narrator who pays no attention to, and even suppresses, the signs of independence in his characters – tendencies that Macmann have developed under Moll's tender care.

Lemuel turns his mind inwards towards himself. When asked something, he bids Macmann shut up that he may think the matter over, but "It usually ended by his saying he did not know" (p. 96). Malone has a tendency to write down his queries: Lemuel sets down the questions Macmann directs to him in a notebook, but this is solely for his own benefit: "Macmann could then be sure he would never hear any more about it" (p. 96). Lemuel appears isolated in himself; he neither heeds nor understands what goes on around him, and he cannot communicate his thoughts in a meaningful way to others. Thus, in contrast to Moll, he does not take the regulations of the place very seriously because he apparently does not know them, and his speech consists of "unintelligible words" (p. 96).

Lemuel appears to suffer mentally, judged by the cries he lets out. His habit of hitting himself with a hammer signals what really takes place in his mind: "But the part he struck most readily . . . was the head, and that is understandable, for it too is a bony part, and sensitive . . . and the seat of all the shit and misery" (p. 97). Lemuel's physical self-punishment only expresses metaphorically how he torments himself by his internal probing.

Lemuel becomes a parallel to Malone in his self-punishment. To underline the relation between them, Malone, shortly after the incident where Lemuel hits himself, describes how he receives "a violent blow on the head" (p. 98). The one who deals him the blow is a visitor who bears every resemblance to Death personified as a gentleman, immaculately dressed in black. His sharp-pointed umbrella, which Malone fears will be thrust into his heart, replaces the traditional sickle. The visitor must be seen as another character or chimera, sprung from Malone's imagination. The narrator externalizes his mental and physical deterioration and pain through this description.

A comparison between the two parallel incidents – Lemuel hitting himself and Malone being struck by personified Death – throws light on the narrator's position in the last part of the narrative. Lemuel flagellates himself and so does Malone, despite his presentation of the visitor as the cause of his troubles. Malone blames "Death" for his suffering, just as the thoughts of impending death may be at the back of Lemuel's unspeakable anguish. Lastly, the identity between the narrator and "Death" unquestionably exists in Malone's case, stressed among other things through the circumstance that the visitor uses his umbrella as Malone his stick (p. 101). In addition, Lemuel emerges towards the end of the novel as a figure of death representing the narrator.

In the last few pages of the novel, Lemuel literally kills off several of his companions. Where Moll personifies the creative aspect, Lemuel represents the destructive element of the Janus-like narrator. Moll believes in the immortality of the *Logos*; Lemuel disbelieves. Moll's role was seen above to be explained through the use of Christian symbolism, which is also used in connection with Lemuel. Hokenson points out that Lemuel is a destructive figure: "the executioner Lemuel becomes keeper to the Son of Man"[36] and he draws attention to various parallels that exist between the life of Christ and Macmann's stay in the asylum. However, Hokenson does not explicitly state that Lemuel represents the narrator and that it is as such that his role as destroyer of the Son of Man or the Word has real meaning.

The nexus between Lemuel and Macmann becomes gradually more pronounced, and the relation between them greatly resembles that of Moran and Molloy in the first part of the trilogy. Lemuel, who is first presented as Macmann's pursuer, becomes his fellow sufferer and at times exchanges roles with him. This is described in the garden incident where he first sets out to drive Macmann back indoors, but then sits down beside him under a bush and lastly remains there while Macmann goes back to his cell on his own. During the excursion episode, all the main characters are grouped in twos and Lemuel forms a pair together with Macmann. The close relation between Lemuel, the narrator, and one of his characters is significant. Lemuel's violence towards Macmann signifies the narrator's self-destruction. Finally, Lemuel leads Macmann towards death.

The journey towards death takes the form of an outing sponsored by rich Lady Pedal, but with Lemuel, whom the Lady takes for one of the patients, in charge of the inmates from the asylum. Hokenson shows how this incident becomes an ironic reversion of the last events in the life of Christ and his resurrection. He also finds that Beckett caricatures the five "prisoners" in Lemuel's keeping "as five stages in the life of Christ".[37] Apart from Macmann, the Son of Man, representing the incarnation of the Word, the text yields little support to this theory. The five inmates bear resemblance to various characters in Beckett's earlier novels. The Saxon, for instance, reminds one of Watt, and the young man who likes to spend his time sitting in the rocking chair resembles Murphy. In addition, the narrator, or Malone, refers to them and Lemuel as his "creatures" (p. 115), a word used earlier by Malone about the characters in his stories (p. 54).

Macmann becomes the last creation in a long row of characters described in earlier novels, and he is the last one in *Malone Dies,* apart from Lemuel, the representative of the narrator. Malone intrudes into the narrative with these final words about him: "Macmann, my last, my possessions, I remember, he is there too, perhaps he sleeps" (p. 117). Compared with the other four that Lemuel takes with him in his boat in the end, Macmann stands out because of his vitality. While the others seem to have submitted themselves to Lemuel's authority, Macmann tries to escape from his company all the time: "Macmann made a bid for freedom. In vain'' (p. 115). Lemuel hits him on the head with a hatchet. Macmann at first resists the last voyage, refusing to die. But eventually he has to give in to Lemuel and disappears with him and the others into the sea of death: "This tangle of grey bodies is they ... They are far out in the bay'' (p. 117). Lemuel, the figure of death, is left unvanquished.

Lemuel represents the destructive aspect of the narrator. He too is seen to disappear before the end, but he departs in triumph with the murderous weapon, the hatchet-pencil with which he has silenced the other characters. In contrast to this ending, the Moll-episode finishes on a more optimistic note. Even if Moll, the narrator-figure, departs, Macmann, the incarnated Word, continues, securing its immortality. Lemuel finishes off the Son of Man or the *Logos*. As an embodiment of death and destruction, he alone remains in complete control of the dead bodies together with which he disappears at the end of the novel on his journey towards annihilation. This last episode in *Malone Dies* underlines the destructive element of art. The narrator becomes a figure of death because he reduces life, squeezing existence into rigid and eternally fixed shapes.

3. The Superfluous Narratee

What characterizes Malone's situation is that he tries to escape from himself by making up stories, but he does not succeed. He constantly ends up talking about himself. In the first ten pages or so of the narrative, Malone does not address himself to a narratee. He speaks to himself, frequently asking questions and answering them as well. When the first "you" appears in the story, Malone obviously does not speak to another person: "A little darkness, in itself, at the time is nothing. You think no more about it and you go on. But I know what darkness is, it accumulates'' (p. 18). In this passage the second person pronoun is quickly replaced by "I''. Malone does not as yet manage to create a distance from himself.

In the next part of the narrative, "you" occurs a few times but the pronoun has the meaning of "one" very often: "That is what you might call taking a reef in your sails'' (p. 26). The narratee becomes more prominent when Malone uses "we''. Malone applies this pronoun in passages where he has succeeded to some extent in shaking himself loose from his own situation and is describing one of his characters: "One day Sapo arrived at the farm earlier than usual. But do we know what time he usually arrived?'' (p. 40). The narrator or Malone here intrudes into the narrative. By describing another character he has taken one step away from himself and with his intruding remark the narrator removes himself still further. Who is this "we" of which Malone speaks? Is it after all just himself, Malone, using "we" instead if "I"? Or is the reference also to another person, the reader, who experiences the narrative together with the narrator? Both of these explanations are valid, and no definite narratee has been established in the cases where "we" is used.

In about the middle of the narrative, "you" is used more in the sense of a narratee, a person spoken to outside the story. It is no longer only a substitute for "one" as was discussed above, but the connections to the narrator are still close. On this occasion Malone again makes himself the topic of his conversation: "Yes, those were the days . . . And you imagine it will be so till the end. But suddenly all begins to rage and roar again, you are lost in the forests . . . till you begin to wonder if you have not died without knowing" (p. 55). Malone dramatizes his own situation, making a "you" enact what he has been through. Nevertheless, even if Malone portrays his own experiences, the story is removed from a personal to a general level. When Malone lets "you" suffer, instead of describing how "I" undergo the pain, he creates a distance from his own tortures. Usually, through the narratee, the narrator wants to bring the reader closer to the proceedings and characters in his story. Here the opposite is the case.

Later in the novel, Malone makes the same application of "you" when telling the story of Macmann, rolling on the ground before he swoons off or dies: "And it was then his hair appeared clearly . . . For when, lying on your stomach . . . you turn over on your back, then there is a sideway movement of the whole body, including the head" (p. 70). Malone shifts the attention from Macmann to "you" with the effect of generalizing Macmann's case. The reader or "you" is brought into the story, taking Macmann's place. This does not result in the reader's identification with Macmann; on the contrary, the reader becomes engaged in the mere mechanics of the movements of rolling on the ground instead of realizing the suffering Macmann is experiencing in this awkward position. Thus the use of the narratee alienates the reader as well as the narrator, from the story.

In the last part of the novel Malone, only a couple of times more, pronouncedly addresses a character apart from himself: "But enough about me. You would think I was relieved to be without my stick. I think I know how I might retrieve it" (p. 84). However, these examples are so few and Malone makes so little out of them, that they may rather serve as the exceptions to the rule that Malone in the whole does not manage to create a narratee who is not himself.

4. Conclusion – *Malone Dies*

The narrator in *Malone Dies* has moved closer to death than the narrators in the first part of the trilogy. This is shown in the way Malone submits to his fate. He is not much concerned with the incentives behind his writing, the questions about why he writes: he merely describes his feelings of compulsion and how his stories seem to rise from his inner darkness.

The narrator uses the Saposcats to exhibit his own frustration as a writer. Like them he experiences an inability to communicate and his senses fail to register external impressions. Accordingly, his inner darkness becomes his field of exploration. The stories, which the narrator creates as a substitute for his limited participation in life, prove a meagre consolation, because they deal with his own desolate situation.

Malone's dying, his bodily disintegration, expresses metaphorically the narrator's growing inability to tell stories. This probably entails references to Beckett's own life. In contrast to most other authors he finds that for him the process of writing grows more difficult over the years.[38] The dying Malone in fact represents a narrator experiencing an evaporation of his creative powers. However, Malone also connects the narrator's role with rebirth, suggesting the immortality of art and the narrator's continued life in his work.

☆

The narrative, describing Malone's dying, consists of stories with different protagonists, reflecting various aspects of the narrator's situation. Mrs Lambert voices Malone's feeling of hopelessness, and the sluggish Sapo mirrors the narrator's frustration at his own mental inertia.

The paradoxical position of the narrator is developed in the symbolism of the novel; to a considerable degree this revolves around the life-death complex. Old Lambert, another representative of the narrator, excels in the sticking of pigs and in talking about his feats afterwards with great vigour despite his age. The ambiguity of both Lambert's and the narrator's task is pointed out; the climax of the killing season is Christmas, which is also the time of "the Saviour's birth . . ." The colour grey recurs throughout the novel, indicating the narrator's middle position between life and death.

Macmann, the character who moves into the centre of the narrator's attention after Sapo has been discarded, marks a further step in the narrator's progress towards complete inability to continue. The narrator's suffering also becomes more prominent in the passage about Macmann. Lastly, Moll and Lemuel in their relation to Macmann exhibit two important aspects of the narrator: his creative ability, his conjuring up of characters and incidents, and his destructivness, his reduction of life to fixity in art.

☆

The narratee plays a rather insignificant part in the novel: the narrator is alone and he does not reckon with any audience outside himself. On the few occasions when he directly addresses another, it is nearly always obvious that he speaks to himself, and he uses the narratee to create distance from his own situation.

The Unnamable

1. Narrator Without Identity

At the very opening of their stories, the narrators in *Molloy* describe their present setting. The narrator in *Malone Dies* rambles on for about three pages before he depicts more accurately the room in which he stays. In *The Unnamable* the narrator hesitates still longer before he gives any description of his whereabouts. About one third into the novel the narrator comes up with the account of the jar where he is then stationed, permanently as it seems.[39] The absurdity of this situation adds to the vagueness of the narrator's whole position.

The uncertainty attached to the narrator's situation reveals his general weakening. The narrator in the last part of the trilogy has moved one step further towards complete exhaustion. This is also emphasized by the narrator's relation to the incentives behind his writing. In the first novel the force behind the narratives is represented by a visitor and by Youdi. In *The Unnamable* the narrator just mentions a "master", who presumably sets him the "pensum" he has to "discharge" (p. 26) before he is free to say what he wants. The relation between the narrator and this apparent incentive behind his story becomes that of a pupil to his school-teacher.

However, even if the master at first may seem to be a decidedly external force, the narrator speaks to him as if created "in my image" (p. 28), which indicates that the master is a chimera of the narrator's imagination. The master functions as a censor to the narrator's words, rather than as their ultimate source of inspiration:

> the words ... have to be ratified by the proper authority ... the messenger goes towards the master, and while the master examines the report, and while the messenger comes back with the verdict, the words continue, the wrong words, until the order arrives, to stop everything ... (p. 87)

The master and the messenger have their parallel in Youdi and Gaber in *Molloy*. The master decides between the right and the wrong words and becomes the guardian of accepted literary taste, and he appears as an internal faculty in the narrator's psyche.

While the "master" becomes the controlling force of the narrator's words, his incentive stems from the "voices".[40] In addition, the narrator mentions the "delegates" (p. 13), or simply "they", who have told him what to speak. The narrator is puzzled by his relation to the voices, and he admits that he does not know how he came into contact with "them". He only knows that he has his knowledge of men from others (p. 13). He speaks the words that come to him, but "No one compels me to" (p. 30). Thus, the narrator presents himself as a medium transmitting the words he receives rather than as an independent being.

Besides speculating on the incentives behind his writing, the narrator in *The Unnamable* wants – like his predecessors in the trilogy – to settle the problem of his identity. In *Molloy* and *Malone Dies* this question is elucidated through various incidents that befall the narrators. The narrator in *The Unnamable* does not illustrate the problem of his identity by what happens to him. Because nothing occurs in his life, he can only *talk* of his concern.

Since the narrator has been left with little else than his voice as the incentives to his writing, it seems logical that he should connect the question of identity with them. The narrator is reduced to a mere head on a torso. He is stripped, not only of external remedies like his stick, but of bodily organs like his arms and his eyelids. The narrator's physical reduction signals his general education: "Not only is the Unnamable nameless; he is placeless, timeless, and he often feels languageless through all his talk".[41] Anyhow, speak he must, and he inevitably links the questions of who he is with the words he utters and the incentives behind them.

At one point the narrator regards himself both as the impetus behind his words and as the one who registers them: "I am Matthew and I am the angel" (p. 17). The analogy here is to Christ as the Word and the first *mentioning* of "the Word" in the angel's prophecy to Mary. Further, the narrator refers to the *recording* of the Word by St. Matthew.

The two-sidedness of the narrator's identity is further stressed in a passage where he states that he is both the words that form "inside" himself as well as the words spoken "outside" himself. But then he goes on to speculate about whether or not he is the partition *between* his inner self and the external world: "I'm the tympanum, on the one hand the mind, on the other the world, I don't belong to either" (p. 100). In that case he is left with no identity at all. He functions just as a transmitter of words.

The question of his identity or rather the fear of not having any, is of great concern to the narrator: "come now, make an effort, at your age, to have no identity, it's a scandal" (p. 94). At this point it is important for the narrator to

136

take on the identity of Worm and Mahood, the characters whose stories he is supposed to tell. But he finds that he "can't stir" (p. 95), which means that he is not able to get a story going. He realizes that while formerly he could easily deceive himself about his own identity, becoming the characters he describes, this is no longer the case: "when I think of the time I've wasted . . . beginning with Murphy . . . when I had me . . . within easy reach . . . rotting with solitude and neglect, till I doubted my own existence" (p. 108). By continually adopting the identity of his characters, the narrator has lost his own, becoming "unnamable", indeed.

Near the end of the novel the Unnamable looks back at his past with regret: "if only I knew if I've lived . . . . impossible to find out" (p. 131). In contrast to the former narrators in the trilogy, the Unnamable does not solve the question of who he is. His stories have caused the loss of his own self, and he can no longer attain any identity through his fictitious characters because he is unable to produce any more stories.

The Unnamable differs from the previous narrators of the trilogy because he wants to talk about himself and not his characters. With Malone, for instance, the opposite is the case. He wants to get away from his decrepit self by talking about others, but he finds that he is constantly returning to his own situation: "The final novel of the trilogy marks an important change in the relationship between the 'I' that creates and the selves it has assumed . . . The latter are no longer welcome diversions".[42]

In *Malone Dies*, the character of Macmann is adopted by the narrator in the shapes of Moll and Lemuel. In *The Unnamable* the characters play the active part. They beset the powerless narrator much against his will:

> Decidedly Basil is becoming important, I'll call him Mahood instead, I prefer that, I'm queer. It was he told me stories about me, lived in my stead, issued forth from me, came back to me, entered back into me, heaped stories on my head. I don't know how it was done. (p. 25)

The character of Basil or Mahood usurps the narrator, forcing him to give voice to their stories.

The Unnamable, when narrating Mahood's story, speaks in the first person, thereby imperceptibly gliding into Mahood's role, taking on his identity. However, at times he manages to create a distance between himself and Mahood, intruding with remarks like "Still Mahood speaking" (p. 37) or "Mahood dixit" (p. 38). But eventually Mahood's voice grows completely silent and the Unnamable may go back again to speaking in his own voice.

Very soon another character, Worm, takes over from Mahood, and he seems to succeed because the Unnamable seems more likely to think that Worm is himself: "I won't be delivered from him, I mean Worm . . . I am he who will never be caught, never delivered, who crawls . . . towards the new day" (p. 55). However, in a little while, the Unnamable is no longer sure of being

Worm, because it is unlikely that Worm, this primitive kind of creature, has any voice with which to speak: "if I were Worm . . . I wouldn't say anything, I'd be Worm" (p. 64).

The Unnamable sees Worm as more in line with his wasted self than for instance Mahood. But being able to think and speak, the narrator has not reached Worm's level yet. He admits that he was Worm "but ill" and he returns to himself "in triumph" (p. 81). The image he at last arrives at, which expresses more truly his conception of himself, is that of "a vast cretinous mouth, red, blubber and slobbering, in solitary confinement, extruding indefatigably . . . the words that obstruct it" (p. 108). At this point the Unnamable seems to be speaking about himself.

The narrator claims that the "cretinous mouth" must be connected to "a body" (p. 108) and also perhaps to "a mind" (p. 108). This image of the narrator comes rather close to the Unnamable's earlier description of himself as a head on a torso placed in a jar. The Unnamable further regards himself as a planet-like ball, moving through space without feeling anything, a totally dead body, but on the move. This emphasizes the sterility of the narrator's situation. He has to continue his narrative, which tells the story of his purposeless undertaking: "it's round that I must revolve, of that I must speak" (p. 23).

In *Malone Dies* there is a sporadic description of the narrator comparing himself to a planet circled by his moon or character and the two of them turning "dead on dead, about poor mankind" *(Malone Dies,* p. 93). In the last part of the trilogy the planet motif comes more to the fore, but with the same underlying idea of the narrator as a dead body whose story can only repeat itself without end.

The idea of the narrator as a planet with the characters circling about him is implicit in the first pages of *The Unnamable*. The narrator has succeeded Malone in the narrative task, and the latter figures in the last novel of the trilogy as a character. Malone is referred to time and again as a character that passes before the narrator with some regularity. The narrator knows nothing about where he comes from or what is his destiny. The same uncertainty pertains to the narrator's own situation. He does not know why he writes and what his writing amounts to: "It is equally possible, I do not deny it, that I too am in perpetual motion, accompanied by Malone, as the earth by its moon" (p. 11). The earth-moon symbolism expresses the narrator's conception of his situation and that of his characters as an eternal and purposeless circling.

In an interview Beckett comments on the process of dissolution which his characters go through in his trilogy: "My people seem to be falling to bits . . . In the last book – 'L'Innommable' – there is complete disintegration. No 'I', no 'Have', no 'being'. No nominative, no accusative, no verb. There's no way to go on".[43] Here Beckett widens the perspective from the narrator's situation to his own. In *The Unnamable* he portrays a narrator who reaches a deadlock from which he cannot extricate himself, and Beckett's comment suggests that it is his own experiences he voices in the novel.

2. Narrative at a Deadlock

The Unnamable contains three main stories in which the protagonist is referred to as first Basil and Mahood, and lastly Worm.[44] The incident in which Worm figures shows quite clearly that it represents the origin, the making, and the nature of narrative: wondering about when his existence started, the narrator compares himself to the fallen Lucifer, and like him he finds himself in an everlasting hell. The prominent feature of Worm's life is silence. Then "a feeble cry" (p. 12) is heard and the narrator is not sure whether it is himself or someone else who has uttered it.

However, this is the beginning of the narrative of which he sees himself at least as transmitter if not inventor. He suspects the sounds which he hears of being a trick to tempt him into adopting the sounds as his own. They are intended as a means to entice him to utter them. The narrator feels that "they", the incentives, pester him to get going and start a narrative.

In the "character" of Worm, the narrator hopes to have found an expression which corresponds to his own self. Worm is a being without sight or hearing at first, the lowest of the low. But Worm, like himself, is beset by sounds and eventually the narrator describes how a "head has grown out of his ear . . . It's a transformer in which sound is turned" (p. 73). The disturbing sounds have made Worm into an organ for hearing, which again needs a head as a kind of resonance box.

The next step in the creation of a narrative is to furnish Worm with the ability to see: "let's leave him his eye too, it's to see with . . . it's to weep with, it's to practise with" (p. 76). The aim is to humanize Worm, and supplied with eyes, he will develop other human faculties in due course. He will be able to think and to suffer, and this will prevent him "from being what he was before" (p. 78). The narrator makes Worm's fate parallel to his own. The Unnamable wants to be left alone, he wants to die, but "they" will not let him. He feels compelled to create the character of Worm, who develops from nothing, a mere worm, to a being with human characteristics.

In his attempts to create the character of Worm, the narrator reveals a fictional device formerly applied in *Molloy* and *Malone Dies*. In these novels, the narrator lets a character pass in front of him or suddenly visit him. The narrator in *The Unnamable* suggests that it might be an idea to make someone or something pass before Worm:

> A presence at last. A visitor, faithful, with his visiting-day, his visiting-hour, never staying too long . . . but just the necessary time for hope to be born, grow, languish and die, say five minutes. (p. 80)

Here it is made clear that the visitor is a means of developing the narrator-protagonist. When someone passes with regularity before Worm, he will hope for his return as a welcome break in his dull existence. This will change Worm into a human being, because he will be forced to respond in an emotional way.

However, the devices the narrator formerly resorted to, no longer work. The Unnamable gives up the idea of a visitor for Worm, because he is the sole inhabitant of his universe. Nothing can be added to Worm's existence: "Here there is no wood, nor any stone ... no vegetables, no minerals, only Worm, kingdom unknown, Worm is there, as it were, as it were" (p. 80).

But the narrator is not yet allowed to leave his task of creating a story about Worm. The incentive behind the narrative, now termed "the master", forces him to continue. The narrator refers to himself in the third person plural: "For they may come back ... having pleaded for years in vain before the master and failed to convince him there is nothing to be done, with Worm, for Worm. Then all will start over again, obviously" (p. 83).

In the subsequent story about Worm the narrator makes a last, painful effort: "they are doing the best they can, with the miserable means at their disposal, a voice, a little light, poor devils" (p. 85). The narrator projects his own problem on to Worm, who suffers from the narrator's attempts to change him into something he is not qualified to be; in the same way, the "master" wields his power over the narrator. Worm is portrayed as a hunted being, whom the narrator hopes in the end to bring "to the wall" (p. 84) and to capture.

Worm has become a character persecuted by the narrator. The idea of the fugitive character and the pursuing narrator occurs in the earlier parts of the trilogy, for instance in Moran's search for Molly and Lemuel's for Macmann. But previously the pursuit resulted in the narrator changing places and becoming one with the character. In *The Unnamable*, Worm is never "captured" by the narrator, who does not succeed in making him a character in the ordinary sense, a being with recognizable human features.

The narrator at last dismisses Worm. He cannot regard him as anything but a fiction. With his meagre life and bleak characteristics, he never develops towards a character who could make readers forget his fictitiousness: "The mistake they make of course is to speak of him as if he really existed, in a specific place, whereas the whole thing is no more than a project for the moment" (p. 89). The narrator has not succeeded in breathing life into his character and there he pinpoints the situation of Worm quite accurately when he says: "Worm will vanish utterly, as if he has never been, which indeed is probably the case" (p. 90).

While the story about Worm concerns the formation and development of fiction, the story about Mahood centres mainly on two issues; the thematic circling of the narrative and the narrator's despair with his own undertaking. As regards the first point, the Unnamable's attempts to speak about Worm or Mahood only result in his talking about himself.

Similarly, the characters undertake journeys which end up where they started. For instance, Mahood, the narrator's "next vice-exister" (p. 31), is described as he reaches the end of his journey towards the home from which he set out. Now Mahood does not proceed in a straight line, but

> in a sharp curve which . . . seemed likely to restore me to my point of departure, or to one adjacent. I must have got embroiled in a kind of inverted spiral . . . which, instead of widening more and more, grew narrower and narrower . . . I should no doubt have had to stop, unless of course I elected to set off again at once in the opposite direction, to unscrew myself as it were, after having screwed myself to a standstill . . . (pp. 32–33)

The image of the spiral which may end in a full stop, expresses very well the narrator's feeling of having arrived at a deadlock.

The second issue in Mahood's story focuses on the narrator's feeling that his strivings are not worth while. Mahood at last arrives home, but he has little regards for his family, and they do not esteem him highly either. They all, however, die of food poisoning so that his last spiralling movements are undertaken in the stench of the rotting bodies of his family. Mahood admits that despite the knowledge that his journey lacks a "desirable goal" (p. 37), the thing for him has been to continue. However, this time the smell and the sight of the dead bodies nearly suffocate him. This incident underlines the narrator's feeling of hopelessness and loathing for his situation, which is a dead end from which he cannot extricate himself.

Nevertheless, the narrative continues, but from this point onwards the characters do not undertake any more journeys. The narrator-protagonist asserts that "this active life is at an end, I do not move and never shall again" (p. 43). From now on the stories about Mahood and Worm are completely lacking in plot. They amount to no more than descriptions of the characters' status.

Lastly, Mahood presents himself as stuck in a jar from which his head protrudes, stationed outside a café. He describes his function as two-fold: He furnishes manure for the lettuce of the owner and he serves as a "kind of landmark" (p. 45) to the customers of the establishment. This description reveals how the narrator considers his own story. Mahood's only "product" at this stage is paralleled by the anal imagery in the earlier parts of the trilogy and later in *The Unnamable* when the narrator says that he will "shit stories" (p. 97). The narrator here expresses what he finds his narrative amounts to.

This description also serves as an ironic comment on the function of fiction or art in contemporary life. The narrator-protagonist becomes the bizarre "landmark" or symbol for a place where people go to have their hunger stilled. He is employed in this society to help stimulate and cater for people's basic needs. This is a consumer's society, a circumstance which is further underlined by the fact that the café is situated near the slaughter house, where "all is killing and eating" (p. 57). The spiritual aspect of existence has been given no room here. The narrator-protagonist produces manure for the lettuce which the customers want, and so his "output" is presented as a waste product which, in its small way, merely contributes to gratify the consumers' appetites.

The eternal continuation of art is suggested as a possibility in *Malone Dies*. In *The Unnamable* Beckett denies his fiction any spiritual value.

3. The Loss of Narratee

To a greater extent than is the case in *Molloy* and *Malone Dies*, critics have commented on the reader's role with regard to *The Unnamable*, i.e. they speak about how they as readers react to the novel. Thus their concern is with the external reader, not the reader spoken to, the narratee, in the book. Abbott, for instance, mentions the pain the reader experiences because his normal expectations are not fulfilled during the reading process. However, in Abbott's case the pain gives way to surprise and delight owing to Beckett's humour.[45]

Abbott touches a problem many readers experience when approaching *The Unnamable*, i.e. that the novel is unreadable. The fact remains that the book does not appeal to the general reader. The references to the narratee in the novel do not help the external reader to identify with the narratee. Most readers feel alienated from the world of the novel.

However, if a distance exists between the external reader and the novel and its narratee, the relation between the narratee and the narrator within the novel appears close. Hesla finds that they are two aspects of the same individual – the Unnamable – and that "In the communion of the written word, writer and reader become one".[46] The unity between narratee and narrator largely explains the distance felt by the external reader. The narrator speaks to and addresses *himself*, and he appears to have no message to impart to the world, but rather to attempt a clarification for himself of his own situation.

The narrator in *The Unnamable* is a reduced being compared to his predecessors in the earlier parts of the trilogy. More than they, he is stripped down to the bare essentials of the human predicament. This circumstance also effects the relation to the narratee. The narrators of *Molloy* and *Malone Dies* pretend *not* to speak about themselves. This is after all the case; the narrator of *The Unnamable* gives over all pretences and talks about himself. He does not hide the fact that the "you" addressed, the narratee, is himself: "Squeeze, squeeze . . . a little longer, this is perhaps about you" (p. 26). It is himself he wants to get out by the squeezing, and the person addressed is unmistakably himself.

However, as the narrative proceeds, the narrator does not manage to keep clear of other characters as a topic for his story. When at times he does not speak of himself, the "you" appears more as a narratee proper, another individual addressed by the narrator: "You wouldn't think it was the same gang as a moment ago, or would you? What can you expect" (p. 89).

On another occasion the distance between narrator and narratee becomes still more marked when the narrator describes himself as performing in a public show and the "you" is presented as one of the audience: "oh you know, who you, oh I suppose the audience . . . it's a public show, you buy your seat . . . you hear a voice, perhaps it's a recitation, that's the show" (p. 99). But "you" soon discovers that he is the only person in the audience and the only listener to the voice, and the situation of the narratee resembles unmistakably that of the narrator pestered by voices. This shows that the narratee is no more than a disguise for the narrator after all.

In the passage referred to above the narratee changes from audience to narrator, thus bringing the relation between narrator and narratee back full circle; in the beginning of the story they are more clearly seen as aspects of the same individual, i.e. the Unnamable. This is further reinforced by a passage not far from the end of the novel where the Unnamable deplores the lack of terms to adequately express his own identity: "you don't know why . . . someone says you, it's the fault of the pronouns, there is no name for me, no pronoun for me, all the trouble comes from that" (pp. 121–122). So when "you" is used, it is actually himself he speaks of.

4. Conclusion – *The Unnamable*

The narrator of *The Unnamable* describes himself as an utterly reduced being. He is stripped of his limbs and he is also mentally exhausted. His weakening makes itself felt in the vagueness with which the setting is presented. The reader has a rather indistinct idea of the narrator's whereabouts. His exhaustion also appears in the description of the incentive to his narrative, mentioned as a "master" in complete control of his pupil, the narrator. The messengers that the "master" makes use of to enforce his will over the narrator are vaguely alluded to either as "they" or "the voices".

The narrator's exhaustion is further apparent in the discussion of his identity. He can no longer conjure up entertaining stories illustrating his preoccupation with this problem, but confines himself to commenting on the question. He finds that he is not able to take on the identity of any fictional character, because he has grown tired of creating masks for himself. But neither can he speak about himself, feeling himself to be devoid of any identity. That the narrator is at the end of his capacities is seen lastly in the way the characters dominate him. He finally wants to talk about himself but they continually intrude into his narrative. But no character represents adequately his real self and to express this, he resorts to an image of himself as a dead planet, with his characters like moons, circling around him, in eternal motion.

☆

In the discussion of the narrative, the story of Worm was seen as an illustration of the origin and development of fiction. In the beginning was Worm, the lowest of creatures, fallen from his heavenly abode like Lucifer, and dwelling in unbroken silence. Then the attempts to make a character of Worm are revealed. He is exposed to sounds and supplied with eyes so that he may develop his human faculties.

Furthermore, the device of launching a story by letting objects and people pass before Worm is revealed; the descriptions of these visitations and Worm's reflections on them will furnish material for the story. However, Worm cannot be brought to life, and his story remains an abortive attempt because it is also the tale of the narrator's frustration and exhaustion.

The story about Mahood circling towards his original point of departure and coming to a standstill there, describes the deadlock the narrator finds himself in. The manure-producing Mahood illustrates another point, i.e. the narrator's low regard for his art and his conception of how art functions in the modern world. It is a mere product to serve the consumer's physical needs devoid of any spiritual value.

☆

The distance between the external reader and the novel was found to have its explanation partly in the close connection between the narrator and the narratee. The narrator wants to interpret his own situation to himself through the narrative process, and he pays little or no attention to the external reader for whom he has a low regard. Thus the narratee addressed is himself.

Conclusion

In Beckett's trilogy the external circumstances, such as the setting and the name of the protagonist, change from one novel to the next. However, thematically the three books are closely related, the same problems being dealt with in each novel to a large extent. Further, a development takes place, metaphorically expressed by the narrator's physical deterioration in the course of the trilogy.

This comparison will first pay attention to the narrator's role in the three books. The separate discussion of the narrator is centred specifically on four problems: the question of the incentive for the narrator's story-telling; the narrator's identity; the problem of communication, and lastly the symbolic meaning of the narrator's physical exhaustion. In this section, the development of each of these problems in the course of the trilogy will be traced.

In *Molloy* the question about the incentive behind the narrator's story figures prominently. Both Molloy and Moran mention external prompters: in Molloy's case there is a visitor who tells him what to do and collects the written pages, while Moran feels himself to be at the beck and call of Gaber and Youdi. The narrator regards the external incentives as forces from outside whose demand is for a conventional kind of narration in keeping with the taste of the public at large.

However, Molloy and Moran are also beset by voices which an inner necessity compels them to follow. Both narrators experience a conflict between the demands of conventional story-telling, ordered by the visitor or Youdi, and narration in keeping with their own conviction and taste, inspired by the voices. The first part of *Molloy* discloses that in his rambling monologue, Molloy follows predominantly the dictates of his inner voice, while in the second part Moran mostly gives in to what he supposes to be Youdi's claim for conventional narrative technique.

In *Malone Dies* the question of the incentives carries less weight. The narrator mentions vaguely some "grown-ups" that force him to continue, but he does not feel any conflict between external and internal incentives. The narrator has almost completely turned towards his inner darkness from which his stories first arise in the form of a noise he feels pressed to interpret. Malone appears weaker and more submissive than the narrators of *Molloy*, and the story his inward prompters impel him to express pays still less attention to traditional narrative form.

The narrator of *The Unnamable* also refers to voices and a "master", but the individuality of the narrator has dwindled to such an extent that he sees himself as a mere vehicle voicing the words that come to him. To heed the demands of conventional art is no longer felt as a vital question and the narrative disregards most of the devices of traditional story-telling.

The above discussion of the incentives reveals how the narrators in *Molloy* experience a conflict as to whether to follow conventional or highly individual laws in their art. The narrators of *Malone Dies* and *The Unnamable* pay less and less attention to conventional demands and become increasingly dominated by the inner voice. The narrative itself suggests this development through a growing vagueness of setting, plot and character.

The question of the narrator's identity is strongly related to the kind of art he produces. In the first part of the trilogy, the narrators oscillate between opposing tendencies in themselves and both make their choice between two ways of existence, which signify two kinds of identity: Molloy spurns the life of a bourgeois and remains an ill-smelling and in every way offensive bum; Moran abandons the loafer's existence in the end.

The identity conflict is expressed through the incidents that befall them, such as Molloy's meeting with the police, but also in the narrative technique. Both Molloy and Moran, when leading the life of social outcasts, express themselves in long monologues that leave a vague impression about time, location and characters. Their style becomes more conventional and easier to comprehend during their periods as decent, ordinary citizens.

Malone's identity conflict does not take the form of a struggle between opposing tendencies. His problem is to avoid the question and to get away from the self. He tries to escape by recounting stories in which he does not figure as the protagonist. But his characters grow to resemble him, struggling with similar problems.

While Molloy and Moran desperately search for their own identity, describing their own adventures, Malone goes to the other extreme, attempting to avoid the self by conjuring up stories about other characters. The problem for the Unnamable is the lack of self. In his search for himself, he discovers that he has lost his identity. The Unnamable does not manage to produce any proper story at all. His abortive attempts fall flat. His tale becomes a mere discourse on his problem. Without identity, he cannot experience anything, and accordingly he has no story to tell.

A usual characteristic of metafiction is the narrator's pronounced concern with his ability to communicate. This problem figures most prominently in the first part of the trilogy. Molloy is worried about his difficulties in making himself understood and describes various incidents where he fails in this respect. His lack of success in verbal communication has its symbolic parallel in his sexual impotence.

Of all the narrators in the trilogy, Moran is the most conventional. He abides by the traditional devices of narration and is not openly concerned with the problem of communication. He manages to tell a story quite well. Thus he apparently succeeds in communicating with his readers, by making them able to follow his story.

Various incidents with his son show that Moran has communication problems as well, but he is not aware of them. Lack of awareness is his problem; he lives on the surface. This is further underlined by the fact that he does not mention any involvement with members of the opposite sex. The question is whether Moran in his garden existence, being out of touch with the deeper layers of life, has any real message to communicate.

Unlike Molloy, Malone does not talk directly about his own failing ability to communicate. Indirectly he shows his concern on this point by comparing himself to the obtuse Sapo, who is completely absorbed in himself, having a minimum of contact with the external world.

The Unnamable has totally withdrawn into his own world. The question of communication does not concern him at all, simply because he has nothing to communicate.

Thus, in the course of the trilogy, the more the narrator's concern with the problem of communication diminishes the more he turns inwards on himself. As the narrator pays less heed to traditional narrative technique, he ceases to worry about being understood. When Moran appears to communicate more successfully, it is because the story he tells about life in his garden lacks depth.

Throughout the trilogy, the narrator's bodily fitness is presented as a symbolic expression of his ability to tell a story. Moran, at one point the healthiest of the narrators, manages to produce a traditional story; but when his legs stiffen and make progress difficult, his story also comes to a standstill. The narrator grows more and more decrepit in the course of the trilogy, while at the same time the story stagnates. In *The Unnamable*, the narrator is reduced to a mere torso. The story disintegrates completely, and the traditional narrative elements of plot, setting and characters disappear in the unceasing flow of words.

When comparing the presentation of the narrative in the three parts of the trilogy, one is struck by the importance of the circle both in connection with the thematic aspect of the three novels and as a narrative device. Molloy ends up where he started, in the vicinity of his mother's room. This fact suggests that his journey is a search for the self. Besides the circle of the main story, the narrative also forms smaller circles: it consists of incidents, illustrating the narrator's identity problem. These are interspersed with passages where the narrator returns more directly to his own situation.

In Molloy's case it is already clear that his quest is also a quest for his identity as a narrator. This becomes more explicit in Moran's case. He also undertakes a circular journey from and to the self. He sets out to pursue Molloy. This may be seen as an image of the narrator in quest of his character who turns out to be himself. Moran merges with the Molloy he pursues, and his style alternates with his shifts in personality.

The close relation between narrator and character is further demonstrated in *Malone Dies*. Malone's story moves, like Molloy's, in smaller circles where the narrator comments on his own situation in-between the incidents. But, in contrast to Molloy's story, the incidents deal with characters other than the narrator. To talk about others is a means for Malone to escape the self which proves futile as indirectly the incidents concern his own situation. Malone circles round this self despite his efforts to avoid doing so.

In *The Unnamable*, to a still greater extent, the significance of the circle both as a technical device and as important for the thematic aspect in the trilogy is seen. In the episodes dealing with Worm, the narrator reveals why he makes use of the trick of letting characters and objects orbit around Worm. To make Worm a recognizable character he has to let him come into contact with characters and objects outside himself; the circle signifies the interaction between the narrator-protagonist and his world.

This device has been employed in the earlier parts of the trilogy, for instance when Molloy's individuality is brought out through his interaction with other characters, such as Lousse and the policeman. It is, however, not until *The Unnamable* that the full significance of the circle motif is recognizable. The sterility of the narrator's situation is suggested when the relation between the narrator-protagonist and the character is described as that of a dead earth circled by its moon.

The thematic significance of the circle is further illuminated in *The Unnamable*. Mahood's circling, like that of the other protagonists in the trilogy, is revealed as a preoccupation with the self, i.e. the self of a narrator of fiction. But Mahood's case stresses the barrenness of this kind of self-centredness as he spirals inwards in ever smaller circles towards a complete standstill.

Another dominating feature in the narrative of the three novels is the conflict of art versus life. In *Molloy* the conflict is primarily presented in terms of setting. Molloy and Moran have the choice between the garden of physical comfort and spiritual death, and an existence of hardship, in agreement with the deeper layers of the self. This conflict implies the choice between conventional fiction, which tries to reproduce reality, and a more controversial, avant-garde "non-figurative" kind of narrative.

In *Malone Dies,* the emphasis is not so much on opposing conceptions of art as on different views of the artist's or the narrator's role: the narrator plays an ambiguous part because he is able to create art that will outlive his own existence at the same time as he destroys life by giving it a fixed form.

Malone Dies expresses this conflict in the ambiguity attached to Big Lambert's pig-sticking. It is also traceable in the symbolic significance of the colour grey, which suggests the narrator's middle position between life and death. Lastly, this conflict is exposed by the difference between the life-giving Moll and the destructive Lemuel, both aspects of the narrator.

In *The Unnamable*, the conflict between life and art experienced by the narrator is projected particularly onto the Worm episode. The narrator is completely exhausted. His self-absorbed narrative has brought him to the end of the line. Nevertheless, he feels forced to continue, and describes his attempts to portray Worm, who does not come alive as a character.

With *The Unnamable*, the conflict between life and art moves to a close; unconventional art has been chosen where the narrator explores the narrative process with the result that the affinity to human life – as can be seen from Worm's example – is reduced to a minimum.

The third central aspect presented in the novels may be expressed by

Prufrock's question in T. S. Eliot's "Love Song": "Would it have been worth it, after all . . ." The answer the trilogy moves towards is "no". The narrator expresses his disgust with his narrative in the anal symbolism in the three books.

Throughout the trilogy the oral and the anal orifices are linked, suggesting the abhorrence with which the narrator regards his product, the Word. In *Malone Dies* the narrator speaks of his poles: "dish and pot" (p. 13), and in the Lemuel episode one just hopes that this brute will not confuse the contents of the two buckets he carries around, sometimes in only one hand, containing the soup and the slops of his patients.

In *The Unnamable* the linking of anal and oral matters is humourously presented: The Unnamable ends up with no other function but to produce manure for his keeper's lettuce. Nevertheless, depite the humour, the narrator's despair is obvious. He considers his narrative of no greater worth than the muck which Macmann carefully exhibits along the sidewalk.

Tracing the references to the narratee in the trilogy one finds a development parallel to that of the narrator. As the narrator turns more and more inwards towards himself, the references to the narratee grow less and less frequent. It becomes more obvious, in the course of the trilogy, that the narrator addresses himself.

In the first part of *Molloy*, an external reader is at times clearly appealed to, though the narrator mostly addresses his speeches to himself. The reader is drawn even less into the narrative in *Malone Dies,* where the calls to the narratee are less frequent. In addition, the narrator quite obviously speaks to himself even when he addresses a "you".

The Unnamable abandons every pretence of speaking to others. The narratee and the narrator are described as aspects of the same individual, i.e. the Unnamable. Thus the inward circling also relates to the situation of the narratee. In the last part of the trilogy his role has dwindled away until he has become a mere part of the narrator's disintegrated self.

E. M. Forster, discussing the difference between people in everyday life and people in books, lists the "main facts in human life" as "birth, food, sleep, love, and death". He further finds that the novelists' approaches to these facts vary; they may try to reproduce them as accurately as possible, exaggerate or ignore them.[47]

Beckett does not fit into any of these three categories. He is as much concerned with the various questions that arise for the narrator when reproducing life in words as with the portrayal of life. In the trilogy he touches nevertheless the "main facts" of existence drawn up by Forster, expressing the writer's position in terms of the basic problems of human life.

However, the narrator in Beckett's trilogy cannot completely turn his back on the question which Forster debates, i.e. the relation between fiction and life. He removes himself further and further from life, circling ever closer to his own situation *qua* narrator. Inevitably, the Beckett narrator realizes the costs of choosing to write about the art of narration instead of life; in the end, he has to face the disintegration of self in his narrative. Beckett's trilogy describes this process in the portrayal of the dying narrator.

The Meaning of Metafiction –
Conclusion

In the Introduction, metafiction was defined as fiction whose primary concern is to express the novelist's vision of experience by exploring the process of its own making. A novelist's vision, or the message he wants to convey, is closely related to the form of his work. When metafictionists write as they do, calling attention to the writing process itself, this is no mere exhibition of craftmanship. Admittedly, this possibility does exist, but Sterne, Nabokov, Barth and Beckett do not limit themselves to the technical aspect of writing fiction. What they have in common is a deep concern for verbal creation and communication. However, their opinions differ as to the possibilities of communication and the making of fiction. Their different conceptions are revealed in their attitudes to the narrator, narrative and narratee in their works.

Sterne's narrator regards his role first and foremost as that of an entertainer. Tristram cherishes an unconquerable belief in his own calling. He may tell the most whimsical of stories, but he nevertheless considers them a boon bestowed on mankind to alleviate suffering. Sterne's narrator subscribes to Horace's idea in *Ars Poetica*, in vogue in the neoclassical period, that art should amuse as well as instruct, and Tristram plays the role of a court jester, calling attention to his bell-furnished cap. With due respect to the lapse of time, he turns up again in Van, Nabokov's circus artist. Some resemblance also exists between Tristram, Henry Burlingame and Harold Bray, the narrators' alter egos in Barth's novels.

However, the narrators of the 20th century novels differ from Sterne's Tristram in that they have less belief in their ability to reach the reader and do not see their roles first and foremost as that of a jester. There exists, on the other hand, no unanimous conception in the modern novels as to what part the narrator should play. Nabokov's ideal narrator combines the artist's intense experience of reality with the scientist's knowledge and precision. Only a synthesis of these qualities can produce art of lasting beauty, which is the aim of Nabokov's narrator. This perfect combination is represented in the joint narratorship of Ada and Van.

Barth also advocates a synthesis of qualities in his ideal narrator, but his aim differs from Nabokov's. The Barthian narrator sets out to save the world from destruction by creating order out of chaos. His task is to find an answer to the apparently insoluble conflicts of existence. This calls, on the narrator's part, for a burning conviction about the importance of his own role and that of art. In addition, the narrator must possess technical competence. Ideally, Barth's narrator should combine the qualities of a saviour and a magician.

While the narrators of the other metafictionists assume recognizable roles, like Sterne's clown and Barth's saviours and tricksters, Beckett's narrators leave a vague impression. Beckett explores the existential consequences for man in the modern world, epitomized by the narrator's situation. The Beckettian narrator experiences an identity crisis which terminates with the complete loss of self. He goes through a process af dehumanization. In the trilogy the narrator's status deteriorates from that of an imbecile bum to a manipulated tool. In *The Unnamable,* the last part of the trilogy, the narrator is presented as "Worm", a mere head on a torso.

The comparison between the novelist's narrator-portrayals shows the degree of attention which is paid to the narrator, but despite a shared concern with communication, their roles vary from one novel to the next. Only few common traits seem to exist between Sterne's entertaining clown, Nabokov's circus artist, Barth's saviours and Beckett's bums.

The four novelists also differ in their conception and presentation of the narrative where especially the question of mimesis is a central issue. Sterne, in common with the modern novelists, is concerned with this problem. In *Tristram Shandy* he debates the question of mimesis through the incidents and controversies of his characters, who must be characterized as ordinary, every-day people despite their idiosyncracies. The disparity between life and art comes out in the conflicting uses of language, which give rise to no end of misunderstandings: the word *bridge* means one thing to Dr Slop and has quite another significance to Uncle Toby. Sterne shows his preoccupation with mimesis through the various ways the characters try to come to terms with reality in their writing or like Uncle Toby in his play war. Tristram opts for a compromise between Toby's exact copying and Walter's a priori approach.

Like Sterne, Nabokov underlines that the hope of attaining an exact correspondence between art and life is an illusion. This is illustrated in *Ada* by, for instance, Kim's photo album, which in this respect corresponds to Toby's play town in *Tristram Shandy.* However, Nabokov shows a more fundamental grasp of the problem of mimesis in fiction by focusing in his narrative on the aspects of time and space. Sterne's novel further illustrates the disparity between fiction and reality by dealing with the problem of time. This is demonstrated in *Tristram Shandy* by Walter's endeavour to keep step in his writing with the development of his son. In *Ada,* Van is much more sophisticated when exhibiting the ambiguity bound up with any conception of reality, not only the fictional one.

Barth is less subtle than Nabokov and Sterne in his handling of the question of mimesis. In *The Sot-Weed Factor* Henry and Eben represent various attitudes to mimesis in art. Like Uncle Toby, Henry prefers an exact copy of reality, whereas Eben resembles Walter with his preconceived notions about art. *Giles Goat-Boy* does not directly debate the question of mimesis, but indirectly the novel shows its preoccupation with the problem. This novel is an allegory of the origin and development of fiction. Thus the story may be read as a tale about George with a basis, though rather remote, in human existence. The second level of the novel has its frame of reference in the world of books.

Beckett also takes up the question of mimesis and, like *Giles Goat-Boy*, his trilogy represents narrative art allegorically. The narrators' quest for identity in *Molloy* signifies a choice of narrative medium between a conventional, mimetic way of narration and an unconventional, non-mimetic approach. The narrator chooses the latter alternative, and in *The Unnamable* this leads to the affinity with life being reduced to a minimum. The novel, lacking story and recognizable characters, does not come alive.

As regards the conception of the narrative in the four novels, the writers share a preoccupation with the question of mimesis. They try to exhibit the disparity between life and art, but choose different means.

Of the four novelists, Sterne devotes most attention to the narratee. Tristram constantly addresses himself to the reader, teasingly or in an appealing way, asking for his understanding and indulgence. By every kind of trick, he lures his narratee into active participation in the act of communication, cf. his leaving a blank page for a drawing of widow Wadman's portrait. In addition, Sterne's narrative supplies examples of accomplished narrators, like Trim, who establish contact with their audience, and impossible ones, like Walter, who fail to make themselves understood. Tristram points out that successful communication depends on the narrator's ability to appeal both to the head and the heart of his audience.

Sterne shows that he wants to reach the average man and woman, and cares not at all about the critic-expert. The narratee in Nabokov's *Ada* is represented by an ideal set, the narrators themselves, and secondly, by the silent observers like "the boor", "the simple-minded reader", and "the scholars", who are all kept at a distance. The narrator could not care less whether his message reaches them or not. He even gives vent to the opinion that more likely than not his intention will be misunderstood, as exemplified in "the editor" 's remarks. Nabokov's narrator is aware of the importance of the reader for the understanding of the narrative. But it is enough for him to have secured one kind of reader, the ideal one, he does not bother about the rest. Despite his self-irony, Barth's narrator has a message he wants to impart to the world, and accordingly the narratee is seen as important in his novels: without the reader, the message loses its point. However, even if Barth's narrator sees the significance of the reader, he has no illusions about the average reader's ability to understand the message. Like Nabokov's Van, he believes that few will grasp the meaning of his work, but unlike Van, Barth's narrator does not write only for a select elite.

Beckett's novels represent an even greater degree of disillusionment with the reader. His narrators do not care very much about creating an art that should try to enlist the attention of the audience. They are gradually overwhelmed by the pointlessness of the world and accordingly also of their own task, but still they feel forced to go on. They become so absorbed in the intricacies of expressing themselves that few efforts are made to secure the readers' attention. A symptom of this is that Beckett's narrator addresses *himself* to a great extent.

This discussion about the narratee shows a change of view regarding the importance of art in the 20th century compared to Sterne's time. Sterne's Tristram hopes to reach the greater part of the educated public of his time. The narrators of Nabokov and Barth face the fact that their readership has shrunk to a chosen few, while Beckett's narrators seem to communicate mostly with themselves.

This comparison reveals that each of the four novelists has his own vision of life, which he presents by exploring the choice of expression open to the narrator. Sterne's narrator wants to arouse laughter as a means of establishing contact with the readers and succeeds to the extent that he makes *Tristram Shandy* one of the wittiest books ever written. Nabokov, on the other hand, has quite another aim with his work. Examining the aesthetic possibility of fiction writing, he creates in *Ada* a novel of intense beauty. The reader is introduced to a fascinating, glittering world where the amalgamation of 19th century aristocratic Russia with 20th century technologically advanced America indicates only one aspect of its richness.

Barth has yet another conception of the narrator's function, which is to create meaning. In *The Sot-Weed Factor* and *Giles Goat-Boy* the reader is invited to join in a quest to seek an answer, not merely to aesthetic problems, but to questions of an existential-religious nature. Beckett's novels also focus on man's existential situation, but ultimately he denies the possibility of salvation through the word, and as little attention is paid to the reader, his books represent a most stimulating mental challenge. Beckett represents a more advanced stage in the development of metafiction than Barth, and therefore the chapter on his trilogy comes last in this study.

The relation between vision and form in the metafictive novel becomes quite clear when the 20th century novels are examined against the background of Sterne's work. Both with regard to the view of life expressed and to its form, *Tristram Shandy* differs most markedly from the later books.

Compared to 20th century narrators, Tristram stands out through his unflagging and conscious attempts to make the readers laugh. Thus the most striking feature of the novel is its humour. Sterne is, however, well aware of the evils of life, being fatally ill himself. But Sterne's narrator nevertheless sees it as his task to make the readers forget the sore realities of life through laughter.

The novels of Nabokov, Barth and Beckett do indeed contain elements of humour. Further, to the degree that it reveals itself as a parody of earlier forms, the metafictive novel has necessarily a satirical aspect. This aspect has been debated only in connection with *Tristram Shandy:* Sterne's Tristram sees it as essential that the narrator should elicit the readers' smiles and good humour. Barth's narrators, for instance, regard themselves first and foremost as saviours, not as entertainers. Tristram, on the other hand, believes that he can communicate his own sense of humour to the readers by writing in a way that makes them laugh. Thus despite his difficulties, Sterne is basically optimistic, which is shown in his positive view of the narrator's function.

Sterne reveals that he is a child of his time by the picture he draws of the middle class society of his day and by debating the question of mimesis within the frames of the characters' ordinary life, for instance their attitudes to language. Sterne's art seems to be founded on a Christian, 18th century view of life, and the author does not question reality or existence as such. Sterne does not venture to consider his fictional world as a universe in its own right, of equal worth to that of a Supreme Creator. His fiction is a means to escape and mitigate the evils of the world, but no alternative to it.

Compared to Sterne's Tristram, the narrators of the 20th century metafiction have much more daring conceptions about their own art. Thus Van considers his fiction an alternative and no copy of the existing world, and Eben in *The Sot-Weed Factor* equates the poet's task with that of a god and considers art a protection against the chaos of existence. The modern metafictionists abandon any attempt to present a picture of "real" life. Nabokov's *Ada*, for instance, resembles science fiction and so does Barth's *Giles Goat-Boy*, and the disparity between life and art is expressed through the use of allegory.

However, not only the novelist's view of his art, but also his general outlook on life has altered since Sterne's time. The modern metafictionists describe a world characterized by conflicts and instability, and inhabited by restless, displaced characters. Nabokov and Barth are less pessimistic than Beckett, who leaves little hope for his narrator-protagonists and their environments. The modern metafictionists have a waning belief in the narrator's role and nourish few illusions of being understood by the world at large.

Metafiction has become a trend in 20th century literature, particularly after the Second World War. William Gass suggests that the metafictionist creates his own universe intact with narrator and reader because he sees the actual world crumbling around him.[1] This is the case with Nabokov who, in most of his novels, turns in disgust from the political intrigues and violence of modern society and creates his own fictional kingdom of exceptional beauty. But not all of the metafictionists succeed so well in escaping from the world into metafiction. Barth shows in Eben's story that it is impossible even for a poet to refuse responsibility for the state of affairs. And the crucifying experiences of Beckett's narrators do not exactly mean a relief from the evils of the world. It may be that metafiction for the 20th century writers represents a way of escape, but it generally does not work so well for them as it did for Sterne.

NOTES

Introduction

1. E. C. Riley, *Cervantes's Theory of the Novel* (Oxford, 1962), p. 46: "Artists turned their glass on the working of art and made works of art out of what they saw". This is a more suitable description of Cervantes's *Exemplary Stories* than of *Don Quixote*.
2. William H. Gass, "Philosophy and the Form of Fiction", *Fiction and the Figures of Life* (New York, 1970), p. 25. This is a collection of essays printed earlier in various publications.
3. Joseph T. Shipley, ed., *Dictionary of World Literary Terms* (London, 1970), pp. 15–16.
4. Larry McCaffery, "The Art of Metafiction: William Gass's *Willie Masters' Lonesome Wife*", *Critique*, XVIII, 1 (1976), 22.
5. John Fletcher and Malcolm Bradbury, "The Introverted Novel", in Malcolm Bradbury and James McFarlane, eds., *Modernism 1890–1930* (Harmondsworth, 1976), pp. 394–395.
6. Robert Scholes, "Metafiction", *The Iowa Review*, I (Fall 1970), 100.
7. —————, "The Fictional Criticism of the Future", *Triquarterly*, XXXIV, 4 (Fall 1975), 237.
8. Stanley Fogel, " 'And All the Little Typtopus': Notes on Language Theory in the Contemporary Experimental Novel", *Modern Fiction Studies*, XX, 3 (Autumn 1974), 328–336. My objection to Fogel's definition also applies to Robert Alter's definition of "the self-conscious novel" (cf. ch. I, note 7).
9. Cf. Kenneth Monkman and J. C. T. Oates, "Towards a Sterne Bibliography: Books and Other Material Displayed at the Sterne Conference", *The Winged Skull*, ed. by Arthur H. Cash and John M. Stedmond (London, 1971), p. 280; Franz-Josef Wickler, *Rabelais und Sterne* (Bonn, 1963); R. F. Brissenden, " 'Trusting to Almighty God': Another look at the composition of *Tristram Shandy*", *The Winged Skull*, p. 262: Northrop Frye, *Anatomy of Criticism* (Princeton, 1971), pp. 311–312.
10. Wayne C. Booth, *The Rhetoric of Fiction* (Chicago, 1961), pp. 224–229. Also the many writers of satire and burlesques such as Swift, Erasmus and Rabelais are referred to by Booth as some of Sterne's literary influences.
11. Robert Alter, *Partial Magic. The Novel as a Self-Conscious Genre* (Berkeley, Los Angeles, London, 1975), p. 89.
12. Bernard Bergonzi, *The Situation of the Novel* (London, 1972), p. 26.
13. Gabriel Josipovici, *The World and the Book. A Study of Modern Fiction* (London, 1971), p. 289. It is interesting to notice that Riley finds a similar recurrence of meta-art in Spanish literature, where "some of the more tricksy devices" of 17th century art came to the fore again two centuries later (cf. *Cervantes's Theory of the Novel*, p. 47).
14. Nathaniel Hawthorne, *The Blithedale Romance, The Works of Nathaniel Hawthorne*, V (Boston and New York, 1888), 409.
15. Cf. my article "Absence of Absolutes: The Reconciled Artist in John Barth's *The Floating Opera*", *Studia Neophilologica*, XLVII, 1 (1975), 53–58.
16. The way in which the 19th century novelist deals with the poet's situation is also illustrated in Walter Scott's *Waverley:* The protagonist acts the role of the poet, but this does not constitute

the main theme of the novel. The narrator comments on his writing and use of sources, but these remarks to the reader do not function as central issues in this novel as it would have done in a metafictional work. Likewise Henry James in *The Portrait of a Lady* focuses on Isabel's fate while hinting only that both Osmond and Ralph in their aesthetic dedication caricature the novelist.

[17] Wolfgang Kayser, *Das Sprachliche Kunstwerk*, Zwölfte Auflage (München, 1967), p. 349.
[18] ――――――, "Wer Erzählt den Roman?" *Zur Poetik des Romans*, ed. by Volker Klotz (Darmstadt, 1969), p. 206.
[19] Cf. for instance, Booth, *The Rhetoric of Fiction*, pp. 151 ff.
[20] "Wer Erzählt den Roman?", p. 203.

Chapter I

[1] Cf. INTRODUCTION for a discussion of the term *metafiction*.
[2] Victor Shklovsky, "Sterne's *Tristram Shandy:* Stylistic Commentary", *Russian Formalist Criticism, Four Essays*, ed. by Lee T. Lemon and Marion J. Reis (Lincoln, 1965) p. 35.
[3] Shklovsky, p. 27.
[4] Shklovsky, p. 30
[5] Cf. for instance Northrop Frye, "Towards Defining an Age of Sensibility", *Journal of English Literary History*, XXIII (1956), 145; Robert Alan Donovan, *The Shaping Vision, Imagination in the English Novel from Defoe to Dickens* (Ithaca, New York, 1966), p. 95; Kenneth E. Harper, "A Russian Critic and *Tristram Shandy*", *Modern Philology*, LII, 2 (November 1954), 94. Because this examination hopes to show that the metafictional aspect is of central importance in Sterne's novel, other critical views will only be referred to when these are relevant to my argument. Lodwick Hartley has drawn up the chief lines of the 20th century criticism on Sterne, finding that the main bulk occurred after 1940, when Sterne was at last generally accepted as a serious writer (cf. *Laurence Sterne in the Twentieth Century. An Essay and a Bibliography of Sternean Studies 1900-1965* (Durham, N.C., 1966), p. 21). Fairly early the critics have noted the Lockean influence on Sterne, and his conception of the association of ideas gave rise to the "assumption that Sterne was the first 'stream-of-consciousness' novelist and that he invented the Proustian method of exploring memory" (cf. Hartley, p. 27). John Traugott goes against this view: "Tristram's associations are conscious and calculated and his characters though surprising do not change". (cf. "Introduction", *Laurence Sterne. A Collection of Critical Essays*, ed. by John Traugott (Englewood Cliffs, N.J., 1968), p. 13). Though the question whether Sterne employs the technique of the stream-of-consciousness has been much debated, several critics regard him as a forerunner of Joyce and Proust. Helene Moglen asserts that he anticipates these writers as well as Virginia Woolf and André Gide, in his scepticism of reason and language and in his wit (cf. "The Philosophical Irony of Laurence Sterne", *Dissertation Abstracts*, XXVII (1966), 184–A). Henri Fluchère mentions another quality which Sterne shares with Proust and Joyce; his self-consciousness as an artist and his preoccupation with time as a personal experience contrary to the traditional view of time as a straight, chronological sequence (cf. *Laurence Sterne: From Tristram to Yorick*, transl. and abr. by Barbara Bray (London, 1965), p. 344).
[6] J. M. Stedmond, *The Comic Art of Laurence Sterne* (Un. of Toronto Press, 1967), p. 133.
[7] Alter, pp. 30–56. This critic considers Sterne's exposure of literary artifice through his parodies of earlier literature. Instead of *metafiction* Alter employs the phrase "the self-conscious novel" which he on p. x of the Preface defines as "a novel that systematically flaunts its own condition of artifice and that by so doing probes into the problematic relationship between real-seeming artifice and reality".
[8] Cash and Stedmond, *The Winged Skull* facing p. 189.
[9] Richard A. Lanham, *Tristram Shandy: The Games of Pleasure* (Berkeley, Los Angeles, London, 1973), p. 13.
[10] Wayne C. Booth, "The Self-Conscious Narrator in Comic Fiction before *Tristram Shandy*", *PLMA*, LXVII, 2 (March 1952), 164–165.

[11] Laurence Sterne, *The Life and Opinions of Tristram Shandy, Gentleman*, ed. by Ian Watt (Boston, 1965), p. 113. Subsequent references are to this edition and page numbers will be given in the text.

[12] Fluchère, p. 344.

[13] Melvyn New, *Laurence Sterne as Satirist. A Reading of "Tristram Shandy"* (Gainesville, 1969), pp. 76–78.

[14] Lewis Perry Curtis, ed., *Letters of Laurence Sterne* (Oxford, 1965), p. 90.

[15] Curtis, p. 143.

[16] Cf. Stedmond, p. 76.

[17] A. R. Towers convincingly argues that though it is made clear that Tristram is merely circumcised by the fall of the window-sash, "Sterne seems to anticipate the modern anthropologists and psycho-analysts who regard circumcision as a ritualistic substitution for the graver deprivation". "Sterne's Cock and Bull Story", *Journal of English Literary History*, XXIV, (1957), 16.

[18] Curtis, p. 232: note 4.

[19] *Tristram Shandy*, p. 411, note 6.

[20] Cf. Stedmond, p. 67.

[21] Robert Alter discusses how Sterne connects "sex as a motif with communication as a theme" in his article "*Tristram Shandy* and the Game of Love", *The American Scholar*, XXXVII, 2 (Spring 1968), 317.

[22] Stedmond, p. 165.

[23] Kayser, "Wer Erzählt den Roman?", p. 215.

[24] Alter, p. 318.

[25] John J. Enck, "John Barth: An Interview", *Wisconsin Studies in Contemporary Literature*, VI, 1 (1965), 6.

[26] Fluchère, p. 59. Cf. also Helene Moglen, "Laurence Sterne and the Contemporary Vision", *The Winged Skull*, p. 61; Robert Gorham Davis, "Sterne and the Delineation of the Modern Novel", *The Winged Skull*, p. 28.

[27] Curtis, p. 74.

[28] R. F. Brissenden, *Virtue in Distress. Studies in the Novel of Sentiment from Richardson to Sade* (Bristol, 1974), p. 188; Shklovsky, pp. 28 ff.

[29] Clarence Tracy holds quite the opposite view on Sterne's use of details and authentic material: "Sterne nevertheless gave the impression that his story was a true one, a genuine family history that might be authenticated by documents just as a biography might". "As Many Chapters as Steps", *The Winged Skull*, p. 105. And similarly Brissenden, who argues that "*Within the confines of the novel Sterne (or Sterne/Tristram) never suggests that his characters are fictions*" (*Virtue in Distress*, p. 207). I find this contradicted by, for instance, Tristram's words that he does not look forward to "that future and dreaded page" (p. 343) when Toby will be dead.

[30] Shklovsky, p. 37.

[31] Fluchère, p. 120.

[32] Cf. for instance Gillian Beer, *The Romance* (London, 1970), p. 14.

[33] Cf. "Introduction".

[34] Gerald Prince uses the term in his article "Notes Towards a Categorization of Fictional 'Narratees' ", *Genre*, IV (March, 1971), 100–105. This corresponds to Wolfgang Iser's expression "the implied reader": cf. his book *Der implizite Leser. Kommunikationsformen des Romans von Bunyan bis Beckett* (München, 1972).

[35] John Preston, *The Created Self: The Reader's Role in Eighteenth-Century Fiction* (London, 1970), p. 205.

[36] Cf. Fluchère, p. 258.

[37] Cf. Alter, p. 322 and Towers, p. 26.

[38] Cf. Graham Petrie, "A Rhetorical Topic in 'Tristram Shandy' ", *The Modern Language Review*, LXV, 2 (April 1970), 266.

[39] On Trim's eloquence, cf. Fluchère, pp. 303 ff.

[40] John Traugott, *Tristram Shandy's World. Sterne's Philosophical Rhetoric* (Berkeley and Los Angeles, 1954), p. 73; Helene Moglen, "Laurence Sterne and the Contemporary Vision", *The Winged Skull*, p. 66; Brissenden, pp. 193–194.

[41] Alter, p. 318.

[42] Iser, p. 57.

158

43 Alter, p. 319. Cf. also Norman N. Holland, "The Laughter of Laurence Sterne", *The Hudson Review*, IX, 3 (Autumn 1956), 427.

44 Preston, p. 164. Cf. also Holland, p. 427; Graham Petrie, "Rhetoric as Fictional Technique in *Tristram Shandy*", *Philological Quarterly*, XLVIII, 4 (October 1969), 479–494.

Chapter II

1 *Speak, Memory. An Autobiography Revisited*, rev. ed. (New York, 1966), p. 290.

2 Vladislav Khodasevich, "On Sirin", *Nabokov. Criticism, reminiscences, translations and tributes*, ed. by Alfred Appel, Jr. and Charles Newman (New York, 1970), p. 97. For more recent criticism, cf. Robert Alter, *Partial Magic. The Novel as a Self-Conscious Genre* (Berkeley, London, Los Angeles, 1975), p. 181; and Julia Bader, *Crystal Land. Artifice in Nabokov's English Novels* (Berkeley, Los Angeles, London, 1972), p. 4.

3 Khodasevich, p. 100.

4 Cf. Alfred Kazin, *Bright Book of Life. American Novelists and Storytellers from Hemingway to Mailer* (Boston and Toronto, 1973), pp. 313—14; Philip Toynbee, "Too much of a good thing", *The Observer* (October 5, 1969), 34; Alfred Weber, "Nabokov's *Ada*: A Style and its Implications", *Recovering Literature*, I, 1 (1972), 63.

5 *Look at the Harlequins!* (New York, 1974), p. 7.

6 *Ada or Ardor: A Family Chronicle* (London: Weidenfeld and Nicolson, 1969), p. 9. All subsequent references are to this edition, and page numbers will be given in the text.

7 *Nabokov*, ed. Appel and Newman, p. 242.

8 Cf. Bobbie Ann Mason, *Nabokov's Garden. A Guide to Ada* (Ann Arbor, 1974), p. 124. This is a valuable contribution to the criticism of *Ada,* clarifying many of the subtle allusions to literature, painting and lepidoptera. But Mason overlooks the fictitiousness of the characters and the metafictional quality of the novel when stating that "*Ada* is about incest" (p. 13) and condemning Van for solipsism and "misuse of nature" (p. 37).

9 Similarly, John Barth finds that instead of trying to minimize the gap between fiction and reality, a "different way to come to terms with the discrepancy between art and the Real Thing is to ... make the artifice part of your point": Cf. Enck, p. 6.

10 This is part of an answer to the critic Jeffrey Leonard and printed in "Supplement" to *Triquarterly*, XVII (Spring 1970), 5.

11 Nancy Anne Zeller in her interesting essay, "The Spiral of Time in *Ada*", presents the theory that the meetings of Van and Ada recur over the years with the regularity of the loops in a spiral. Cf. *A Book of Things about Vladimir Nabokov*, ed. by Carl R. Proffer (Ann Arbor, 1974), pp. 280–290.

12 John O. Stark asserts that Van's and Ada's moments of ardour "escape the clutches of time because they produce ecstasy"; *The Literature of Exhaustion. Borges, Nabokov, and Barth* (Durham, N.C., 1974) p. 86. He does not make it sufficiently clear that these moments are preserved because the narrator frees himself from them adequately enough to reproduce them in art.

13 Cf. Carl R. Proffer, "*Ada* as Wonderland: A Glossary of Allusions to Russian Literature", *A Book of Things about Vladimir Nabokov*, p. 251. Cf. also Robert Alter who explains the relation between *Ada* and Andrew Marvell's "The Garden" in "Nabokov's Ardor", *Commentary*, XLVIII, 2 (August 1969), 47–50; and Herbert Grabes who refers to among others Sergej T. Aksakov and François Chateaubriand as some of the literary sources of the book, in *Erfundene Biographien. Vladimir Nabokovs englische Romane* (Tübingen, 1975), p. 67.

14 When asked about his use of incest in *Ada*, Nabokov gave the following answer: "If I had used incest for the purpose of representing a possible road to happiness or misfortune, I would have been a best-selling didactician dealing in general ideas. Actually I don't give a damn for incest one way or another": Cf. Vladimir Nabokov, *Strong Opinions* (New York, 1973), pp. 122–3.

15 *Strong Opinions*, p. 116.

16 *Strong Opinions*, pp. 47–8.

17 *Strong Opinions*, p. 41. Cf. also, p. 18: "I don't think that an artist should bother about his audience. His best audience is the person he sees in his shaving mirror every morning."

Chapter III

[1] Annie Le Rebeller, "A Spectatorial Sceptic: An Interview with John Barth", *Annales De L'Université De Toulouse-Le Mirail*, XI (1975), 109.

[2] Frank Gado, ed., "John Barth", *First Person Conversations on Writers & Writing* (New York, 1973), p. 132.

[3] John Barth, *The End of the Road* (Harmondsworth, 1971), p. 116.

[4] John Barth, "The Literature of Exhaustion", *The Atlantic Monthly*, 220 (August 1967), 33.

[5] Barth's use of literary and historical sources has brought forth a great deal of criticism. On the one hand, the novel has been regarded as a satire on previous literature, for instance the classical epic and the 18th century novel (cf. Philip E. Diser, "The Historical Ebenezer Cooke", *Critique*, X, 3 (1968), 48–59; Charles B. Harris, *Contemporary American Novelists of the Absurd* (New Haven, Conn., 1971); Russel H. Miller, "*The Sot-Weed Factor*: A Contemporary Mock-Epic", *Critique*, VIII, 2 (1965–66), 88–100; Earl Rovit, "The Novel as Parody: John Barth", *Critique*, VI, 2 (Fall 1963), 77–85. On the other hand, *The Sot-Weed Factor* has been considered a parody of the writing of history and historical theory (cf. Brian W. Dippie, " 'His Visage Wild; His Form Exotick': Indian Themes and Cultural Guilt in John Barth's *The Sot-Weed Factor*", *American Quarterly*, XXI, 1 (Spring 1969), 113–121; Barbara C. Ewell, "John Barth: The Artist of History", *The Southern Literary Journal*, V (Spring 1973), 32–46; Richard Boyd Hauck, *A Cheerful Nihilism. Confidence and "The Absurd" in American Humorous Fiction* (London, 1971); Alan Holder, " 'What Marvelous Plot . . . Was Afoot?' History in Barth's *The Sot-Weed Factor*", *American Quarterly*, XX, 3 (Fall 1968), 596–604; Gordon E. Slethaug, "Barth's Refutation of the Idea of Progress", *Critique*, XIII, 3 (1972), 11–29). On the whole, this criticism affords valuable information, which this study has made ample use of (cf. the following notes to this chapter), but its range is limited and several aspects of the novel are left untouched.

  Some of the critics who endeavour to find an over-all pattern in *The Sot-Weed Factor* concentrate on Eben's existential quest (cf. Jerry H. Bryant, *The Open Decision. The Contemporary American Novel and its Intellectual Background* (London, 1970); Richard W. Noland, "John Barth and the Novel of Comic Nihilism", *Wisconsin Studies in Contemporary Literature*, VII, 3 (Autumn 1966), 239–257; John C. Stubbs, "John Barth as a Novelist of Ideas: The Themes of Value and Identity", *Critique*, VIII, 2 (Winter 1965–66), 101–116). Others point to the problem of opposites as the major theme of the novel; cf. John O. Stark. *The Literature of Exhaustion. Borges, Nabokov, and Barth.* (Durham, N. C., 1974); Jac Tharpe, *John Barth. The Comic Sublimity of Paradox* (London and Amsterdam, 1974). Especially the latter criticism approaches a central issue of the work, but leaves several problems unanswered or half-answered, just like the existential criticism. In my opinion, the question of opposites has to be seen in relation to the metafictional aspect. This examination hopes to show that, for instance, Eben's dreams and Henry's ambiguous role cannot be fully accounted for if not regarded in the metafictional perspective.

[6] Tony Tanner, *City of Words. American Fiction 1950–1970.* (London, 1971), p. 242.

[7] Frank D. McConnel, *Four Postwar American Novelists* (Chicago and London, 1977), p. 138.

[8] Diser, pp. 48–59. This critic compares the evidence of the life of the original Ebenezer Cooke, who lived in the early eighteenth century, with Barth's presentation of Eben in his novel. He shows that the quotations from the poem in the book are lifted more or less *verbatim* from Cooke's poem.

[9] John Barth, *The Sot-Weed Factor*, rev.ed. (New York: Doubleday, 1967), p. 741. Subsequent quotations refer to this edition and page numbers will be given in the text.

[10] Holder, p. 600.

[11] Holder, p. 604.

[12] Barth, *The End of the Road*, p. 116.

[13] Hauck, p. 227.

[14] Enck, p. 13.

[15] Enck, p. 6.

[16] Eben-Anna-Henry and Anna-Eben-Joan form the most significant sexual triangles in *The Sot-Weed Factor*; one of the racial triangles consists of Henry (representing predominantly the white race) and his two Indian half-brothers; a political as well as a racial triumvirate is made up of Quassapelagh (Indian), Drepacca (Negro) and Chicamec (partly white and partly Indian).

[17] One of the peaks of Parnassus was sacred to Apollo, the other to Dionysus (cf. Paul Harvey, ed., *The Oxford Companion to English Literature*, 4th ed., (Oxford, 1967) p. 618). Eben's dream indicates the polarity between Apollonian and Dionysian art which constitutes the central conflict in the novel. A well-known use of this opposition is Nietzsche's description of the Apollonian and Dionysian trends in art and literature; cf. Friedrich W. Nietzsche, *Die Geburt der Tragödie aus dem Geiste der Musik* (Leipzig, 1941 (1872)).

[18] Cf. Dagobert D. Runes, ed., *Dictionary of Philosophy* (Totowa, 1972) p. 264.

[19] Cf. references above to Holder's article and to the author's alleged flirtations with Clio *(The Sot-Weed Factor*, p. 743).

[20] Cf. Miller, pp. 88–100; Evelyn Glaser-Wöhrer, *An Analysis of John Barth's Weltanschauung: His View of Life and Literature* (Salzburg, 1977), pp. 57 ff.

[21] Gado, p. 125.

[22] Campbell Tatham, "The Gilesian Monomyth: Some Remarks on the Structure of *Giles Goat-Boy"*, *Genre*, III, 1 (March 1970), 365 ff.; David Morrell, *John Barth: An Introduction* (University Park and London, 1976), pp. 61–64.

[23] Raymond M. Olderman, "The Grail Knight Goes to College", *Beyond the Waste Land: A Study of the American Novel in the Nineteen-Sixties* (New Haven and London, 1972), pp. 76 ff.

[24] Joe David Bellamy, "Algebra and Fire: An Interview with John Barth", *Falcon*, IV (1972), 7. Cf. also John J. Enck, "John Barth: An Interview", 12.

[25] John W. Tilton, *"Giles Goat-Boy*: An Interpretation", *Bucknell Review*, XVIII, 1 (Spring 1970), 94.

[26] *ibid.*, p. 103.

[27] Robert Scholes, *The Fabulators* (New York, 1967), p. 153; Morrell, *John Barth*, p. 70; Hauck, pp. 230 ff.

[28] One finds occasional remarks about the metafictional quality of *Giles Goat-Boy*. Charles B. Harris states, for instance, in his essay that the novel "is not about the world but about the ways we *talk* about the world". Cf. "George's Illumination: Unity in *Giles Goat-Boy"*, *Studies in the Novel*, VIII, 1 (Spring 1976), 181. McConnell finds that Barth constructs "before the reader's eyes, as it were, a primal fiction, a myth . . ." *(Four Postwar American Novellsts*, p. 142).

[29] John Barth, *Giles Goat-Boy or, The Revised New Syllabus* (New York: Doubleday, 1966), p. IX. Subsequent quotations refer to this edition and page numbers will be given in parenthesis in the text.

[30] Morrell, *John Barth*, p. 65–66.

[31] John Barth, "Author's Note", *Lost in the Funhouse* (London, 1969), p. x.

[32] Tanner, p. 249.

[33] Tilton, p. 98.

[34] Beverly Gross, "The Anti-Novels of John Barth", *Chicago Review*, XX, 3 (November 1968), 95. – "Author" is written in quotation marks, to distinguish Harold Bray from the actual author, John Barth. As the discussion will reveal, his role as author overlaps with the functions usually assigned to the narrator, like intrusion and omniscience.

[35] Wordsworth gives vent to a similar conception in his "Preface to *Lyrical Ballads"*. He answers his own question "What is a poet?" with this definition: "He is a man speaking to men: a man, it is true, endued with more lively sensibility, more enthusiasm and tenderness, who has a greater knowledge of human nature, and a more comprehensive soul . . ." Quoted from M. H. Abrams et al., eds., *The Norton Anthology of English Literature*, 3rd ed., II (New York, 1974), 133.

[36] Barth, "The Literature of Exhaustion", 30.

[37] T. S. Eliot, "Tradition and the Individual Talent", *The Norton Anthology*, 2199.

11

Chapter IV

1 Edward Lucie-Smith, *Movements in Art Since 1945* (London, 1975), p. 8.
2 Vivian Mercier, *Beckett/Beckett* (New York, 1977), pp. 95 ff.
3 Despite the bulk and the diversity of the critical response to Beckett, some general trends make themselves felt. Of the mainly biographical studies, one may mention, in addition to Mercier's book, John Fletcher, *Samuel Beckett's Art* (London, 1967) and Deirdre Bair, *Samuel Beckett: A Biography* (London, 1978). Perhaps the greater part of the criticism deals with Beckett's work in relation to its sources. Fletcher, for instance, discusses some of the literary influences while the connection between Beckett and philosophy is debated in works like John Pilling, *Samuel Beckett* (London, 1976) and Raili Elovaara, *The Problem of Identity in Samuel Beckett's Prose. An Approach from Philosophies of Existence* (Helsinki, 1976). Psychoanalytical criticism forms a third kind of approach to Beckett, for instance G. C. Barnard, *Samuel Beckett. A New Approach: A Study of the Novels and Plays* (London, 1970) and Norma Lorre Goodrich, "Molloy's Musa Mater", *Literature Symposium*, III (January 1970), 31–53. Lastly, criticism has paid attention to the formal aspect of Beckett's work; the present study belongs to this category.
4 Michael Robinson, *The Long Sonata of the Dead. A Study of Samuel Beckett* (London, 1969), p. 17.
5 Robinson, p. 145.
6 H. Porter Abbott, *The Fiction of Samuel Beckett. Form and Effect* (London, 1973), p. 99 and p. 114.
7 Hanna Case Copeland, *Art and Artist in the Works of Samuel Beckett* (The Hague and Paris, 1975), p. 89 and p. 107.
8 Dina Sherzer, *Structure De La Trilogie De Beckett: Molloy, Malone Meurt, L'Innommable* (The Hague and Paris, 1976), pp. 15–17.
9 Gerald L. Bruns, "The Storyteller and the Problem of Language in Samuel Beckett's Fiction", *Modern Language Quarterly*, XXX, 2 (June 1969), 267; Wolfgang Iser, *The Implied Reader. Patterns of Communication in Prose Fiction from Bunyan to Beckett* (Princeton, N.J., 1973), p. 174.
10 The trilogy was originally written in French during the years 1946–49. The French editions of *Molloy* and *Malone Meurt* appeared in Paris in 1951 while *L'Innommable* was published in 1953. The English translation of *Molloy* was published in 1955 while *Malone Dies* and *The Unnamable* appeared in English in 1956 and in 1958 respectively. While Beckett had a strong hand in the working out of the English translation of *Molloy*, he undertook the translation of *Malone Dies* and *The Unnamable* entirely himself; cf. Bair, pp. 405–488.
11 Quotation taken from Ruby Cohn, *Back to Beckett* (Princeton, N.J., 1973), p. 112.
12 Samuel Beckett, *Molloy* (London: Calder and Boyars, 1966), p. 8. Subsequent references are to this edition. Page numbers will be given in parenthesis in the text.
13 Abbott, p. 110; Frederick J. Hoffman, *Samuel Beckett. The Language of Self* (London, 1967), p. 128; Iser, p. 264.
14 Sherzer, p. 15.
15 Copeland, p. 120.
16 Ursula Dreysse, *Realität als Aufgabe. Eine Untersuchung über Aufbaugesetze und Gehalte des Romanwerks von Samuel Beckett* (Berlin, Zürich, 1970), p. 41.
17 Sherzer, p. 40.
18 Dina Sherzer has examined very accurately how the narrator in *Molloy*, I, sabotages, as she calls it, the usual way of telling a story: "le narrateur utilise un certain nombre de techniques (disjonctions, asyndète [omitting connectives], non-élaboration, contradictions, dilatations) qui ont pour résultat la *dislocation du récit*"; Sherzer, p. 35.
19 David H. Hesla mentions how *Molloy*, I, contains references to "other narratives of travel and quest" such as "the *Aeneid,* the *Odyssey*, Jesus' entry into Jerusalem and his subsequent passion, *Pilgrim's Progress, Through the Looking-Glass,* and Goethe's *Faust*"; Cf. "Being, Thinking, Telling, and Loving. The Couple in Beckett's Fiction", *Samuel Beckett: The Art of Rhetoric*, eds. by Edouard Morot – Sir et al. (Valencia, 1976), p. 15. This adds to the metafictive quality of the novel.

[20] Edith Kern, "Moran – Molloy: The Hero as Author", *Twentieth Century Interpretations of Molloy, Malone Dies, The Unnamable*, ed. by J. D. O'Hara (Englewood Cliffs, N. J., 1970) pp. 43–44.

[21] Cf. Abbott, p. 100.

[22] Sherzer, p. 50 and p. 53.

[23] David H. Hesla, *The Shape of Chaos. An Interpretation of the Art of Samuel Beckett* (Minneapolis, 1971), p. 98.

[24] Raymond Federman, «Samuel Beckett: The Liar's Paradox,» *Samuel Beckett: The Art of Rhetoric*, eds. Edouard Morot – Sir et al., p. 123. Cf. also Francis Doherty, *Samuel Beckett* (London, 1971), p. 50.

[25] Jan Hokenson, "A Stuttering *Logos*: Biblical Paradigms in Beckett's Trilogy", *James Joyce Quarterly*, VIII, 2 (Summer 1971), 295–6.

[26] Several critics have discussed the similarity between Moran and Molloy and how the one forms the counterpart of the other, without mentioning the metafictional aspect. Cf. for instance Doherty, p. 51, and Cohn, p. 86. David Hayman explains the relationship in Freudian terms whereby Molloy represents the id or the libido and Moran the superego; cf. "*Molloy* or the Quest for Meaninglessness: A Global Interpretation", *Samuel Beckett Now*, ed. by Melvin J. Friedman (Chicago and London, 1970), pp. 148–9.

[27] Samuel Beckett, *Malone Dies* (London: Calder and Boyars, 1975), p. 11. Subsequent quotations refer to this edition, page numbers will be given in the text.

[28] Copeland, p. 122.

[29] Samuel Beckett, *Proust. And three Dialogues. Samuel Beckett & Georges Duthuit*, (London, 1965), p. 86.

[30] Dreysse, p. 93.

[31] Robinson, p. 172.

[32] Sherzer, p. 62.

[33] Bair, pp. 376–77.

[34] Cf. Jan Hokenson, pp. 293 ff.: Beckett's use of the Gospel according to Saint John is taken up by Hokenson, but the implications of the Moll incidents are not debated.

[35] According to the Book of Proverbs (XXXI, 1–9), Lemuel was a king instructed by his mother to be a defender and spokesman for the dumb and the dying; Beckett's Lemuel must be seen as an ironic reversal of his biblical prototype.

[36] Hokenson, p. 302.

[37] Hokenson, p. 302.

[38] Israel Shenker, "Moody Man of Letters. A Portrait of Samuel Beckett, Author of the Puzzling 'Waiting For Godot' ", *The New York Times*, May 6, 1956, Sec. 2, 1.

[39] Samuel Beckett, *The Unnamable* (London: Calder and Boyars, 1975), pp. 43 ff. Subsequent quotations refer to this edition and page numbers will be given in parenthesis in the text.

[40] Robert Martin Adams points to the circumstance that Beckett himself asserts that he hears voices, whose words he uses in his narratives. Cf. Adams, *Afterjoyce. Studies in Fiction After Ulysses* (New York, 1977), p. 106.

[41] Cohn, p. 100.

[42] Robinson, p. 195.

[43] Shenker, p. 1 and p. 3.

[44] Cf. Hokenson, p. 306: Basil, Mahood and Worm are seen to represent "three stages in the now archetypal *Homo Logos*: Lord, Man, Worm".

[45] Abbott, p. 135. Cf. also Alvin J. Seltzer, *Chaos in the Novel. The Novel in Chaos* (London, 1974), p. 222.

[46] Hesla, "Being", p. 20.

[47] E.M. Forster, *Aspects of the Novel* (London, 1974), p. 33.

The Meaning of Metafiction – Conclusion

[1] Gass, pp. 23–24.

BIBLIOGRAPHY

Laurence Sterne

Primary Sources

The Life and Opinions of Tristram Shandy, Gentleman. Ed. by Ian Watt. Boston: Houghton Mifflin, 1965.
A Sentimental Journey Through France and Italy. London: Oxford Univ. Press, 1963.

Secondary Sources

Alter, Robert. "Sterne and the Nostalgia for Reality", *Partial Magic. The Novel as a Self-Conscious Genre.* Berkeley, London, Los Angeles, 1975, pp. 30–56.
——————. "*Tristram Shandy* and the Game of Love", *The American Scholar,* XXXVII, 2 (Spring 1968), 316–323.
Booth, Wayne C. "The Self-Conscious Narrator in Comic Fiction before *Tristram Shandy*", *PMLA,* LXVII, 2 (March 1952), 163–185.
Brissenden, R. F. " 'Trusting to Almighty God': Another look at the composition of *Tristram Shandy*", *The Winged Skull.* Ed. by Arthur H. Cash and John M. Stedmond. London, 1971, pp. 253–268.
——————. *Virtue in Distress. Studies in the Novel of Sentiment from Richardson to Sade.* Bristol, 1974.
Curtis, Lewis Perry, ed. *Letters of Laurence Sterne.* Oxford, 1965.
Davis, Robert Gorham. "Sterne and the Delineation of the Modern Novel", *The Winged Skull.* Ed. by Arthur H. Cash and John M. Stedmond. London, 1971, pp. 21–41.
Donovan, Robert Alan. *The Shaping Vision, Imagination in the English Novel from Defoe to Dickens.* Ithaca, New York, 1966.
Fluchère, Henry. *Laurence Sterne: From Tristram to Yorick. An Interpretation of Tristram Shandy.* Trans. and abr. by Barbara Bray. New York and Toronto, 1965.
Frye, Northrop. "Towards Defining an Age of Sensibility", *Journal of English Literary History,* XXIII (1956), 144–152.
Harper, Kenneth E. "A Russian Critic and *Tristram Shandy*", *Modern Philology,* LII, 2 (November 1954), 92–99.
Holland, Norman N. "The Laughter of Laurence Sterne", *The Hudson Review,* IX, 3 (Autumn 1956), 422–430.

Lanham, Richard A. *Tristram Shandy: The Games of Pleasure*. Berkeley, Los Angeles, London, 1973.

Moglen, Helene. "The Philosophical Irony of Laurence Sterne", *Dissertation Abstracts*, XXVII (1966), 184–A.

———. "Laurence Sterne and the Contemporary Vision", *The Winged Skull*. Ed. by Arthur H. Cash and John M. Stedmond. London, 1971, pp. 59–74.

New, Melvyn. *Laurence Sterne as Satirist. A Reading of "Tristram Shandy"*. Gainesville, 1969.

Petrie, Graham. "A Rhetorical Topic in 'Tristram Shandy' ", *The Modern Language Review*, LXV, 2 (April 1970), 261–266.

———. "Rhetoric as Fictional Technique in *Tristram Shandy*", *Philological Quarterly*, XLVIII, 4 (October 1969), 479–494.

Preston, John. *The Created Self: The Reader's Role in Eighteenth-Century Fiction*. London, 1970.

Shklovsky, Victor. "Sterne's *Tristram Shandy*: Stylistic Commentary", *Russian Formalist Criticism, Four Essays*. Ed. by Lee T. Lemon and Marion J. Reis. Lincoln, 1965, pp. 25 57.

Stedmond, J. M. *The Comic Art of Laurence Sterne*. Un. of Toronto Press, 1967.

Towers, A. R. "Sterne's Cock and Bull Story", *Journal of English Literary History*, XXIV (1957), 12–29.

Tracy, Clarence. "As Many Chapters as Steps", *The Winged Skull*. Ed. by Arthur H. Cash and John M. Stedmond. London, 1971, pp. 97–111.

Traugott, John, ed. "Introduction", *Laurence Sterne. A Collection of Critical Essays*. Englewood Cliffs, N.J., 1968, pp. 1–20.

———. *Tristram Shandy's World. Sterne's Philosophical Rhetoric*. Berkeley and Los Angeles, 1954.

Wickler, Franz-Josef. *Rabelais und Sterne*. Bonn, 1963.

Bibliography

Dyson, A. E., ed. *The English Novel. Select Bibliographical Guides*. London: Oxford Univ. Press, 1974.

Lodwick, Hartley. *Laurence Sterne in the Twentieth Century. An Essay and a Bibliography of Sternean Studies 1900–1965*. Durham, N.C., 1966.

Monkman, Kenneth, and J. C. T. Oates, "Towards a Sterne Bibliography: Books and Other Material Displayed at the Sterne Conference", *The Winged Skull*. Ed. by Arthur H. Cash and John M. Stedmond. London, 1971, pp. 279–310.

Vladimir Nabokov

Primary Sources

Ada or Ardor: A Family Chronicle. London: Weidenfeld and Nicolson, 1969.
Bend Sinister. New York: New Directions, 1959.
Lolita. London: Weidenfeld and Nicolson, 1955.
Look at the Harlequins! New York: McGraw Hill, 1974.
Pale Fire. London: Weidenfeld and Nicolson, 1962.

Pnin. New York: Doubleday, 1957.
The Real Life of Sebastian Knight. New York: New Directions, 1941.
Transparent Things. New York: McGraw Hill, 1972.

Secondary Sources

Aksakov, Sergej T., and François Chateaubriand. *Erfundene Biographien. Vladimir Nabokovs englische Romane*. Tübingen, 1975.
Alter, Robert. "Nabokov's Ardor", *Commentary*, XLVIII, 2 (August 1969), 47–50.
——————. "Nabokov's Game of Worlds", *Partial Magic. The Novel as a Self-Conscious Genre*. Berkeley, London, Los Angeles, 1975, pp. 180–217.
Bader, Julia. *Crystal Land. Artifice in Nabokov's English Novels*. Berkeley, Los Angeles, London, 1972.
Kazin, Alfred. "A Personal Sense of Time. Nabokov and Other Exiles", *Bright Book of Life. American Novelists and Storytellers from Hemingway to Mailer*. Boston and Toronto, 1973, pp. 283–317.
Khodasevich, Vladislav. "On Sirin", *Nabokov. Criticism, reminiscences, translations and tributes*. Ed. by Alfred Appel, Jr. and Charles Newman. New York, 1970, pp. 96–101.
Mason, Bobbie Ann. *Nabokov's Garden. A Guide to Ada*. Ann Arbor, 1974.
Nabokov, Vladimir. "Jeffrey Leonard", *Triquarterly. Supplement*. XVII (Spring 1970), 5–6.
——————. *Speak, Memory. An Autobiography Revisited*. Rev. ed. New York, 1966.
——————. *Strong Opinions*. New York, 1973.
Proffer, Carl R., ed. "*Ada* as Wonderland: A Glossary of Allusions to Russian Literature", *A Book of Things about Vladimir Nabokov*. Ann Arbor, Michigan, 1974, pp. 249–279.
Stark, John O. *The Literature of Exhaustion. Borges, Nabokov, and Barth*. Durham, N.C., 1974.
Toynbee, Philip. "Too much of a good thing", *The Observer*. October 5, 1969, 34.
Weber, Alfred. "Nabokov's *Ada*: A Style and its Implications", *Recovering Literature*, I, 1 (1972), 54–65.
Zeller, Nancy Anne. "The Spiral of Time in *Ada*", *A Book of Things about Vladimir Nabokov*. Ed. by Carl R. Proffer. Ann Arbor, 1974, pp. 280–290.

John Barth

Primary Sources

Chimera. New York: Random House, 1972.
The End of the Road. Harmondsworth: Penguin, 1971.
The Floating Opera. Rev. ed. New York: Doubleday, 1967.
Giles Goat-Boy or, The Revised New Syllabus. New York: Doubleday, 1966.
Lost in the Funhouse. London: Secker and Warburg, 1969.
The Sot-Weed Factor. Rev.ed. New York: Doubleday, 1967.

Secondary Sources

Barth, John. "The Literature of Exhaustion", *The Atlantic Monthly*, 222 (August 1967), 29–34.
Bellamy, Joe David. "Algebra and Fire: An Interview with John Barth", *Falcon*, IV (Spring 1972), 5–15.
Bryant, Jerry H. *The Open Decision. The Contemporary American Novel and its Intellectual Background*. London, 1970.
Christensen, Inger Aarseth. "Absence of Absolutes: The Reconciled Artist in John Barth's *The Floating Opera*", *Studia Neophilologica*, XVLII, 1 (1975), 53–68.
Dippie, Brian W. " 'His Visage Wild; His Form Exotick': Indian Themes and Cultural Guilt in John Barth's *The Sot-Weed Factor*". *American Quarterly*, XXI, 1 (Spring 1969), 113–121.
Diser, Philip E. "The Historical Ebenezer Cooke", *Critique*, X, 3 (1968), 48–59.
Enck, John J. "John Barth: An Interview", *Wisconsin Studies in Contemporary Literature*, VI, 1 (1965), 3–14
Ewell, Barbara C. "John Barth: The Artist of History". *The Southern Literary Journal*, V (Spring 1973), 32–46.
Gado, Frank, ed. "John Barth", *First Person Conversations on Writers and Writing*. New York, 1973.
Glaser-Wöhrer, Evelyn. *An Analysis of John Barth's Weltanschauung. His View of Life and Literature*. Salzburg, 1977.
Gross, Beverly. "The Anti-Novels of John Barth", *Chicago Review*, xx, 3 (November 1968), 95–109.
Harris, Charles B. *Contemporary American Novelists of the Absurd*. New Haven, Conn., 1971.
——————. "George's Illumination: Unity in *Giles Goat-Boy*", *Studies in the Novel*, VIII, 1 (Spring 1976), 172–184.
Hauck, Richard Boyd. *A Cheerful Nihilism. Confidence and "The Absurd" in American Humorous Fiction*. Bloomington and London, 1971.
Holder, Alan. " 'What Marvelous Plot . . . Was Afoot?' History In Barth's *The Sot-Weed Factor*", *American Quarterly*, XX, 3 (Fall 1968), 598–604.
Le Rebeller, Annie. "A Spectatorial Sceptic: An Interview with John Barth", *Annales De L'Université de Toulouse Le Mirail*, XI (1975), 93–110.
McConnell, Frank D. "John Barth and the Key to the Treasure", *Four Postwar American Novelists*. Chicago and London, 1977, pp. 108–158.
Miller, Russel H. *"The Sot-Weed Factor:* A Contemporary Mock-Epic", *Critique*, VIII, 2 (1965–66), 88–100.
Morrell, David. *John Barth: An Introduction*. University Park and London, 1976.
Noland, Richard W. "John Barth and the Novel of Comic Nihilism". *Wisconsin Studies in Contemporary Literature*, VII, 3 (Autumn 1966), 239–257.
Olderman, Raymond M. "The Grail Knight Goes to College", *Beyond the Waste Land: A Study of the American Novel in the Nineteen-Sixties*. New Haven and London, 1972, pp. 72–93.
Rovit, Earl. "The Novel as Parody: John Barth". *Critique*, VI, 2 (Fall 1963), 77–85.
Scholes, Robert. "Fabulation and Epic Vision", *The Fabulators*. New York, 1967, pp. 135–173.
Slethaug, Gordon E. "Barth's Refutation of the Idea of Progress". *Critique*, XIII, 3 (1972), 11–29.
Stark, John O. *The Literature of Exhaustion. Borges, Nabokov, and Barth*. Durham, N.C., 1974.

Stubbs, John C. "John Barth as a Novelist of Ideas: The Themes of Value and Identity". *Critique*, VIII, 2 (Winter 1965–66), 239–257.

Tatham, Campbell. "The Gilesian Monomyth: Some Remarks on the Structure of *Giles Goat-Boy*", *Genre*, III, 1 (March 1970), 364–375.

Tharpe, Jac. *John Barth. The Comic Sublimity of Paradox*. London and Amsterdam, 1974.

Tilton, John W. "*Giles Goat-Boy:* An Interpretation", *Bucknell Review*, XVIII, 1 (Spring 1970), 92–119.

Bibliography

Vine, Richard Allan. *John Barth: An Annotated Bibliography*. Metuchen, N. J., 1977.

Weixlmann, Joseph. *John Barth: A Descriptive Primary and Annotated Secondary Bibliography, Including a Descriptive Catalogue of Manuscript Holdings in United States Libraries*. New York and London: Garland Publishing, 1976.

Samuel Beckett

Primary Sources

Malone Dies. London: Calder and Boyars, 1975.
Molloy. London: Calder and Boyars, 1966.
Murphy. New York: Grove Press, 1957.
The Unnamable. London: Calder and Boyars, 1975.
Watt. New York: Grove Press, 1959.

Secondary Sources

Abbott, H. Porter. *The Fiction of Samuel Beckett. Form and Effect*. London, 1973.

Bair, Deirdre. *Samuel Beckett: A Biography*. London, 1978.

Barnard., G. C. *Samuel Beckett. A New Approach: A Study of the Novels and Plays*. London, 1970.

Beckett, Samuel. *Proust. And three Dialogues. Samuel Beckett & Georges Duthuit*. London, 1965.

Bruns, Gerald L. "The Storyteller and the Problem of Language in Samuel Beckett's Fiction", *Modern Language Quarterly*, XXX, 2 (June 1969), 265–281.

Cohn, Ruby. *Back to Beckett*. Princeton, N. J., 1973.

Copeland, Hannah Case. *Art and Artist in the Works of Samuel Beckett*. The Hague and Paris, 1975.

Doherty, Francis. *Samuel Beckett*. London, 1971.

Dreysse, Ursula. *Realität als Aufgabe. Eine Untersuchung über Aufbaugesetze und Gehalte des Romanwerks von Samuel Beckett*. Berlin, Zürich, 1970.

Elovaara, Raili. *The Problem of Identity in Samuel Beckett's Prose. An Approach from Philosophies of Existence*. Helsinki, 1976.

Federman, Raymond. "Samuel Beckett: The Liar's Paradox", *Samuel Beckett: The Art of Rhetoric*. Ed. by Edouard Morot-Sir et al. Valencia, 1976, pp. 119–141.

Fletcher, John. *Samuel Beckett's Art*. London, 1967.

Goodrich, Norma Lorre. "Molloy's Musa Mater", *Literature Symposium*, III (January 1970), 31–53.

Hayman, David. "*Molloy* or the Quest for Meaninglessness: A Global Interpretation", *Samuel Beckett Now*. Ed. by Melvin J. Friedman. Chicago and London, 1970, pp. 129–156.

Hesla, David H. *The Shape of Chaos. An Interpretation of the Art of Samuel Beckett*. Minneapolis, 1971.

——————. "Being, Thinking, Telling, and Loving. The Couple in Beckett's Fiction", *Samuel Beckett: The Art of Rhetoric*. Ed. by Edouard Morot-Sir et al. Valencia, 1976, pp. 11–23.

Hoffmann, Frederick J. *Samuel Beckett. The Language of Self*. London, 1967.

Hokenson, Jan. "A Stuttering *Logos*: Biblical Paradigms in Beckett's Trilogy", *James Joyce Quarterly*, VIII, 2 (Summer 1971), 293–310.

Iser, Wolfgang *The Implied Reader. Patterns of Communication in Prose Fiction from Bunyan to Beckett*. Princeton, N.J., 1973. Orig.tit. *Der implizite Leser*.

Kern, Edith. "Moran – Molloy: The Hero as Author", *Twentieth Century Interpretations of Molloy, Malone, Dies, The Unnamable*. Ed. by J.D. O'Hara. Englewood Cliffs, N.J., 1970, pp. 35–45.

Mercier, Vivian. *Beckett/Beckett*. New York, 1977.

Pilling, John. *Samuel Beckett*. London, 1976.

Robinson, Michael. *The Long Sonata of the Dead. A Study of Samuel Beckett*. London, 1969.

Shenker, Israel. "Moody Man of Letters. A Portrait of Samuel Beckett, Author of the Puzzling 'Waiting For Godot' ", *The New York Times*, May 6, 1956, Sec. 2, 1 and 3.

Sherzer, Dina. *Structure De La Trilogie De Beckett: Molloy, Malone Meurt, L'Innomable*. The Hague and Paris, 1976.

Other Fictional Work

Hawthorne, Nathaniel. *The Blithedale Romance. The Works of Nathaniel Hawthorne*. Vol. V. Boston and New York, 1888.

James, Henry. *The Portrait of a Lady*. New York, 1881.

Scott, Walter. *Waverley*. Harmondsworth, 1972.

General Criticism

Adams, Robert Martin. *Afterjoyce. Studies in Fiction After Ulysses*. New York, 1977.

Alter, Robert. *Partial Magic. The Novel as a Self-Conscious Genre*. Berkeley, Los Angeles, London, 1975.

Bergonzi, Bernard. *The Situation of the Novel*. London, 1972.

Beer, Gillian. *The Romance*. London, 1970.

Booth, Wayne C. *The Rhetoric of Fiction*. Chicago, 1961.

Eliot, T. S. "Tradition and the Individual Talent", *The Norton Anthology of English Literature*, II. Ed. by M. H. Abrams et al. New York, 1974, 2198–2205.

Fletcher, John, and Malcolm Bradbury. "The Introverted Novel", *Modernism 1890–1930*. Ed. by Malcolm Bradbury and James McFarlane. Harmondsworth, 1976, pp. 394–395.

Fogel, Stanley. " 'And All the Little Typtopus': Notes on Language Theory in the Contemporary Experimental Novel", *Modern Fiction Studies*, XX, 2 (Autumn 1974), 328–336.

Forster, E. M. *Aspects of the Novel*. London, 1974.

Frye, Northrop. *Anatomy of Criticism*. Princeton, 1971.

Gass, William H. "Philosophy and the Form of Fiction", *Fiction and the Figures of Life*. New York, 1970. pp. 3–26.

Harvey, Paul, ed. *The Oxford Companion to English Literature*. 4th ed. Oxford, 1967.

Iser, Wolfgang. *Der implizite Leser. Kommunikationsformen des Romans von Bunyan bis Beckett*. München, 1972.

Josipovici, Gabriel. *The World and the Book. A Study of Modern Fiction*. London, 1971.

Kayser, Wolfgang, "Wer Erzählt den Roman?" *Zur Poetik des Romans*. Ed. by Volker Klotz. Darmstadt, 1969, pp. 197–216.

—————. *Das Sprachliche Kunstwerk*. Zwölfte Auflage. München, 1967.

Lucie-Smith, Edward. *Movements in Art Since 1945*. London, 1975.

McCaffery, Larry. "The Art of Metafiction: William Gass's *Willie Masters' Lonesome Wife*", *Critique*, XVIII, 1 (1976), 21–34.

Nietzsche, Friedrich W. *Die Geburt der Tragödie aus dem Geiste der Musik*. Leipzig, 1941 (1872).

Prince, Gerald. "Notes Towards a Categorization of Fictional 'Narratees' ", *Genre*, IV (March 1971), 100–106.

Riley, E. C. *Cervantes's Theory of the Novel*. Oxford, 1962.

Scholes, Robert. "The Fictional Criticism of the Future", *Triquarterly*, XXXIV, 4 (Fall 1975), 233–247.

—————. "Metafiction", *The Iowa Review*, I (Fall 1970), 100–115.

Seltzer, Alvin J. *Chaos in the Novel. The Novel in Chaos*. London, 1974.

Tanner, Tony. *City of Words. American Fiction 1950–1970*. London, 1971.

Whitaker, Thomas R. *Fields of Play in Modern Drama*. Princeton, N. J., 1977.

Index